Ethnic Citizenship Regimes

Palgrave Politics of Identity and Citizenship Series

Series Editors: **Varun Uberoi**, University of Oxford; **Nasar Meer**, University of Southampton and **Tariq Modood**, University of Bristol.

The politics of identity and citizenship has assumed increasing importance as our polities have become significantly more culturally, ethnically and religiously diverse. Different types of scholars, including philosophers, sociologists, political scientists and historians, make contributions to this field, and this series showcases a variety of innovative contributions. Focusing on a range of different countries, and utilizing the insights of different disciplines, the series helps to illuminate an increasingly controversial area of research, and titles in the series will be of interest to a number of audiences, including scholars, students and other interested individuals.

Titles include:

Derek McGhee
SECURITY, CITIZENSHIP AND HUMAN RIGHTS
Shared Values in Uncertain Times

Nasar Meer
CITIZENSHIP, IDENTITY AND THE POLITICS OF MULTICULTURALISM
The Rise of Muslim Consciousness

Ganesh Nathan
SOCIAL FREEDOM IN A MULTICULTURAL STATE
Towards a Theory of Intercultural Justice

Michel Seymour (*editor*)
THE PLURAL STATES OF RECOGNITION

Palgrave Politics of Identity and Citizenship Series
Series Standing Order ISBN 978–0–230–24901–1 (hardback)
(*outside North America only*)

You can receive future titles in this series as they are published by placing a standing order. Please contact your bookseller or, in case of difficulty, write to us at the address below with your name and address, the title of the series and the ISBN quoted above.

Customer Services Department, Macmillan Distribution Ltd, Houndmills, Basingstoke, Hampshire RG21 6XS, England

Ethnic Citizenship Regimes

Europeanization, Post-war Migration and Redressing Past Wrongs

Aleksandra Maatsch
Jean Monnet Centre for European Studies, University of Bremen, Germany

First published 2011 by
PALGRAVE MACMILLAN

Palgrave Macmillan in the UK is an imprint of Macmillan Publishers Limited,
registered in England, company number 785998, of Houndmills, Basingstoke,
Hampshire RG21 6XS.

Palgrave Macmillan in the US is a division of St Martin's Press LLC,
175 Fifth Avenue, New York, NY 10010.

Palgrave Macmillan is the global academic imprint of the above companies
and has companies and representatives throughout the world.

Palgrave® and Macmillan® are registered trademarks in the United States,
the United Kingdom, Europe and other countries.

ISBN: 978–0–230–28424–1 hardback

This book is printed on paper suitable for recycling and made from fully
managed and sustained forest sources. Logging, pulping and manufacturing
processes are expected to conform to the environmental regulations of the
country of origin.

A catalogue record for this book is available from the British Library.

Library of Congress Cataloging-in-Publication Data

Maatsch, Aleksandra, 1979–
    Ethnic citizenship regimes : Europeanization, post-war migration and
redressing past wrongs / Aleksandra Maatsch.
        p. cm.—(Palgrave politics of identity and citizenship series)
    Includes index.
    ISBN 978–0–230–28424–1
    1. Citizenship – Europe. 2. Naturalization – Europe. 3. Assimilation
(Sociology) – Europe. I. Title. II. Series.

JF801.M23 2011
323.6094—dc22   2011005250

10 9 8 7 6 5 4 3 2 1
20 19 18 17 16 15 14 13 12 11

Printed and bound in Great Britain by
CPI Antony Rowe, Chippenham and Eastbourne

Contents

Acknowledgements

I would like to express special thanks to Professors Ulrike Liebert and Rainer Bauböck, who inspired my academic interests and commented very thoroughly on the final draft of my book. I also wish to thank my ConstEPS project fellows (and affiliates) and good friends at the same time: Kathrin Packham, Tatjana Evas, Dr Petra Rakušanova, Dr Alexander Gattig, Sönke Maatsch, Samba Diop, Ewelina Pawlak, Joanna Serdyńska, Dr Katarzyna Gajewska and Anja Vedder. You have created a very stimulating research environment that I will greatly miss. I am particularly indebted to Anna Horvath, who helped me with conducting the empirical analysis of the Hungarian parliamentary debates.

This book would not have been completed in such a short period of time without the financial support of the *Volkswagen Stiftung*, which not only supported me with a scholarship but also offered additional funds for the German language courses that allowed me to conduct independently the analysis of the German parliamentary debates.

Many chapters of this book have greatly benefited from the discussions held during various workshops and conferences, particularly those organized within the CONNEX network. I would like to mention the European Research Colloquium, organized over two years (2005–2006) by Professor Ronald Holzhacker, as well as the workshop 'Research Design and Methods', organized at the European University Institute in 2007 by Professors Tanja Börzel and Adrienne Héritier.

Finally, I would like to thank my family members, who supported me emotionally: my mother and Andrzej, and first and foremost my husband, Sönke.

Figures

Tables

1
Citizenship in a Migratory World

Introduction

In a migratory world, citizenship is no longer a symbol of exclusivity and permanence; rather, it has become portable, exchangeable and multiple. As Kim Barry observed, 'Migration decouples citizenship and residence disrupting tidy conceptions of nation-states as bounded territorial entities with fixed populations of citizens. Today states are constituted increasingly by large numbers of resident noncitizens as well as non-resident, external citizens' (Barry, 2006, pp. 17–18). As a consequence, the 'transnationalized' national citizenship that crystallized under the impact of migration became distinctively extraterritorial and non-residential, for immigrants residing outside their states are simultaneously subject to the legislation of multiple sovereigns.

However, states, migrants and the EU institutions approach these new trends from very different perspectives (Bauböck, 2005a). States still want to maintain some control over migration but at the same time to foster democracy at the national level. Migrants wish for more open borders, easier and faster naturalization procedures and a wider tolerance for dual citizenship (Bader, 2005b). Concomitantly, the EU institutions are interested in developing a more democratic European Union promoting citizens' participation.

These different perspectives can only be reconciled successfully if we approach national citizenship as an already transnationalized phenomenon (Bauböck, 2010). Every immigrant in a receiving state is at the same time an emigrant from a sending state, which implies

1

that sending and receiving state citizenships are two sides of the same coin. As a consequence, migrants usually maintain links with a sending and a receiving state and strive to remain attached to both national publics (Koslowski, 2005). States and EU institutions aimed at strengthening democracy and participation at the national and the EU level need to acknowledge that for migrants, and especially for the first generation, there is a trade-off between naturalizing in a state of residence and losing citizen status in a state of origin. The first generation is usually still emotionally, politically or economically attached to the country of origin and therefore remains reluctant to give up citizenship of the sending state – if that is the price of naturalizing in the state of residence (Bader, 2005a). Therefore, in the European Union, both emigrant and immigrant sides of citizenship need to be taken into consideration (Koslowski, 2000).

This book sheds more light on the processes that have transformed national citizenship of the European Union's member states and explains the legislative changes that have taken place in these states. National citizenship in a migratory world is still 'the last bastion of states' sovereignty' (Brubaker, 1992), meaning that the EU institutions cannot exercise any direct influence on national citizenship legislation in the EU member states. On the other hand, the process of political integration in the EU, international human rights development and globalization are claimed to have indirectly challenged states' exclusive competences in that legal area (Soysal, 1994; Liebert, 2004; Isin and Turner, 2007; Lavanex, 2007; Liebert, 2007; Kuisma, 2008). As a consequence of these processes a number of questions arise: what kind of national citizenship has developed in the member states of the European Union? Which principles have informed it? Which factors have triggered the legislative reforms?

Citizenship: definition of the research subject

In this book, if not stated otherwise, I refer to 'citizenship law' as a set of legal normative rules regulating entitlement to citizenship, including dual and quasi-citizenship as well as the loss of citizenship.

In general terms, citizenship consists of a formal relationship between an individual and a state and is usually associated with specific rights and duties. The concept of citizenship has been analysed in many dimensions: narrowly, as a legal status (Brubaker, 1992;

Bauböck *et al.*, 2006) and widely, as a set of rights (Marshall, 1949) and as a 'practiced individual's engagement' (Barry, 2006). Defined narrowly, citizenship concerns the legal relation between an individual and a state, enshrined in domestic law. It is formal and official and 'its formalization and codification are themselves social phenomena, with sociologically interesting effects' (Brubaker, 1992). On the other hand, citizenship can also be defined as a set of civil, political and social rights that have come to be associated with citizenship in a historical process. Defined in ideational terms, citizenship serves as a foundation for the way people think about themselves as members of a given political community. In that respect, an ideational dimension of citizenship very often overlaps with the notion of nationality.

This book adopts a narrow definition of citizenship. It takes a top-down perspective in order to establish *whether* and *how* citizenship legislation and policies evolve, and what were the motivations and goals of policymakers when drafting citizenship laws in their countries. For the purpose of this research, citizenship shall be defined as *a legal status that binds a person to a particular state under the provisions of domestic law, regulated by specific legal norms concerning acquisition and loss of this status.*

Distinguishing between both terms, that is, nationality and citizenship, is important not only for conceptual but also for normative reasons. In some languages nationality is an ambiguous term denoting membership in an ethnocultural community or national citizenship (Bauböck, 2005c). The concept of nationality is also used to distinguish multinational from single-nation states. Citizenship, on the other hand, refers to a legal link between an individual and a sovereign state, which can also become a significant component of an individual's identity. However, it needs to be acknowledged that in some languages, such as German or Polish, the terms 'nationality' and 'citizenship' are used as equivalents.

Citizenship conceptualized as a legal status of a person is a thicker concept than nationality because it can embrace various types of communities. For instance, in multinational states such as Canada, holders of national citizenship are at the same time members of different national groups. It is important to acknowledge that *not all* nations have established states and *not all* states are composed of one nation only. On the other hand, citizenship is a narrower concept than nationality due to the fact that it is associated with a self-governing community. Autocratic regimes that do not have the institutions of popular government do not fulfil that condition. Their citizens do not enjoy the basic citizens' right of self-government, and hence they constitute citizens only in a very limited sense (Bauböck, 2005c).

Normative dimension of citizenship

Citizenship is a 'Janus-faced' phenomenon evoking both inclusionary and exclusionary practices that specify the terms of membership in a given state (Lister, 2003; Benhabib, 2004; Calder *et al.*, 2010). In doing so, citizenship establishes clear rules that define who obtains and loses the status of a citizen and under what conditions. With respect to citizens, citizenship not only grants rights but also constrains their powers in two different ways (Perczyński and Vink, 2002). At the individual level, citizenship imposes duties and obligations towards the state and the community. At the societal level, citizenship manifests both an inclusionary and an exclusionary nature. These two mechanisms have become the source of a major tension between the conceptions of democracy and citizenship. For instance, Greek democracy introduced a very narrow and exclusive conception of who could become a citizen, while entirely excluding migrants, women and slaves. On the other hand, modern democracies seek to establish more egalitarian criteria for citizenship acquisition and loss. Although the principle of *jus sanguinis* continues to play a role, liberal states have made it possible for non-nationals to naturalize on the *jus soli* basis, which clearly distinguishes these states from their ancient Greek predecessor. As a result, the definition of citizenship depends strongly on how democracy is conceptualized.

The definition of a liberal state adopted in this book draws mostly on the approaches of Joseph Carens (1992) and Ruth Rubio-Marin (2000, 2006), who argued that 'states claiming to be committed to liberal democracy ought to regard as full members of their organized political community all those who reside in their territory as permanent residents' (Rubio-Marin, 2000, p. 20). A system is a liberal democracy not only when its procedures and principles are democratic but, first and foremost, when it is democratic towards everyone who is subject to its rules. For example, in the view of many theories of democracy, state X can, in fact, be democratic if it has democratic institutions but its national citizenship is acquired only on the *jus sanguinis* basis. This state would continue to be regarded as democratic even though its law did not allow immigrants to naturalize. However, the theory of liberal democracy introduced more demanding criteria (Kymlicka and Norman, 1994; Kymlicka, 1995). Its fundamental assumption is that individual liberty is maximized when all permanent residents in a state, being subject to its rules, are considered equal, regardless of their cultural or ethnic background (Chwaszcza, 2009). From that perspective, those who bear the burdens (for instance, taxation) in their state of residence should also be entitled to the rights and benefits that the status of citizenship offers (Dahl, 1989). Forbidding these rights in the name of protecting a homogeneous ethnic or cultural identity in a state is in conflict with liberal principles.

What kind of citizenship does liberal democracy envisage? Joppke and Morawska (2003) have identified three basic indicators for liberal citizenship: first, resurgence of the territorial, *jus soli* citizenship; second, increasing toleration for dual citizenship in receiving states (in sending states dual citizenship is an indicator for ethnicization; see also Kovacs, 2006; Górny and Koryś, 2007); and, third, *de facto* multiculturalism, which means that 'to be a member in a state no longer connotes membership in a particular cultural or political community. The only culture that citizens share is a political culture of liberalism itself' (Joppke and Morawska, 2003, p. 19).

The republican approach differs from liberalism by acknowledging the right of a self-governing community to introduce various naturalization requirements, mostly of a socio-political nature. This is due to the fact that membership in a community constitutes a special value for republicans (Honohan, 2010). Hence members of a community are entitled to make sure that the new citizens will become active members. A good example to show the difference between liberalism and republicanism is a language test (Shorten, 2010). According to Carens, asking for a certain degree of cultural assimilation is problematic, though not impermissible. As Carens argued, hegemony of one language in most of the states is neither a good nor a bad thing (Carens, 2000). On the one hand, this fact does not preclude provision of some services in the immigrants' language, for instance, educational or medical services. Therefore, it is justifiable for republicans, like Rubio-Marin (2000), to support and encourage immigrants to learn the language of the national majority so that the immigrants increase their possibilities of having access to various economic, social, cultural and political opportunities.

Rubio-Marin takes Carens' argument further, claiming that naturalization of immigrants *could* actually be conditioned on some degree of knowledge of the official language. First, given the fact that in most countries there is one language used in the public sphere, mastering that language is a necessary condition for immigrants to become conscious participants of political and social life in that country. Second, even if an immigrant decided not to engage in political life, she would feel alienated on a daily basis without at least a basic knowledge of the language. As a consequence, the difference between the positions of Carens and Rubio-Marin is that Carens emphasized equality of rights and opportunities for immigrants, which very often are conditioned by the knowledge of the language, while Rubio-Marin prioritized participation or 'active citizenship'. However, both argue in favour of non-conditional and automatic naturalization.

Citizenship as an empirical research subject

Empirically, citizenship can be researched in two different ways: first, in a top-down perspective, focusing on how and why policymakers tailor citizenship in a specific way; second, in a bottom-up perspective, investigating the meaning individuals assign to citizenship. The latter approach is therefore more concerned with individuals' perception of citizenship practice, analysing, for instance, individuals' reasons to naturalize in a receiving state.

The top-down approach explains the legal and policy changes concerning national citizenship. It focuses on institutions in order to establish either meaningful regularities in the area of national citizenship laws in different states or the incentives of politicians, lawyers and policymakers. Scholars researching citizenship from that perspective tend to define citizenship narrowly, as a legal bond between an individual and a state regulated by national legislation. This is because the top-down process of policy and law-making focuses on one dimension of citizenship: its acquisition and loss.

Within that approach citizenship can be also researched in a historical perspective. This stream of research draws on the by now classical thesis by T. H. Marshall (1949), who argued that citizenship provides an individual with three types of rights: civil, social and political. Civil rights concern, for instance, negative rights, such as protection against the abuse of power by governments, or freedom of speech. Social rights comprise entitlement to social services, such as education, a free health system or a pension. Finally, political rights concern a right to vote and to be elected. Marshall argued that in England the development of citizenship rights was sequential: first, the civil rights were developed, then the political and finally the social rights. According to Marshall, the development of citizenship rights was a functional process. The critics of Marshall's theory usually pointed to the Anglocentrism and evolutionism of his theory (Mann, 1987). According to Michael Mann (1987), the sequential development of rights as envisaged by Marshall could not be observed in any state other than the United Kingdom.

Objectives of this study

In the last few years the comparative literature on national citizenship has devoted a lot of attention to the issue of liberal convergence of national citizenship laws in Europe and worldwide, assuming that national citizenship legislation is becoming not only more similar (convergent) but also more liberal (Hansen and Weil, 2001; Weil, 2001; Howard, 2005). National citizenship legislation regulating entitlement to and loss of citizenship is a 'hard case' for studying convergence due to the fact that the sovereign states exercise an almost unconditional right to define the terms of membership in their polities. In other words, there is no authority higher than a state itself to decide on its national citizenship law. The European institutions, such as the European Commission or the Council of Europe, can only exercise a very limited influence over national legal provisions on entitlement to citizenship (see Chapter 6).

However, in the contemporary literature on the subject there is no agreement that liberal convergence has occurred. Moreover, those scholars who have identified liberal convergence in national citizenship legislation have attributed it to very different factors, for instance, to the impact of international human rights (Soysal, 1994; Faist, 2007) or the absence of radical right-wing parties (Howard, 2005). On the other hand, most recent comparative studies are more sceptical and argue that (liberal) convergence is very limited or has not taken place at all (Bauböck *et al.*, 2006). The findings in this book suggest that, although legislation regulating entitlement to citizenship of the European states became more similar (convergent) in many aspects, liberal convergence did not take place.

This book aspires to contribute to the debate by establishing the direction of legal changes in selected case studies (Germany, Hungary and Poland), and, moreover, by identifying the factors and mechanisms that explain the reforms of national legislation. This book does not cover in equal depth national citizenship legislation in all the European Union's member states. The analysis is limited to the three aforementioned states, but the book also makes references to further European countries. However, the major aspiration of this book is to use the in-depth analysis of legislative reforms introduced in the three states under study in order to verify and identify new mechanisms responsible for legislative convergence and divergence. These mechanisms can later be tested on a broader set of countries. The period of investigation covers approximately 20 years (1985–2007), during which time national citizenship legislation in the selected states has undergone very significant changes. The research questions posed by this study are:

1. What kind of tendency (convergence, divergence) can we observe if we compare national citizenship legislation in Germany, Hungary and Poland in the period 1985–2007?
2. How can we explain the legislative reforms in these states?

Liberal convergence means that the legislation of different states approaches a common, predefined standard, for instance, 'liberal citizenship'. That development can also take place in an opposite direction when the legislation of the states under study becomes illiberal. Convergence, on the other hand, implies narrowing of differences between policies or laws over time. In that case legislation of the states under study becomes similar, but the direction of change varies in these states. It means that some states reach common standards in the course of, for instance, liberalizing reforms, while other states arrive at the same *status quo* after introducing de-liberalizing reforms.

In the comparative citizenship literature there are four major approaches to comparatively explaining convergence and divergence of national citizenship legislation (see Table 1.1). This section presents

Table 1.1 Popular approaches comparatively explaining convergence and divergence of national citizenship legislation

Explanatory factor	Author(s)	Expectation
Divergence		
Different nationhood conceptions	Brubaker (1992)	National citizenship legislation in D, HU and PL should remain ethnic due to shifted borders' experience and large kin minorities abroad.
Post-war migration experience	Weil (2001)	Germany as a receiving state should be oriented on immigrants' inclusion, whilst Hungary and Poland, as sending states, should be oriented on external Diaspora's inclusion.
Convergence		
Top-down Europeanization	Checkel (1999, 2001), Vink (2001, 2002)	Europeanization of the national legislation in Germany should be stronger than in Hungary and Poland, due to the fact that Germany was longer exposed to the EU norms and standards.
Parallel path-dependencies	Hansen and Weil (2001)	Convergence is caused by domestic factors only, no horizontal observation or coordination between the states under study.

Source: Own compilation.

them in a rather compact way, but a detailed analysis can be found in Chapter 2 of this book. According to the first approach (Brubaker, 1992), national citizenship legislation diverges due to different conceptions of nationhood; that is, states with an ethnic conception of nationhood, such as Germany, have an ethnic citizenship legislation, while states with a civic conception of nationhood, for instance France, also have a civic citizenship legislation. According to Brubaker, conception of nationhood and citizenship legislation are closely linked to each other, and therefore states with different conceptions of nationhood will not develop a similar citizenship legislation.

Brubaker's theory was challenged from two different angles. First, referring frequently to the German case, it was demonstrated that conception of nationhood is not the major factor informing citizenship legislation (Joppke and Morawska, 2003; Faist, 2007). Germany, despite having a long history of ethnic conception of nationhood, de-ethnicized its national citizenship legislation in the late 1990s. Second, as other scholars pointed out (Kemp, 2002; Liebich, 2007), ethnic citizenship legislation does not need to be brought about by the ethnic conception of nationhood as such. Rather, as the example of the post-communist Central European states demonstrates, ethnic citizenship legislation can be introduced with the aim of compensating nationals who find themselves abroad due to shifting borders or political persecution. Kinship politics was forbidden in the Soviet bloc, hence, for the newly established democratic elites it was a moral obligation to redress the past wrongs (Liebich, 2007):

> A peculiarity of the new EU states is that citizenship laws and related provisions are formulated with the intention of redressing past wrongs. The compensatory or restitutional function – Wiedergutmachung – is particularly strong with respect to the recent communist past, though it extends to earlier periods as well. (Liebich, 2007, p. 15)

In the light of Brubaker's theory it can be expected that Germany, Hungary and Poland, as states with long traditions of the ethnic conception of nationhood, will also have ethnic citizenship legislation. In the process of nation-building that took place in the nineteenth century, these states developed an ethnic understanding of national identity (Kohn, 1944; Gellner, 1993; Brubaker, 1996). This means that the collective identity in these states was defined by culture, language and in some respects also religion (mostly in Poland). The experience of shifting borders in the twentieth century,[1] leaving large numbers of nationals outside the state territory, is believed to have strengthened the ethnic understanding of nationhood in these three states. This case selection aims to demonstrate that conception of nationhood fails to explain divergence of national citizenship legislation. Contrary to expectations, the analysis conducted in this book shows that national citizenship legislation in the analysed kin-states ceased to be informed by the ethnic conception of nationhood. Rather, the factor that fosters ethnicization of the legislation is a willingness to address and compensate past wrongs.

The second popular approach attributes divergence to the post-war migration experience (Joppke, 2001; Weil, 2001). Migration is said to have an impact on the national citizenship legislation when a legal tradition is perceived to fulfil the interests of the state in terms of migration.[2] As a consequence, receiving states tend to be concerned with immigrants' inclusion, for instance, by liberalizing naturalization requirements. On the other hand, sending states strive to maintain links with their external Diasporas, quite often fostering the possession of dual citizenship in that group.

Germany is traditionally classified as a receiving state, and Hungary and Poland as sending states. As a consequence, German legislation should be concerned with immigrants' inclusion and integration, while the Polish and Hungarian legislations should be focused, first and foremost, on maintaining links with the emigrants (external Diasporas) abroad. The analysis conducted in this book illustrates that migration pattern is indeed the second factor explaining divergence of national citizenship legislation in Germany, Hungary and Poland.

The two popular approaches explaining convergence of national citizenship legislation point towards external (top-down Europeanization) and domestic factors (parallel path-dependencies). According to the first approach (Checkel, 1999, 2001a, b; Vink, 2001, 2002), convergence of national citizenship legislation is expected to be caused by the top-down impact of the European institutions. The second approach attributes convergence exclusively to domestic factors. As Hansen and Weil argued (2001), it is domestic politics that has a decisive impact on national citizenship legislation. According to the authors, national citizenship legislation in Western European states has undergone a process not just of convergence, but of liberal convergence. In their view, that process was an effect of the Western European states' response to a common challenge: a need to integrate the long-term residents and the second generation of immigrants. The reforms in the Western European states were not coordinated or copied from the neighbours; rather, the reforms were conducted independently in each state as 'parallel path-dependencies'.

Scholars analysing vertical Europeanization of national citizenship expected that convergence of national citizenship legislation would be induced by an external factor influencing all the EU member states in the same way. They also assumed that, with the minor exception of the EU conditionality concerning some of the new EU member states, compliance with the legal standards promoted by the EU and the pan-European institutions (such as the Council of Europe) would be voluntary, given the fact that the EU has no formal competences in that area. Applying these assumptions to the selected cases, one would expect that Germany, having been exposed for a long time to the top-down impact of the European norms, would be more likely than Hungary and Poland to apply the EU norms voluntarily to national citizenship legislation. On the other hand, it might be expected that vertical Europeanization of national citizenship legislation in Hungary and Poland would be more prominent if conditionality came into play.

Nonetheless, the existing empirical research has not produced much evidence supporting the thesis that convergence of national citizenship legislation is induced by vertical Europeanization. Rather, as the most prominent scholars in that area concluded (Checkel, 1999, 2001a; Vink, 2001, 2002), there is *de facto* no vertical Europeanization of national citizenship legislation to be observed. This book confirms that thesis by demonstrating that vertical Europeanization was indeed very limited. However, contrary to that expectation, the new member states were voluntarily more oriented than Germany towards the norms promoted by the Council of Europe.[3]

The second approach attributes convergence exclusively to domestic factors. According to Hansen and Weil (2001), in reforming citizenship legislation national politicians are informed by the current trends in domestic politics and their own conception of the national or party interest. A liberal convergence of citizenship legislation across the Western European receiving states was caused, according to Hansen and Weil, by the fact that these states faced the same challenge, namely, large-scale immigration, and that they adopted similar legislative arrangements in order to respond to that challenge. However, as Hansen and Weil argued, the liberal convergence among these states was not caused by observation or copying of the legislation in the neighbouring states.

The 'parallel-path dependency' approach can be criticized for being too quick in heralding the liberal convergence of national citizenship legislation in Western European states. First, the scope of Hansen and Weil's analysis was too narrow[4] to draw conclusions referring to the whole of citizenship legislation in each state. Second, as one of the most recent studies showed (Bauböck *et al.*, 2007), there is no overall liberal convergence of national citizenship legislation. Rather, even within the legislation of one state, it is possible to observe several different tendencies. Therefore, if 'path-dependency' explained convergence, it would be expected that the tendencies in German, Hungarian and Polish domestic politics would be decisive for policy formation in these states, leading eventually to legislative convergence among them. However, this book demonstrates that, while national contemporary politics and political actors' interests played a role, though not the dominant role, they did not lead to liberal convergence. In fact, *liberal* convergence did not take place at all, but only convergence. Moreover, the empirical analysis conducted in this book demonstrates that convergence was mainly due to the horizontal observation of other states' legislative practices.

This book puts forward two hypotheses explaining divergence of national citizenship legislation and one hypothesis explaining convergence:

Divergence 1: redressing past wrongs
- *Divergence of national citizenship legislation is caused by legislative practices aiming to redress past wrongs.*

Divergence 2: post-war migration experience
- *Divergence of national citizenship legislation can be explained by migration experience: sending states are concerned with inclusion of external Diasporas, while receiving states are concerned with inclusion of immigrants (long-term permanent residents).*

Convergence: horizontal norm diffusion
- *Horizontal diffusion of international and EU norms leads to convergence of national citizenship legislation in the EU member states.*

In order to test these hypotheses, this book conducts a comparative analysis of national legislation regulating entitlement to national citizenship, loss of citizenship and special statuses (see Chapter 3 for more details), namely:

- Modes of citizenship acquisition at birth: *jus sanguinis* at birth, *jus soli* at birth

- Modes of citizenship acquisition after birth: residence-based citizenship acquisition, family-based transfers, socialization-based acquisitions, affinity-based
- National citizenship loss
- Statuses: dual citizenship and quasi-citizenship.

The empirical analysis addresses two questions:

1. What kind of legislative changes were introduced in the states under study in the time-period from the late 1980s to 2007?
2. How can we explain these changes?

In order to answer these two questions this book employs an eclectic methodological approach, comprising a comparative analysis of national legislation (1) and a comparative qualitative and quantitative discourse analysis of parliamentary debates (2). The aim of the comparative analysis of the legal provisions is to identify the major trends in the legislative reforms in Germany, Hungary and Poland. This analysis provides an answer to the first 'What' question. On the other hand, the comparative discourse analysis of the parliamentary plenary debates targets the 'Why' question by providing the reasons that lay behind the legislative changes. The parliamentary discourse analysis was conducted both qualitatively and quantitatively by using the 'Atlas.ti' software.

The comparative analysis of the legal provisions demonstrated that there is no overall tendency in the development of national citizenship legislation. It was established that legal convergence occurred only in the legislation regulating conditions for naturalization, family-based acquisition and the loss of citizenship. Legal divergence, on the other hand, occurred in the *jus soli* citizenship acquisition, ethnic preferences in citizenship policies and dual citizenship. The comparative parliamentary discourse analysis established that the major factor fostering legal convergence in the analysed states was a horizontal diffusion of norms, manifested by the observation and copying of other states' legislative practices (Chapter 3 presents in detail the approach of this study).

This book aims to contribute both to the comparative citizenship literature and to Europeanization studies. Although the core of the analysis conducted here is limited to the legislative citizenship reforms in Germany, Hungary and Poland, the book also refers to the relevant legislative trends in the whole group of the EU member states. Comparative citizenship studies have, until now, focused predominantly on the Western European states, while neglecting the new EU member states. Moreover, the scholarship analysing Europeanization of national citizenship has focused on the top-down processes of norm distribution, underestimating the importance of horizontal processes. This book aims to fill that gap. It compares the legislative reforms in a very specific and still under-researched group of states, namely, kin-states. A comparative analysis of the European kin-states' citizenship legislation can be considered an important contribution to citizenship studies. Second, it has been a common practice in the comparative citizenship literature to analyse the new and old EU member states' legislation separately. This book breaks with this tradition, assuming that certain mechanisms of legislative change characteristic of both the new and the old EU member states can be established by means of comparative analysis. Finally, this book also contributes to the Europeanization literature by providing new insights into horizontal processes of norm distribution.

Outline of the chapters

Chapter 1 introduces the subject of the study and the guiding research questions: (i) What kind of legislative changes were introduced in the states under study in the time-period from the late 1980s to 2007? (ii) How can we explain these changes? In this book national citizenship is defined narrowly as a legal status that binds a person to a particular state under the provisions of domestic law, regulated by specific legal norms concerning acquisition and loss of this status. This chapter introduces the dependent variable of the study, defined here as different modes of national citizenship acquisition and loss as well as statuses:

- Modes of citizenship acquisition at birth: *jus sanguinis* at birth, *jus soli* at birth
- Modes of citizenship acquisition after birth: residence-based citizenship acquisition, family-based transfers, socialization-based acquisitions, affinity-based

- National citizenship loss
- Statuses: dual citizenship and quasi-citizenship

The chapter also elaborates the hypotheses of this study: it is argued that convergence of national citizenship legislation can be explained by horizontal diffusion of international and EU norms, while divergence can be explained by (i) a need to redress past wrongs and (ii) sending or receiving states' migration experiences.

Chapter 2 presents selected contributions to the debate on the direction and causes of changes in national citizenship legislation in Europe and worldwide. The chapter is structured by three schools: historical institutionalism, rational choice institutionalism and sociological institutionalism. According to historical institutionalists (Brubaker, 1992), divergence can be explained by path-dependency: states with an ethnic conception of nationhood also have ethnic citizenship legislation. The rational choice-motivated studies[5] explained changes in citizenship legislation by distribution of power among political parties and their political interests. According to the most prominent scholar representing this approach (Joppke, 2001; Joppke and Morawska, 2003), the impact of international norms is usually overestimated. State actors act as gatekeepers who implement those international norms that correspond with their interests. The third strand, sociological institutionalism, explained legislative convergence and divergence by the impact of international human rights norms (Soysal, 1994) or top-down Europeanization (Checkel, 1999, 2001a; Vink, 2001). The last group of scholars noted that until now the vertical impact of the EU institutions has not been particularly successful in this policy-area.

Chapter 3 presents the comparative framework and methods of this study. The approach taken by this book combines legislative analysis with comparative qualitative and quantitative discourse analysis of the national parliamentary (plenary) debates. Drawing on the NATAC-project classification (Bauböck *et al.*, 2006), the dependent variable is operationalized as different modes of national citizenship acquisition and loss as well as statuses. The analysis of these modes is conducted separately for each state under study within the time frame 1985–2007. The findings are assessed on a two-dimensional scale measuring ethnicization–de-ethnicization and liberalization–de-liberalization of legislation. This part of the empirical analysis allows comparison of the development of citizenship legislation in the three states under study. The comparative exploration of plenary parliamentary debates devoted to national citizenship reforms allows both qualitative and quantitative analysis of the policy formation process. The discourse analysis was conducted using the Atlas.ti software. This book contributes to the existing literature with an in-depth (qualitative and quantitative) analysis of the legislative process and the parliamentary discourse accompanying it. This approach is original, for most existing studies are limited to an analysis of nationality laws and address citizenship policymaking only superficially, if at all. Furthermore, the book tests the hypotheses on the East–West divide in Europe.

Chapter 4 focuses on legislative reforms of national citizenship in Germany, Hungary and Poland. The comparative legislative analysis conducted in this chapter established two major trends. First, Hungarian and Polish legislation developed according to a similar pattern, but German legislation followed a different one. However, the common developments in Hungarian and Polish law did not lead to liberalization, but rather to de-liberalization and ethnicization. Second, the only case of legislative convergence concerned the laws regulating naturalization of immigrants. In that case, the laws in Hungary and Poland became more similar to those of Germany and other Western European states.

Chapter 5 presents findings from the discourse analysis of the parliamentary (plenary) debates on national citizenship law reforms in Germany, Hungary and Poland. Divergence, concerning *jus soli* at birth, cultural acquisitions, quasi and dual citizenship, was explained here by migration experience and communist heritage. Specifically, German legislation followed the pattern of a receiving state and concentrated on the inclusion of long-term immigrants. Hungarian and Polish legislation developed according to the pattern of a sending state, aiming to maintain links with the Diaspora. The ethnicization of Hungarian and Polish legislation had a compensatory function and was triggered by recent experience with communism.

Convergence, concerning residence and socialization-based acquisitions as well as family-transfers, was brought about by horizontal Europeanization of national citizenship legislation manifested by references to other states' legal practices. This finding challenges the state of the art in the literature. According to Hansen and Weil

(2001), legal convergence is an effect of 'parallel path-dependencies', not of learning from or copying other states' best practices in that area.

Chapter 6 closely examines the vertical and horizontal Europeanization of national citizenship laws in Germany, Hungary and Poland. The major mechanism of the European standards' diffusion in this area was established as horizontal, rather than vertical, Europeanization. As a result of horizontal Europeanization, national citizenship laws of the EU member states are becoming more similar, but not necessarily more liberal. Finally, the chapter demonstrates that Europeanization is also possible in policy-areas where the EU has no formal competences.

Chapter 7 summarizes the findings, draws conclusions on how far they can be generalized and about the limitations of the present analysis, and presents open questions and suggestions for future research.

2
Comparative Citizenship Research: Competing Accounts Explaining Convergence and Divergence

Three schools of comparative citizenship research

The empirical research on national citizenship can be classified according to the three stances of institutionalism theory (Hall and Taylor, 1996; Schmidt and Radaelli, 2004; Schmidt, 2005): historical institutionalism (Brubaker, Favell, Weil, Faist and Howard), rational choice-inspired institutionalism[1] (Joppke) and sociological institutionalism (Soysal, Checkel, Vink and Lavanex). Historical institutionalism explains the outcomes by the historical origins of institutions or the logic of 'path-dependence'. Historical institutionalism stresses the importance of sequencing, unintended consequences and contextuality of interests. That approach has been criticized mostly for being historically deterministic, tending to emphasize structures and processes but ignoring actors, or particular single events, which also trigger a change.

Rational choice institutionalism assumes that actors have fixed preferences and that their actions are oriented towards maximizing their utility. Rational choice institutionalism has been criticized for being static; that is, by assuming fixed and rationally defined preferences it is difficult to account for policy change or explain why institutions or actors change over time.

Sociological institutionalism perceives political institutions as socially constructed and culturally framed. Cultural institutions define preferences and identities of actors who act according to the 'logic of appropriateness'. In these respects sociological institutionalism contradicts the rational choice theory, because it assumes that norms and identities constituting interests are embedded in culture and not, as rational choice scholars argue, exogenous to culture. Cultural institutionalism has been criticized for being unable to provide parsimonious findings that could be generalized over a larger number of cases. Furthermore, like other approaches within institutionalism, it has also been accused of determinism; cultural in that case.

The next sections of this chapter will present these three approaches in more detail. Most of the contributions presented in this chapter are considered particularly important due to their impact on comparative citizenship studies (Brubaker, 1992; Checkel, 1999; Aleinikoff and Klusmeyer, 2000, 2001). The chapter begins by presenting the historical institutionalist approach (Brubaker, 1992; Aleinikoff and Klusmeyer, 2000; Favell, 2001; Weil, 2001; Howard, 2006; Faist, 2007), then the rational choice (Joppke and Morawska, 2003; Howard, 2006) and the sociological institutionalism (Soysal, 1994; Checkel, 1999, 2001a; Vink, 2001).

Historical institutionalism

Comparative citizenship research has its roots in historical institutionalism, which is still a very popular approach in this discipline. Scholars working in this tradition point to the importance of 'path-dependency', defined as adherence to a specific nationhood tradition, emigration or immigration heritage, or experience with democracy (Janoski, 2009).

The modern debate in citizenship studies was triggered in the early 1990s (1992) by Rogers Brubaker. In the book *Citizenship and Nationhood in France and Germany* Brubaker argued that divergence in citizenship regimes can be explained by cultural conceptions of nationhood. Brubaker demonstrated that there is a correlation between the conception of nationhood in a given state and its citizenship legislation. According to Brubaker, the German conception of nationhood is defined by blood-ties (*jus sanguinis* principle), which is also reflected in German citizenship legislation, which excludes foreigners who do not have the German blood-ties but who could nevertheless have been born and raised on German territory. On the other hand, German law grants ethnic Germans born outside the territory of the state a privileged access to German citizenship. In France the conception of nationhood is defined by the territoriality principle (*jus soli*). As a consequence, the rules concerning acquisition and loss of national citizenship favour those who were born on French territory, whether or not they have French blood-ties.

Brubaker's contribution certainly enjoys a 'first-mover' advantage: the empirical studies that followed his publication would always refer to his thesis, whether the authors agreed with it or not. However, since the mid-1990s the link between conception of nationhood, on the one hand, and national citizenship legislation, on the other, has become significantly weaker in many states, with Germany being the best example (Joppke, 1999; Checkel, 2001a; Joppke and Morawska, 2003). If national citizenship reforms ceased to be informed predominantly by national identities (or, using Brubaker's terminology, a conception of nationhood), which factor(s) explain the change?

Rival hypotheses were also suggested within historical institutionalism. According to Favell (2001), these are not cultural concepts of nationhood but, rather, different 'dominant public philosophies' that inform policymaking in each state. A 'public philosophy' was defined as a common, general vision of a state, including institutionalized relations among actors. 'In each country' – Favell argues – 'there was a need to resolve a large national consensus that reconciled an acceptable "new" vision of the contemporary society with the culture, traditions and myths of an "old" nation' (2001, p. 246). In France the consensus was based on republicanism, which implied an ethnically and religiously neutral definition of the public sphere. In Great Britain it was the idea of multiculturalism that served the same purpose.

The role of a perennial concept of nationhood, so prominent in Brubaker's writing, is only symbolic for Favell. He argued that the British and French 'public philosophies' were challenged by large-scale migration. The 'public philosophies' could no longer be changed in such a way as to incorporate the migrants' perception of the public sphere. According to Favell, pressure from EU institutions and international organizations could not be successful, due to the low legitimacy of these institutions: 'But however rational European propositions are, there is also an enormous shortfall in legitimacy at this level. No attempt has been made to fashion a concerted vision that might be able to build a *European* public consensus on minority and migration questions' (Favell, 2001, p. 249). According to Favell, the prevalence of 'path-dependency' prevents implementation of international human rights standards: 'it is the power of path-dependency that blocks internal adaptation [of international norms] and responsiveness to these problems' (2001, p. 241). Nonetheless, Favell's argument raises an important concern. Namely, it is problematic to demonstrate empirically how highly abstract concepts such as 'public philosophy' inform legal or policy change; finding sound empirical indicators for such concepts remains very challenging.

For the same reason Aleinikoff and Klusmeyer (2001) rejected abstract, theoretical concepts as explanatory factors. They argued that: 'Choices among citizenship rules are usually shaped more by historical experience, existing cultural norms, and expedient political calculations than by deduction from abstract principle or compelling reasons of legal consistency' (2001, p. 2). In their comparative study they examined the interplay between the domestic setting and the international norms. Having analysed three different groups of states, that is: (i) immigration states (United States, Australia), (ii) emerging states (Baltic States) and (iii) traditional, ethnic states (Japan and Israel), Aleinikoff and Klusmeyer demonstrated that a specific type of statehood and prior experience with migration are decisive in shaping national citizenship policy.

In the same volume, Weil established that national citizenship legislation of the analysed 25 industrialized, liberal–democratic states became similar in many aspects despite different national legal traditions (2001). Weil identified three factors leading to legislative convergence: (i) influence of democratic values, (ii) stability of borders and (iii) experience with immigration. Weil's findings not only contributed to the debate on convergence of citizenship legislation in Europe but also challenged Brubaker's thesis by demonstrating the lack of causal link between conception of nationhood and citizenship legislation. According to Weil, 'Each state's law is simultaneously influenced by its judicial traditions, nation-state building, examples from abroad, and the role played by migration (emigration and immigration) or the presence of minorities. Divergence between the nationality laws of different countries has sometimes been presented as reflecting varying essential or dominant conceptions of the nation (Brubaker, 1992) which they are not' (Weil, 2001,

p. 18). Rather, the differences and similarities between the citizenship legislations of particular states can be eventually explained by two factors: (i) legal path-dependency and (ii) long-term migration experience (emigration or immigration).

In the same volume, Christian Joppke recognized legal path-dependency as a factor explaining differences and similarities in national citizenship legislation (2001). Drawing on the German case, Joppke argued that, since the end of World War II, the national judiciary has played an important role in resolving public controversies and in safeguarding citizens' and minorities' rights. The German 'constitutional patriotism' is a strong example of this tendency. For that reason the liberalization of citizenship legislation in post-war Germany can be explained by the trends established by the national judiciary.[2]

In the book *Towards a European Nationality: Citizenship, Immigration and Nationality Law in the EU*, Hansen and Weil (2001) examined further the process of convergence in national citizenship legislation. The book compares selected aspects of national citizenship legislation in the old EU-15 member states and establishes that in some areas, for instance naturalization requirements, the legislation of the states under study became not only similar but also more liberal. According to the authors, Western European states liberalized their laws in order to include the second generation of immigrants, already born and raised on their territories. The process of liberal convergence was, therefore, an effect of Western European states' response to a common challenge: integration of long-term immigrants. The second factor fostering liberal convergence was the modern conception of liberal democracy. According to Hansen and Weil, it provided the Western European states with normative justification for introduction of legislative reforms. The introduction of the reforms was not internationally coordinated; rather, the legislatures or executives in the analysed states introduced the liberalizing reforms independently of each other. Hansen and Weil (2001) named this process 'parallel path-dependencies' in order to stress the fact that no copying or learning from the best practices took place among the analysed Western European states. This book challenges Hansen's and Weil's argument; on the one hand, it confirms the thesis that migration experience has an impact on national citizenship legislation; on the other, it demonstrates that the legal reforms were not fostered by parallel path-dependencies but, rather, by mutual observation of the states and learning from their practices.[3]

The comparative study by Marc Morje Howard (2006) explains liberal convergence of citizenship legislation in the Western European EU member states by a combination of long and short-term factors. According to Howard, the variation in citizenship legislation of the Western European states can be explained by two long-term factors: (i) prior experience as a colonial power and (ii) whether or not a state became a democracy in the nineteenth century. In his view, ex-colonial powers and early democratizers were most likely to establish an inclusive model of national citizenship based on civic, rather than ethnic, ties. Furthermore, ex-colonial powers usually do not have difficulties with the integration of immigrants into their societies. As a consequence, the study demonstrates that early democratizers and ex-colonial powers, namely, the United Kingdom, Ireland, France and Belgium, have developed the most liberal citizenship regimes.

According to Howard, these two variables explain the 'starting point' or a long-term tendency. But how do we account for the fact that some liberal states continue to liberalize their citizenship legislation while others make it more restrictive? Howard argues that the modifying factor explaining this phenomenon is radical right-wing parties' mobilization on citizenship and immigration policy (Howard, 2010). Radical right-wing parties constitute powerful veto-players; therefore, a liberal or left-wing government is very often unable to introduce liberalizing reforms. Paradoxically, in the countries where the radical right is strong, national citizenship legislation can be liberalized if a government *does not* initiate a public debate on that issue. As Howard argued: 'this brings us to a larger paradox, if not a serious normative problem: in terms of issues dealing with immigration and citizenship, a non-democratic, elite-driven process may lead to more liberal outcomes, whereas a genuine popular involvement can result in more restrictive laws and institutions. [...] The great challenge, particularly in the EU, will be for elites to surmount the much-criticized "democratic deficit", while avoiding the trap of populism' (2006, p. 451).

The selection of explanatory variables in Howard's study can raise some objections. First, it is not a rule that early democracies are more consolidated than post-World War II democracies, Greece being an example here. Although Greece had already established a democratic regime in the mid-nineteenth century, it collapsed entirely during the autocratic Junta regime after World War II. Germany, on the other hand, was a totalitarian state before World War II, but nowadays it is one of the most stable and consolidated democracies in Europe. Second, hypotheses about long-term causal effects are in general very hard to verify because there are many other proximate causes that have also had an impact on the outcome.

Another study by the same author (Howard, 2005), presenting a comparison of citizenship legislation in the EU-25, confirmed the hypothesis that there is no overall liberal convergence of national citizenship legislation in the EU member states. In the light of Howard's findings, there are varying national traditions that prevent legal convergence. A 'citizenship policy index', examining long-term development in the analysed states, was based on three components: (i) whether or not a state grants *jus soli* at birth to children of non-citizens, (ii) the difficulty of naturalization requirements, in particular the mandatory length of residency, and (iii) whether or not a state allows naturalized immigrants to hold dual citizenship. Arithmetical quantification of the findings allowed the states to be clustered into three categories: restrictive, medium and liberal states. Austria has been classified as a state with a restrictive citizenship legislation, Italy and Germany as medium, and the United Kingdom and the Netherlands as liberal states. States where the citizenship legislation had been liberalized within the last 20 years were: Germany, Italy, Luxembourg, Finland, Sweden and the Netherlands. Other old EU member states liberalized their citizenship legislature only very minimally, if at all.

Regarding the new EU member states, only Lithuania and Slovenia were classified as restrictive states, while all the other new EU member states were clustered into the 'medium' group. Interestingly, Estonia and Latvia, which exclude more than a quarter of their residents from national citizenship,[4] were not classified as 'restrictive states'. That classification contradicts the existing Organisation for Security and Co-operation in Europe's (OSCE) or the Commission's reports on these states[5] but also shows the importance of the selection of significant indicators. If indicators fail to measure the analysed phenomenon, the results are also automatically questionable. In the most recent publication (2009) Howard corrected the components of the Citizenship Policy Index (CPI). He specified that only dual citizenship for immigrants is an indicator of liberalization in the new EU member states. In previous publications Howard did not differentiate between dual citizenship for immigrants and emigrants, which eventually led to incorrect classification of the new EU member states. As other empirical studies have already demonstrated (for instance NATAC 2), the new EU member states usually allow emigrants, but not immigrants, to possess dual citizenship in order to maintain links with the external diasporas. According to the recent studies (Kovacs, 2006; Górny and Koryś, 2007; Howard, 2009) this practice makes national citizenship legislation more ethnic but not more liberal.

Finally, the last study representing the path-dependency approach discussed in this sub-chapter concerns what has been until now the most substantial contribution to comparative citizenship studies (Bauböck *et al.*, 2007). The book was based on the NATAC project (Bauböck *et al.*, 2006), which operationalized all the possible modes of national citizenship acquisition and loss, allowing a very systematic analysis to be conducted of the legal changes introduced over the last two decades in the old and new EU member states. The goal of the NATAC 1 project was to map systematically the legislative changes introduced in the old EU member states. NATAC 2, on the other hand, contributed to the field with both a presentation and an interpretation of the legal reforms introduced since the late 1980s in the new EU member states. The direction of the legal reforms introduced in the new EU member states was explained by the path-dependency mechanism, and more precisely by the type of statehood 'inherited' after the fall of communism. The authors identified four different types of statehood formations among the new EU member states: restored states (Baltic States), states with histories of shifted borders (Hungary and Poland), post-partition states (Czech Republic, Slovakia and Slovenia) and Mediterranean post-imperial states (Malta, Cyprus). For instance, the Baltic States claimed continuity with the statehood formation preceding the Soviet incorporation. For that reason national citizenship was granted only to persons born in the Baltic States, as well as their offspring, before the annexation to the Soviet Union. The ethnic Russians who arrived in the Baltic States during the Soviet times were excluded from national citizenship.[6] Similarly, in all the other groups a specific type of statehood formation was also reflected in the national citizenship legislation.

As this sub-chapter demonstrates, citizenship research embedded in the historical institutionalist tradition contributed very extensively to the field. The selection of explanatory variables within that approach is quite broad; however, all of the explanatory factors traditionally point towards some sort of institutional 'path-dependency'. This account is, on the one hand, very parsimonious; on the other hand, it can be limiting, since the recent reforms of national citizenship legislations cannot always be explained by the long-term variables.

Eclectic approaches drawing on rational choice institutionalism

Rational choice institutionalism is underrepresented in national citizenship studies. Relatively few scholars have explained the outcomes of national citizenship reforms with models drawing on actors' fixed preferences and utility maximization. In most cases, these are rather eclectic explanatory models incorporating some rational choice assumptions or hypotheses explaining actors' preference formation (Joppke, 2001; Ette, 2003; Joppke and Morawska, 2003; Joppke, 2005a, b). The most prominent scholar representing this eclectic approach is Christian Joppke.

Christian Joppke (2001; Joppke and Morawska, 2003) argued that scholars analysing the impact of international norms on national citizenship laws of the EU member states (i.e., Jasemin Soysal) usually disregard the role of state actors in the process. This is a mistake, in his view, because state actors act as gatekeepers who constantly regulate the adoption of external norms and condition it on their partisan interest. In other words, nation states adopt as many international norms as is in the interest of the state actors. A distribution of power among political parties, and the interests of a parliamentarian majority, is often the explanatory factor for policy change.

Joppke claimed that, given the special role that state actors play in the process of policy change, both extreme positions in citizenship literature, represented by Rogers Brubaker and Jasemin Soysal, are mistaken. According to Joppke, Brubaker was wrong because national citizenship policies change according to political parties' preferences. Hence, there is not always a path-dependent process to be observed. Joppke also disagreed with Soysal, claiming that the impact of international norms is dependent on state actors' interests and their preferences at a given moment. In his view state actors would act irrationally, willing to give up their control over national citizenship, which is 'a last bastion of state's sovereignty'.

This stream of research has been more successful than historical institutionalism in providing an explanation for the short-term reforms of national citizenship legislation. Scholars such as Joppke have demonstrated that political actors, not just institutions, also have a decisive impact on national citizenship legislation. On the other hand, the assumption that actors act as informed by their preferences proved to be very deterministic; as sociological institutionalism has demonstrated, domestic actors' preferences do not explain each and every reform of national citizenship.

Sociological institutionalism

Sociological institutionalism unites diverse approaches in national citizenship studies. On the one hand there is a universalistic approach, and on the other a constructivist research on Europeanization and EU-ization of national citizenship. These approaches are united by acknowledging the mechanisms of 'social learning' and 'logic of appropriateness' but differ with respect to factors triggering policy change (March and Olsen, 2004; Hay, 2006). Namely, for universalists the major explanatory factor is the impact of international norms, while for constructivists it is the EU norms. This sub-chapter presents first the studies representing the universalistic approach.

In the book *Limits of Citizenship: Migrants and Postnational Membership in Europe*, Jasemin Soysal argued that international human rights have acquired the role that national citizenship used to have; namely, they grant and protect individuals' rights (1994). Having compared different ways in which European states incorporate immigrants, Soysal claimed that liberalization of the law takes place due to the discourse on human rights. According to Soysal, the rights that non-citizen immigrants enjoy are not much different from citizens' rights. In her view, this is due to the fact that nation states have become nothing more than instruments responsible for implementing international human rights conventions and norms. She argued that the model of citizenship emerging from that discourse is strongly post-national and transnational: 'my analysis of the incorporation of guest workers in Europe reveals a shift in the major organizing principle of membership in contemporary policies:

the logic of personhood supersedes the logic of national citizenship. This trend is informed by a dialectical tension between national citizenship and the universal human rights. Individual rights and obligations, which were historically located in the nation-state, have increasingly moved to a universalistic plane, transcending the boundaries of particular nation-states' (Soysal, 1994, p. 164).

The criticism that Soysal's thesis received was twofold (Joppke, 1999, 2001). It has been noted, first of all, that international human rights are not really external to the nation states. The global space is rather abstract, and hence human rights cannot be attributed to a particular agency. Many of these norms also gave foundations to the political systems of liberal democracies. From that perspective, nation states cannot be perceived solely as 'enemies' of human rights. On the contrary, historically they have contributed to their development.

Second, as long as migration pressure does indeed influence national citizenship laws and policies, the role of state actors cannot be disregarded. Citizenship is an important aspect of state sovereignty, and therefore states will continue to participate in the process of national citizenship development, simultaneously liberalizing it and constraining its openness. In empirical research it is, therefore, crucial to acknowledge the sources of influence and the motives that go with it. For instance, liberalization of citizenship can indeed weaken the role of nation states. Similarly, convergence along international standards can also take place due to rational, interests-based or vote-seeking motivations of political actors. Furthermore, international human rights can be used strategically by political actors in order to enhance their position, or, on the other hand, they can be pursued out of deep conviction and commitment.

One of the recent publications by Joppke (2007) develops the argument further by arguing that integration policies in the West European states are influenced by two conflicting types of liberalism: Rawlsian liberalism (Rawls, 1999), emphasizing equality and individual rights, and repressive liberalism, 'coercing individuals, as well as communities they are part of, to release their self-producing and -regulating capacities, as an alternative to redistribution and public welfare that fiscally diminished states can no longer deliver' (Joppke, 2007, p. 16). According to Joppke, implementation of integration policies does not reflect the traditional national models: multiculturalism (the Netherlands), 'assimilationism' (France) and 'segregationism'

(Germany). The Netherlands, to the contrary, introduced the most repressive policy and Germany the least repressive one. In his view the difference between Western European states that introduce mandatory integration policies and the United States or Australia, where integration policies are voluntary, is that the United States and Australia recruit a highly skilled workforce, while Western Europe receives unskilled migrants, the majority of whom are refugees.

The debate between Soysal and Joppke illustrates that, although international human rights have become more influential in citizenship legislation, the role of the nation state actors cannot be underestimated in the process of transposition of international human rights. As Joppke demonstrated, the question is not only whether or not states adopt international norms, but also why. For instance, nation-state actors can adopt international norms due to both strategic reasons and deep ideological conviction. For that reason, empirical analysis should not prematurely exclude nation-state actors.

So far most of the empirical studies dealing with Europeanization of national citizenship have focused on vertical integration (Checkel, 1999, 2001; Vink, 2001; Dell'Olio, 2005), which is understood as top-down implementation of norms. At the same time, very little attention has been devoted to potential horizontal Europeanization of national citizenship, defined as norm diffusion from one member state to another.[7]

Jeffrey T. Checkel established that the failure of the reform aiming at liberalization of German citizenship law can be attributed to the incompatibility of the norms developed by the Council of Europe, on the one hand, and a deeply rooted ethnic identity in Germany, on the other (Checkel, 1999). Ironically, a few months after the publication of the article, Germany ratified a new, more liberal national citizenship law.[8] In the article from 2001 Checkel again adopted a vertical, top-down approach and examined whether the German political elites, when reforming the national citizenship law, were informed by the norms enshrined in the conventions of the Council of Europe. He established that the German law drafters were not informed by the Council of Europe's norms. Rather, he argued, the outcome is more likely to be explained by the endogenous, demographic and domestic political factors.

In a follow-up article by Maarten Vink (2001), the same approach was adopted in order to analyse the debate on dual citizenship in the Netherlands. Drawing on the results of analysis of the parliamentary debates, Vink established that neither the Council of Europe nor the European Union had an impact on the Dutch dual citizenship law. Vink acknowledged that national citizenship policy is probably the last to be Europeanized, given its silence in the issues of state sovereignty. He argued, however, that, if the European Court of Justice (ECJ) established a more permissive approach towards dual citizenship, this would certainly be reflected in national citizenship legislation.

We are confronted with two questions in regard to Europeanization of national citizenship. First, is Europeanization of citizenship possible only as a result of vertical top-down processes? Second, are horizontal Europeanization processes possible even if the ECJ does not show more activism in the area of national citizenship?

A case study by Lavanex (2007) shows that indirect Europeanization can often come into play. This can occur in policy-areas where the EU *acquis* consists of a small number of binding policy instruments. Lavanex established, by analysing asylum policy, that the vaguely defined common rules on asylum have not prevented the EU member states from exchanging information and working in a horizontal perspective with the aim of developing a common approach towards the issue. As a consequence, Lavanex disagreed with Vink (2002), who argued that the Dutch debate on asylum law reforms did not bear any traces of Europeanization because the Dutch politicians referred to the German asylum law more often than to the EU *acquis*. According to Lavanex: '[...] the need to adapt to Germany would not have been there without the transformative impact of the Schengen and Dublin conventions on the German reforms, therefore pointing at the interdependence and multiple feed-back loops of Europeanization process in the different member states. [...] The transformative impact of European cooperation consists not only of the vertical effects of European rules on an individual member state but also horizontal repercussions of domestic changes on other interdependent member states, even when the latter no longer refer explicitly to the European sources of a particular provision' (Lavanex, 2007, p. 314).

Referring back to the two questions posed above, the empirical findings of Lavanex illustrate that horizontal Europeanization can come into play when the EU *acquis* is very generally defined or has a limited binding power. In the case of national citizenship, the potential legal impact of the EU and the Council of Europe is indeed very vague, as this book will later illustrate, given both the substance and the binding instruments. As a consequence, it can be expected that the impact of the EU legal acts (here: treaties) and the Council of Europe's conventions will be slight, which has already been illustrated by Checkel's and Vink's findings. What is nonetheless worth examining is whether, in the case of national citizenship, indirect, horizontal Europeanization was more intensive, generating more policy convergence than vertical Europeanization.

Conclusions

This chapter presented three different explanatory approaches in comparative citizenship studies, namely: historical institutionalism, the rational choice-motivated approach and sociological institutionalism. The first approach has the longest tradition; it explains changes in national citizenship legislation by path-dependent social mechanisms, for instance nationhood tradition (Brubaker, 1992). The second approach draws on rational choice assumptions, bringing the preferences of actors, mostly political parties, into play. Within the third approach one can identify a universalistic and an EU-oriented stance. The first stresses the impact of international norms; the second, EU norms and institutions. Both stances draw, however, on the 'logic of appropriateness'.

As regards the methodological approach of comparative citizenship studies, there is a lot of variety. There are both case and large-n studies, focusing predominantly on the old (Western European) EU member states, and to a lesser extent on the new EU members and other regions in the world. Immigration states have also received more attention than emigration states. Most of the comparative and case studies map and, at the same time, attempt to explain the analysed legislative changes within one of the presented theoretical approaches. Consequently, the explanatory factors are both long-term (predominantly within historical institutionalism) and short-term. Regarding the conceptualization of the subject of the study (the dependent variable), the existing studies analysed citizenship legislation in very general terms, without specifying the different modes of citizenship acquisition or loss, focusing on a selected aspect of national citizenship legislation, for instance dual citizenship or on a wider range of legally defined modes of citizenship acquisition and loss.

3
National Parliaments As Deliberative Bodies

Introduction

According to Blondel (1973, p. 2), 'Legislatures pose perhaps the most fascinating problem of all structures of government, for they have been and continue to be both the most decried and the most revered, the most hoped for and often the least successful institution in contemporary governments.' In the contemporary European Union, this statement is still up to date: parliaments are widely recognized as important institutions responsible for the quality of representation and deliberation in modern democratic states. Yet, the very performance of parliaments is often critically perceived. Against that background, this chapter targets two questions: (i) how do national parliaments discuss legislation? (ii) how to analyse parliamentary discourse comparatively. The first part of the chapter discusses functions of national parliaments and their formal modes of communication and discussion; the second part gives an overview of the methodological approach of this study regarding comparative legislative and parliamentary discourse analysis.

Patterns of communication in national parliaments

National parliaments constitute the most important formal discussion arena in modern democratic states. The major function of parliaments is to deliberate and produce legislation: while the executive is responsible for governing a state, parliaments provide the legal framework for political, social and economic activities. The second function of parliaments is representation. In modern representative democracies parliamentarians are elected by citizens in order to represent their interests in the legislative process. This study, focusing on parliaments as a discussion arena, targets the following questions: How do parliaments deliberate citizenship legislation? Who are the actors involved? What kind of arguments do they use? Whose interests do the legislatures claim to represent?

The representative function of parliaments has a younger tradition than law-making. In the early phase of modern parliamentarism (the mid-nineteenth century) parliamentarians had a noble background and were also elected by noble persons. The introduction of popular suffrage at the beginning of the twentieth century as well as the consolidation of European democracies after World War II increased the importance of parliaments' representative function. As a consequence, in contemporary democratic states parliaments are supposed to represent and accommodate the variety of social, political and economic interests. Parliamentary debates, as arenas where different interests or arguments are articulated and debated, began to receive more public and scholarly attention in the post-World War II period.

The fulfilment of the representative and the legislative functions proved to be challenging for modern parliaments. The complexity of contemporary law led to an increase in the competences of legislatures: as many studies demonstrated, the share of parliamentarians with a legal background increased significantly over recent decades (Blondel, 1973). On the one hand, professionals are most likely to produce high-quality legislation, but, on the other, they are often perceived as technocrats who do not really represent the society.

In general, national parliaments deliberate legislation in each democratic state; however, the way in which this process takes place varies significantly across the states. This section presents the major forms of formal communication in parliaments. Communication in parliaments is influenced by their structure. In democratic states members of national parliaments are elected anew for each legislative term, lasting from four to five years. The size of national parliaments, regarding the number of members, differs across the states. For instance, in Poland Sejm has 460 parliamentarians and Senat 100 senators. The German Bundestag has 598 seats (and 24 overhang mandates) and the Bundesrat 69 seats, while the Hungarian parliament (one chamber) has 386 parliamentarians. National parliaments are composed of one or two chambers; the bicameral system is more popular in federal or large states. The pattern of communication and deliberation between both chambers depends on the competences that both chambers have in the legislative process.

The forms and frequency of communication in parliaments are also strictly formalized. Given the intensity of meetings, the early studies demonstrated that there is a correlation between the intensity of meetings and the level of democratization; namely, parliaments in consolidated democracies meet more often than those in democratizing states (Blondel, 1973). Parliaments' sittings can be either spread unevenly over the legislation period or concentrated in regular 'blocks'. Although there is also variation across the states, we can identify four common formal activities, namely: written questions, public debates on a bill, public debates on questions not necessarily related to any legal act, and public debates on budget. Written questions are part of formalized communication between legislatures and executives but also among legislatures themselves. Some written questions can be discussed during plenary sessions as well, usually at the end of a discussion devoted to a bill. Public debates on a bill constitute the core of parliamentary work. The debates take place during plenary sessions that are recorded and broadcast on television. It is also a common practice of contemporary parliaments to make plenary debates available in a written form, for instance on a parliament's web page.

Apart from the aforementioned activities, there are also formalized committee meetings. In each national parliament there are a number of specialized commissions whose aim is to develop and discuss various projects of the legislation. Meetings in committees precede plenary session and usually do not have a public character. As a consequence, even if there is a record of the committees' work, it is not presented to the public like plenary debates. The initial phase of the legislative process is, therefore, not fully transparent.

Parliamentary debates: analysing political discourse

Most comparative citizenship studies have compared legislative reforms without explaining them. This book develops the analysis one step further by identifying factors that fostered or blocked the reforms in the three states under study. Explanatory citizenship studies rely on different sources of inference, the most popular ones being: expert interviews (Checkel, 1999), analysis of parliamentary (plenary) debates (Vink, 2001; Faist, 2007) and media analysis (Faist, 2007; Bauder, 2008; Diez and Squire, 2008). This research employs a comparative content analysis of the parliamentary (plenary) debates on national citizenship legislation.

Parliaments are one of the most important institutions in representative democracies; they tailor national legislation, represent different interests and exercise a strong impact on public opinion formation (Liebert, 1995). Due to the high legitimacy of national parliaments, their competences in EU politics were recently also significantly strengthened (O'Brennan and Raunio, 2007). Despite the declining role of political parties in Europe, parliamentary debates constitute the most important arena of political discussion and continue to be an important source of political information for the voters (Eriksen and Fossum, 2002).

Parliamentary debates, according to Wodak and van Dijk (2000), are classified under political discourse and can be defined as: 'a formal gathering of a group of elected representatives, members of various political parties, engaging in a discussion about what collective action or policy to undertake concerning an issue of public concern' (Wodak and van Dijk, 2000, p. 53). The public opinion formation role of the plenary debates was significantly reinforced by the media (Chilton, 2004). The plenary debates are no longer exclusive meetings held behind closed doors; rather, they became open to the public in each and every EU member state. They are not only well reported on television but also easily accessible on the Internet. Parliamentarians are aware that by means of the mass media their speeches target a very large, often even a transnational, audience (Wodak and van Dijk, 2000, p. 13).

> Among the many genres of political discourse, [...] parliamentary debates [...] symbolise democratic discussion, decision making and power. [...] Parliamentary debates feature opinions based on different ideologies, and formulated against the background of different interests as represented by members of parliament (MPs) of different political parties. And as representatives, MPs are expected to voice their opinions of the citizens and organisations

about immigration and ethnic affairs. Parliamentary speeches are delivered for the record and are strictly normalized [...].

Finally, parliamentary debates constitute arenas where national citizenship is tailored in both a legal and a symbolic sense; namely, these are parliamentarians who formulate and reformulate the social meaning of national citizenship, or boundaries of the 'we-community', transformed afterwards through national media to society. For these reasons national parliaments remain crucial actors in citizenship policymaking (Vink, 2005, p. 21):

> [...] the actual output, in terms of domestic public policy, is explained most directly by looking at the parliamentary debate, in that it is, after all, the national parliament that has to approve new laws. Looking at the arguments used by national MPs in these debates allows the evidence for counterfactual, domestic considerations. Secondly, one could assume (perhaps naively) that parliamentary debates are in a sense a residual of wider societal debates, in that MPs have a clear electoral interest in voicing the concerns of their voters and to pick up on these debates. Thus, focusing on parliamentary politics should also enable us to pin down domestic change and resilience in these specific issues beyond the arena of the parliament.

Furthermore, the speeches delivered in the parliament are officially binding for the parliamentarians. In contrast, an interview for academic purposes lacks the element of institutional control: parliamentarians are in an informal situation and present their opinions free from institutional pressure. Finally, given the time frame of this research, namely, 20 years, it would be impossible to conduct interviews with all the actors involved.

Media analysis, on the other hand, offers a more diverse discussion arena than parliamentary debates: in the media there are not only political, but also various social, actors to be found. Furthermore, media allow all these actors to 'communicate' with each other and to confront each other's opinions. However, when it comes to such sophisticated topics as national citizenship, media analysis is not always the best source of empirical inquiry. Media reporting depends heavily on how salient the topic is: first, the coverage is influenced by external events of global or international importance that can marginalize the domestic topic; second, if a certain issue is of low social importance, the coverage of the media will not be high. As various comparative studies have demonstrated (Faist, 2007; Górny and Koryś, 2007), German media covered the national citizenship reform quite extensively, while in Poland the reform of the Polish citizenship law was ignored despite a very intensive parliamentary discussion. As a result, the empirical material offered by the media may often be too superficial to establish and analyse the positions of different political and social actors.

Plenary debates as a source of empirical enquiry

The German, Hungarian and Polish parliamentary debates on national citizenship law were selected from the time-period between 1985 and 2007, during which the national citizenship laws underwent thorough reforms. Parliamentary debates that took place in that period were available on the Internet,[1] which allowed careful screening before composing the final sample.

The sample was composed of plenary debates only. Plenary debates constitute a popular form of debating legislation in Germany, Hungary and Poland. They are organized as wide discussion forums in which all the parliamentarians can take part, raise issues and exchange opinions. Moreover, the discussion is not limited to formal questions prepared and sent in advance to the drafters of the law. Rather, discussions taking place during plenary debates evolve spontaneously due to the fact that parliamentarians can react, for example by asking questions, to the speeches of their colleagues. Also, speeches are also not independent of each other, although many parliamentarians prepare the speech-text in advance, but acknowledge and react to arguments stated in previous speeches.

One could minimize the importance of the plenary debates in Germany, Hungary and Poland by saying that they are dominated by the executive and strong party discipline. Moreover, discussions also take place in other bodies, such as parliamentary committees or expert hearings, which may reflect a much broader view than that presented in the plenary debates. Indeed, party discipline has an impact on the success or failure of a discussed bill. However, although the analysis of party discipline is important for explaining the outcome of the vote, it does not provide any answer with respect to the arguments that were used by opponents and proponents of a bill. Hence, it does not allow us to establish *why* a given bill was rejected or accepted.

Committee meetings and expert hearings constitute important discussion forums in addition to plenary debates, and ideally should also be included in the analysis. Unfortunately, in the three countries under study the minutes of committee meetings and expert hearings are neither recorded nor available to the public in a similar manner to plenary debates. However, given the fact that these gatherings are closed to the public, the plenary debates acquire a special meaning. The parliamentarians are aware that their plenary speech-acts will target a larger audience either directly or through the media. Therefore, the arguments they refer to in the discussion are of high public importance.

The analysis was based on the most important debates that took place before the voting. In most cases it was the second or third reading of a proposed bill, depending on which debate had a richer content (judged by variety of actors and length). The selection strategy also aimed to ensure that participation of parliamentarians, from both large and small parties as well as unaffiliated, was high. It was important to cover the complexity of the parliamentary discourse in each state, including the voices of small parties as well as the opinions of unaffiliated parliamentarians. Only substantial debates fulfilling these criteria entered the final sample.

The selected debates were intended to cover the diversity of national citizenship legislation (all modes of citizenship acquisition and loss as well as statuses). The selection aimed to cover those debates that preceded the most important legal reforms within the analysed time-period. In these respects the German sample provided the richest research material, and Poland and Hungary much less in comparison.

In all, the entire sample amounts to over 1,000 pages of parliamentary debates. The languages of the selected parliamentary debates were German, Hungarian and Polish. However, the coding of the debates was conducted in English. Due to the author's insufficient knowledge of Hungarian, the debates in that country were coded with the help of a native speaker, who was trained beforehand in the application of the coding scheme.

In each country the debates on citizenship legislation took place in a slightly different time-period. In Germany it was a period from 1989 to 2006, in Hungary from 1993 to 2005 and in Poland from 1999 to 2007. This is due to the fact that the legislative reforms had a different dynamic in each state. This book attempted to capture that by comparing the laws before and after the reforms. During the analysed time-period, in each state under study, various components of national citizenship legislation have undergone only one major change.

Comparative approach of this study

The methodology of this book moves away from the dominant approach applied in comparative citizenship literature, namely, an analysis of citizenship legislation either as comparative or as case studies. Both have contributed to the literature with a systematic analysis of citizenship legislation, making it possible to establish in what direction the legislation develops and whether these changes are convergent or divergent across Europe (the most comprehensive comparison concerning the old and new member states was conducted within the framework of the NATAC project; see Bauböck *et al.*, 2006, 2007). This book extends the scope of analysis in order to answer the 'why' question, namely *why* the particular legislative reforms were introduced in the countries under study. As a consequence, the methodological approach of this book comprises, on the one hand, comparative legislative analysis, and, on the other, comparative qualitative and quantitative discourse analysis. Consequently, the empirical inferences were based on, first, the legislation concerning national citizenship law in Germany, Hungary and Poland and, second, plenary debates in the national parliaments devoted to reforms of citizenship legislation.

As already argued, the goal of the legislative analysis was to compare the legislative reforms in Germany, Hungary and Poland. On the other hand, the analysis of the parliamentary debates in these countries identified the actors and arguments that fostered these reforms. The legislation used in the analysis was originally compiled for this book. The German and the Polish legal acts were analysed in the original language, and the Hungarian ones in the official English translation. The legal acts that lacked an official English translation were analysed by a native Hungarian-speaking PhD student.[2] Drawing on the NATAC project approach, the dependent variable of this study was operationalized as *different modes of national citizenship acquisition and loss as well as statuses*, namely:

- Birth-right based modes of citizenship acquisition: *jus soli* and *jus sanguinis*
- Residence-based acquisition
- Family-transfer
- Affinity-based acquisition
- Dual citizenship (status)
- Loss of citizenship and
- Quasi-citizenship (status).

We can identify two birth-based modes of citizenship acquisition: *jus sanguinis* at birth and *jus soli* at birth. *Jus sanguinis* is a 'descent entitlement', meaning that citizenship is inherited from parent(s). *Jus soli*, on the other hand, is a 'territorial entitlement', implying that a person acquires citizenship of a given country by being born on its territory. In both cases citizenship is acquired automatically at birth. The *jus sanguinis* and *jus soli* principles coexist with each other in all the EU member states (Bauböck *et al.*, 2006). However, in most countries the *jus soli* principle applies exclusively to foundlings (children who were found in a state and whose citizenship is unknown or unspecified) or stateless persons, and only a few European states (i.e. France and Germany) have introduced *jus soli* at birth for the second generation of immigrants. The analysis concentrates predominantly on the second case, as statelessness remains relatively rare and is already regulated to a large extent by international law. Furthermore, an introduction of the *jus soli* at birth for the second generation of immigrants constitutes a strong indicator of liberalization.

The residence-based mode of citizenship acquisition is a non-automatic, territorial entitlement. It is applicable to permanent residents who want to naturalize in the country of residence. The standard requirement in the EU member states is a certain period of legal residence as well as additional conditions, such as a language test or proof of no criminal record. Family-transfer is a facilitated, non-automatic mode of citizenship acquisition within a family. It concerns cases of citizenship transfer from a citizen of a given state, as well as a naturalized immigrant, to a spouse and children. In most of the EU member states citizenship acquisition within a family is facilitated regarding, for instance, the required period of residence.

Affinity-based citizenship acquisition applies to *de facto* foreigners who can demonstrate ethnic ties with a state whose citizenship they intend to acquire. This mode of citizenship acquisition is not present in all the EU member states; it usually can be found in states having significant diasporas abroad. The nature of the ethnic tie is defined, in a more or less precise way, in the legislation of a given state, usually referring to such elements as a common cultural, linguistic, historical or religious heritage. It is important to note that affinity-based citizenship acquisition differs from a reacquisition procedure in that it is usually not necessary for the applicants to demonstrate that they themselves or their descendants were the citizens of the state in which they want to naturalize.

Dual citizenship is a status that can be acquired at birth, on the basis of (i) the *jus soli* or (ii) the *jus sanguinis* principle in the country, as well as through (iii) naturalization of immigrants in the receiving state and naturalization of the emigrants and their offspring offered by the sending state (Hansen and Weil, 2002; Hailbronner, 2003). In the first case the second citizenship is acquired automatically at birth on the basis of the *jus soli* principle, while in the second case the status is also acquired automatically at birth but due to mixed parentage. Finally, in the third case, immigrants acquire the second citizenship due to naturalization in a receiving state, or emigrants and their offspring are allowed either to maintain or to acquire (sometimes also reacquire) the citizenship of a sending state, held afterwards together with the citizenship acquired in the other state. These two cases of dual citizenship acquisition should be treated asymmetrically: there are countries that permit dual nationality only for immigrants as well as countries that tolerate it only among emigrants.

Citizenship loss can have either a voluntary or a discretionary character. Most EU member states allow voluntary citizenship renunciation as long as the persons concerned will not be stateless; that is, they intend to acquire citizenship of another state and do not want to be, or cannot become, dual citizens.

Finally, quasi-citizenship (Fowler, 2004) is a partial citizenship status, concerning some selected rights associated with national citizenship, usually excluding political rights (both active and passive). Quasi-citizenship should be distinguished from denizenship; the first is an external status, while the latter is an internal status that concerns only long-term residents (Hammar, 1990). Quasi-citizenship has an extraterritorial nature, meaning that a state grants its co-ethnics, who are citizens of other states, some selected citizenship provisions. This status is not equal to possession of national citizenship, even though states issue official documents.

This study introduces a two-dimensional scale in order to assess the modes of citizenship acquisition and loss discussed above, as well as the two statuses. The scale measures the level of liberalization and ethnicization of national citizenship legislation (see Figure 3.1). As already noted in this chapter, these two dimensions do not overlap with each other, and for that reason they should be treated separately. The categories used in the scale have an analytic nature (Evans and Heath, 1995); that is, they do not intend to represent normative models of national citizenship but rather help to distinguish between two kinds

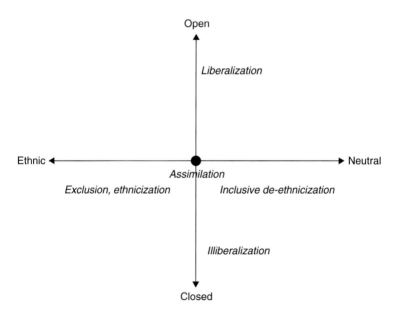

Figure 3.1 National citizenship on a two-dimensional scale
Source: Own illustration.

of legislative reforms, on the one hand liberalizing–de-liberalizing, and on the other hand ethnicizing–de-ethnicizing, the law.

In the horizontal dimension the scale stretches from open to closed citizenship, and in the vertical dimension from ethnic to neutral. The first dimension measures to what extent a given national citizenship law is free from socio-political and economical barriers. Practically speaking, this dimension measures how difficult it is for a foreigner to naturalize in a given state. For instance, the civic model of citizenship, requiring some level of linguistic integration and respect for the basic normative, democratic principles of the West European states, is located on the lower part of the axis. As Joppke rightly noted (2007), there is a tendency emerging in the Western European states to require respect for liberal values (i.e. equality) in a coercive manner, namely by means of a mandatory language or integration test. On the other hand, liberalizing practices leading to an open citizenship are those that make naturalization easier and faster.

The second dimension stretches from ethnic, through assimilatory, to neutral national citizenship and measures how privileged the ethnic entitlement is to national citizenship. In this dimension ethnicity, understood as a specific cultural or religious distinctiveness that constitutes a basis for collective identity building, is a barrier to naturalization. In other words, this dimension measures how ethnically exclusive or ethnically blind a given citizenship law is.

After assessing the legislative reforms on the two-dimensional scale, it is possible to establish whether the states under study developed in a similar or a different direction. The legislative development can take the form of: (i) liberal convergence, (ii) convergence or (iii) divergence. Liberal convergence means that different states' legislation reached a common, normatively predefined standard (Hansen and Weil, 2001). That development can also take place in an opposite direction when legislation of the states under study becomes illiberal. Convergence, on the other hand, implies narrowing of differences between policies or laws over time. In that case legislation of the states under study becomes similar, but the direction of change varies in these states. It means that some states reach the common standards in the course of, for instance, liberalizing reforms, while other states arrive at the same *status quo* after having introduced de-liberalizing reforms. Figure 3.2 illustrates the difference between convergence and liberal convergence.

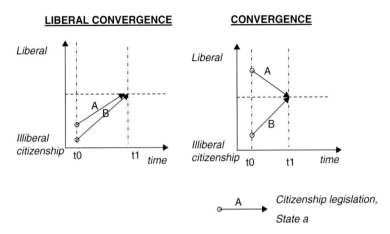

Figure 3.2   Liberal convergence and convergence
Source: Own illustration.

The first figure is a graphical presentation of liberal convergence. The X axis represents time, and the Y axis the level of national citizenship liberalization. The arrows (A and B) represent citizenship legislation in two different states. The figure presents a development in the time-period from t0 to t1. We can see that the legislation of both states developed in the same direction (more liberal national citizenship) and eventually reached the same standard.

The second figure represents convergence, defined in this book as narrowing of differences between citizenship legislation of two (or more) different states. In this figure national citizenship legislation of two different states, A and B, narrowed down and reached the same standard. However, in contrast to the first figure, the direction of legislative change in the second figure was different: state A de-liberalized its legislation while state B liberalized it. As a consequence, national citizenship legislation of these states reached the same standard, though in the course of different processes. Finally, it is also possible that the development of national citizenship legislation in different states does not reveal any regularity. This is the process of legislative divergence.

As already argued, the analysis of the parliamentary plenary debates in Germany, Hungary and Poland identified the actors and arguments that fostered reforms of citizenship legislation. This methodological approach is an original combination of content and Critical Discourse Analysis (CDA).[3] Content analysis allowed the findings to be quantified, for example by counting actors or topics (Krippendorff, 2004). On the other hand, application of the qualitative CDA analysis made it possible to establish *how* and *why* specific categories or argumentative strategies were used (Dryzek, 1990; Wodak and Meyer, 2001).

The analysis was conducted using the Atlas.ti software. The unit of the analysis was a statement given by a participant of a plenary debate. Within each statement the following elements were identified: (i) actor's affiliation (i.e. political party), (ii) subject of the statement – one of the predefined modes of national citizenship acquisition and loss as well as statuses, (iii) type of statement (positive, negative or descriptive) and (iv) justification. The categories 'actors' and 'justifications' were inductively coded, while the categories 'subject of a statement' and 'type of a statement' were coded according to a predefined list. Statements that did not contain one of the predefined subjects were not coded at all. The results were analysed in both a qualitative and a quantitative way.

Comparative and case study analysis in citizenship literature

In the citizenship literature both case studies and comparative research projects are well represented. Case studies traditionally analyse one legislative reform or a sequence of reforms within a longer period of time in a given state (George and Bennett, 2005). Comparative citizenship studies usually do not exceed 20 cases, and can be designed as long or short-term comparisons. This paragraph will discuss the methodology of case studies and comparative projects and present the trade-off between small and large-n research designs. Finally, this discussion will introduce the methodological approach of this book.

Case studies are oriented on either theory-testing or theory-building (Checkel, 1999, 2001; Vink, 2001; Faist, 2004; Kovacs, 2006; Górny and Koryś, 2007). A very good example of a theory-building case study is the article 'The politics of dual citizenship in Hungary' by Maria Kovacs (2006). Having analysed political and public debates on dual citizenship in Hungary, Kovacs arrived at the conclusion that, contrary to well-established opinion in the literature, dual citizenship is not always an indicator of national citizenship liberalization. Rather, depending on whether the addressee groups are immigrants or co-ethnics living abroad, dual citizenship can be an indicator of either national citizenship liberalization or ethnicization. In the context of receiving states (immigration states), tolerance of dual citizenship is a liberalizing practice, while in the sending states (emigration states), or states with shifted borders, dual citizenship is an ethnicizing practice.

The greatest asset of comparative studies is a strong generalizability power that makes them adequate for both theory-testing and theory-generating (see Fowler, 2004). Moreover, only comparative studies allow us to establish tendencies in a larger number of states. Obviously, comparative studies, especially large-n, are not free from potential pitfalls. The most frequent shortcoming of comparative citizenship studies is the lack of a systematic comparative pattern. In such cases citizenship legislation of a given state is treated as one analytic unit without distinguishing between different modes of naturalization, which can eventually lead to oversimplification of the results. The first comprehensive comparative study that thoroughly operationalized all the modes of citizenship acquisition and loss was the already mentioned NATAC project (Bauböck *et al.*, 2006). The very precise approach of the NATAC project contributed substantially to the field by offering the first highly detailed comparison of citizenship legislation in the old EU member states.

In the large-n citizenship studies it is particularly difficult to narrow down the focus of the analysis (Sartori, 1984). On the one hand, only a thorough analysis of all the modes of citizenship acquisition and loss in the analysed states can give us a full picture; on the other hand, conducting such a detailed analysis in large-n studies can often be impossible. In such cases it is important to select those modes of citizenship acquisition and loss that are necessary to answer the research question. This problem will be illustrated here using the example of Howard's comparative study (Howard, 2006). The comparative research design was based on the following three indicators of national citizenship liberalization: (i) presence of *jus soli* at birth, (ii) length of residence period required for naturalization and (iii) tolerance of dual citizenship. The German case illustrates that these three indicators are not sufficient to determine how liberal national citizenship law is in a given state. The legislative reform introduced in the late 1990s in Germany shortened the residence period required for naturalization from 15 to 8 years. However, the reformed law also introduced new naturalization requirements, namely a language and integration test, making access to citizenship more difficult. Applying the three indicators, one could find the reformed German legislation very liberal, while the assessment of the introduced legal changes remains *de facto* more complicated. Secondly, 'tolerance of dual citizenship' cannot always be regarded as an indicator of liberalization. As the literature on the new EU member states demonstrates, dual citizenship can equally well be an indicator of de-liberalization (Kovacs, 2006; Górny and Koryś, 2007).

The last issue to be tackled in this section is scaling. Comparative studies traditionally assess changes in national citizenship legislation as either liberalizing–de-liberalizing or ethnicizing–de-ethnicizing (Joppke and Morawska, 2003; Howard, 2006). In fact, these two dimensions are independent of each other. As an example, not all de-liberalizing practices are automatically ethnic; for instance, a security clause (no criminal record) or financial requirements (a person must have permanent employment in order to naturalize) have nothing to do with ethnicity but nonetheless constitute a barrier to naturalization.

Summary

This chapter discussed the major functions of national parliaments as well as their role in the legislative process. The development of the two major functions, that is, law-making and representation, was presented in a historical perspective. The major focus of the chapter concentrated on different patterns of communication and deliberation in national parliaments. The guiding questions were: (i) how do national parliaments discuss legislation? (ii) how to analyse parliamentary discourse comparatively.

This chapter also presented the comparative methodological approach of this book. In order to explain the direction and causes of national citizenship reforms, this study combined legislative analysis with comparative qualitative and quantitative discourse analysis of national parliamentary (plenary) debates. The first part of the empirical analysis established the direction of legal changes in Germany, Hungary and Poland, while the comparative analysis of parliamentary plenary debates allowed identification of the causes for introduction of specific legislative changes in the analysed states.

4
Legislative Reforms of National Citizenship: Patterns of Convergence and Divergence in Germany, Hungary and Poland (1985–2007)

Introduction

This chapter presents a comparative legal analysis of the national citizenship reforms enacted in Germany, Hungary and Poland from the late 1980s until 2007. The aim of this chapter is not only to describe legal reforms but also to show a trend in these changes. In order to achieve that aim, the findings will be evaluated on a two-dimensional scale, measuring liberalization and ethnicization of the enacted laws (see Chapter 2). This will also allow us to establish whether the reformed laws correspond with a particular, normative model of national citizenship.

In the contemporary literature on citizenship legislation one can often find an assumption that the laws of the democratic states are nowadays becoming more similar and more liberal (Hansen and Weil, 2001; Bauböck *et al.*, 2006; Howard, 2006). The 'liberal convergence hypothesis' has been particularly popular among scholars analysing the European Union's member states. Liberal convergence implies that, despite the lack of EU harmonization in that area, national citizenship laws of the member states begin to reflect the same, liberal normative model of national citizenship.

Major trends in national citizenship legislation of the EU-27 since the early 1980s

This sub-chapter presents major trends in national citizenship legislation enacted in the EU-27 since the early 1980s. It presents the directions of legislative changes and their socio-political context. National citizenship legislation of the old and new EU member states developed along different trajectories. National citizenship of the EU-15 states was predominantly shaped by receiving states' experiences with large-scale immigration in the post-World War II period. On the other hand, the new member states are sending states, often with large, historical Diasporas abroad. The literature identifies two sets of factors that framed the context of legislative reforms in the old and new EU member states. In the old EU member states these were acceptance of immigrants as a permanent phenomenon and politicization of immigration policies (Vink and de Groot, 2010). It was widely acknowledged that immigrants, mostly the first and the second generation of guest-workers, would not return to their countries of origin as previously expected. Finally, increasing social antipathy toward immigrants, as well as economic problems, led to strong politicization of national citizenship policies in Western Europe. In the new EU member states the socio-political framework of reforms was defined by the fall of communism: reforms enacted since the early 1990s were meant to redress the communist past (Liebich, 2009).

Vink and de Groot (2010) identified six major trends in national citizenship legislation of the old EU member states. Although they limited their empirical analysis to Western European states, the findings are in some respects relevant to the new EU member states as well. These six trends are: implementation of gender equality, convergence between countries with *jus soli* and *jus sanguinis*, acceptance of multiple citizenship, introduction of language and integration tests, stronger emphasis on the principle of avoiding statelessness, and a more significant role of membership in the EU.

Implementation of gender equality finalized in the Western European member states in the mid-1980s (Lister, 2003; Vink and de Groot, 2010) and in the new EU member states in the early 1990s (Bauböck, 2009). The reforms focused predominantly on the status of men and women and the rights of children born out of wedlock.

Regarding citizenship transfer between spouses, women were allowed to keep their national citizenship after marrying a foreigner and also to transfer their citizenship to a child. A child born out of wedlock can acquire citizenship from her father after an official acknowledgement of paternity, which is only a simple administrative procedure. Adopted children automatically acquire citizenship from their parents once the adoption process is completed.

According to Vink and de Groot (2010), we can observe convergence between countries with *jus soli* and *jus sanguinis* as dominant principles of citizenship acquisition (Reiter, 2008). In this process, traditional *jus sanguinis* countries, such as Germany, introduce *jus soli* for the second or third generation of immigrants, while traditional *jus soli* countries, such as Ireland or Great Britain, limit the application of that principle by introducing some additional residence requirements (Tyler, 2010). In Great Britain it was the Nationality Act of 1981 and in Ireland the amendment of 2005 that limited the applicability of the *jus soli* principle.

In the new EU member states this trend is absent. None of these states have introduced automatic *jus soli* at birth citizenship acquisition for children of foreign parents (Howard, 2009). Rather, since the beginning of the 1990s, the national citizenship legislation of the new EU member states has introduced more restrictive naturalization requirements for foreigners. Furthermore, the new EU member states engaged in kinship politics that facilitated access of emigrants or Diasporas to national citizenship, manifested by tolerance of dual citizenship or quasi-citizenship status in these two groups (Bauböck *et al.*, 2009; Howard, 2009). On the other hand, Vink and de Groot (2010) noted that kinship politics is not necessarily a feature of the new EU member states' citizenship politics. In their opinion, it can be observed that, while Northern European states are more concerned with inclusion of immigrants, Southern (and Central) European states focus on inclusion of emigrants. This discrepancy can be explained by migration experience but also by statehood formation (Bauböck *et al.*, 2009). For instance, states with shifted borders tend to be inclined to focus on the inclusion of Diasporas.

The third trend concerns wider acceptance of multiple citizenship in Western Europe, manifested by abolition or liberalization of rules regarding renunciation of citizenship in cases of naturalization in another country (Vink and de Groot, 2010). In the new EU member states this trend manifests itself differently. On the one hand, the new EU member states tolerate multiple citizenship if their citizen naturalized in another EU member state (after residence-based or family-transfer citizenship acquisition at birth) or acquired citizenship of another state automatically at birth (the second parent is a citizen of another EU member state). On the other hand, these rules do not apply to immigrant third-country nationals.[1]

In the last decade the old EU member states introduced the so-called civic integration measures, such as language or integration tests (Kostakopoulou, 2001, 2010). In the new EU member states this trend has still not developed, but we can observe that some states, such as Hungary, have already introduced some of these measures, while others debate them (Poland). Civic integration became a new strategy of immigrants' integration in Europe. It is based on a premise that a successfully integrated person should be economically, politically and socially (recognition of liberal values, language proficiency etc.) integrated into the host state. In her recent contribution, Sara Wallace Goodman (2010) developed a systematic, theory-based classification of civic integration measures. She proposed a two-dimensional comparative scale measuring rules regarding citizenship acquisition (from restrictive to liberal) and depth of required integration (from thick to thin). In contrast to Vink and de Groot (2010), Goodman (2010) argued that a deeper analysis of civic integration measures disconfirms the convergence thesis. In her view, there are four different strategies to be observed among the old EU member states. Prohibitive states (Austria, Denmark and Germany) combine exclusive citizenship access with very demanding civic requirements, enabling states (Belgium, Finland and Ireland) have liberal rules concerning citizenship acquisition and low civic requirements, insular states (Italy, Greece and Spain) that only recently became receiving states combine restrictive citizenship access with low civic requirements, and conditional states (the Netherlands, France and the United Kingdom) combine liberal criteria for citizenship acquisition with demanding civic requirements. In the case of insular states civic requirements are not necessary: access to national citizenship is already very difficult. On the other hand, conditional states introduce demanding civic requirements in order to correct their liberal access to citizenship.

The fifth trend concerns a stronger emphasis on the principle of avoiding statelessness, in both old and new EU member states, though with the exception of the Baltic States. As Vink and de Groot noted (2010), the principle of avoiding statelessness was already being taken more seriously in the national legislation of the old EU member states in the 1980s. In the new EU member states national legislation concerning statelessness and renunciation of national citizenship was reformed in the early 1990s. The communist past played a significant role in these reforms. During that period people were involuntarily deprived of national citizenship for political reasons. Therefore, the young Central European democracies found it very important to reform the laws regulating citizenship renunciation and prevention of statelessness (more details are provided in Chapters 4 and 5 of this book). As already mentioned, the Baltic States constitute an exception to this trend. After regaining independence, the Baltic States, in an act of rejection of the Soviet past, decided to reinstall citizenship legislation from the pre-Soviet period. In practice, this decision implied, for instance, that those persons who had not had Latvian citizenship since before 1940 – or whose parents had not been Latvian citizens before 1940 – did not acquire Latvian citizenship in the 1990s. This definition of citizenship was extremely problematic in two of the Baltic States, namely Estonia and Latvia, which had received in the post-World War II period a large number of ethnic Russians. In the light of the reformed law, ethnic Russians, even if born on the territory of the Baltic States, are immigrant foreigners. Due to EU accession conditionality, national citizenship legislation of the Baltic States liberalized a little. However, according to experts, naturalization requirements are still very high, concerning both residence requirements and language tests (Järve, 2009; Krūma, 2009a, b). As a consequence, it has been noted that the number of naturalizations is still far from satisfactory in these states.

The sixth trend is a growing influence of EU membership on national citizenship legislation in the member states (Vink and de Groot, 2010). Although national citizenship legislation still remains within the exclusive competences of the EU member states, the indirect impact of the EU can already be observed in both the old and the new EU member states. First, there is a bilateral tolerance of dual citizenship between the EU member states. Second, Article 10 EC stipulates that the principle of solidarity is violated when a member state grants citizenship to an important part of the population of a non-EU state without first consulting with Brussels. However, recent legislative practices of Hungary, Poland and Romania in this area illustrate that this principle is difficult to enforce (Chapters 4 and 5 of this book provide more details on this issue).

This short section presented the major trends in national citizenship legislation of the EU member states observed since the early 1980s. The findings illustrate that there is no overall convergence among the old and new EU member states. Rather, there are a few trends that allow us to establish some regularities. However, these regularities do not clearly point toward liberalization or de-liberalization of citizenship. As a consequence, the overall picture of national citizenship legislation in the EU-27 remains complex.

Germany: decline of an ethnic citizenship regime

In comparison with Hungary and Poland, and also with most of the EU-15 member states, Germany has introduced many – and radical – legislative changes in the area of national citizenship legislation in the last 15 years (Waldrauch, 2006a). This section will introduce them shortly and identify the dominant trends.

As regards *jus sanguinis* at birth attribution, there have been no radical changes introduced since the late 1980s. The Citizenship Act (StAG)[2] provides that German citizenship can be obtained through descent by a child of a German parent. However, when only the father is a German citizen, acknowledgement or determination of paternity is required.[3] In 2000 an exception was introduced: if both a child and his German parent were born abroad after 31 December 1999 and the parent had a permanent residence abroad at the time, the child would not acquire German citizenship unless he would otherwise be stateless or the parent notified the German diplomatic representation of her child's birth.[4]

In all the EU states it is sufficient if one parent is a citizen of a given state. From this perspective, the German law represents the dominant tendency in the EU. The Austrian law is the most illiberal in these respects: it does not provide automatic citizenship acquisition for a child born out of wedlock to an Austrian father and a foreign mother. Children born out of wedlock can only obtain Austrian citizenship if their mothers are Austrian citizens.[5] This practice is not common in the EU: most of the EU member states introduced gender-blind rules of citizenship acquisition, also applying to children born out of wedlock (Bauböck *et al.*, 2006). In sum, the German law regulating *jus sanguinis* at birth has not changed a lot during the period of study. The only amendment, introduced in 2000, was aimed at limiting applicability of the *jus sanguinis* principle for the third generation of Germans born abroad. In this respect, the amendment clearly decreases the dominance of the *jus sanguinis* principle in the German law, to the benefit of *jus soli*-based acquisitions.

The *jus soli* at birth citizenship acquisition, still very rare in the EU, was introduced in Germany on 1 January 2000 and slightly amended on 1 January 2005.[6] It stipulates that the second generation of immigrants, that is, persons born to foreign parents on German territory, are entitled to acquire German citizenship automatically at birth if one parent has resided legally in Germany for eight years. The residence titles differ according to the category of citizens: the EU citizen has to be a permanent resident in Germany if she/he wants her/his child to obtain German citizenship at birth, the EEA states' citizens need to have equal status to the EU citizens, and third-country nationals have to have a settlement permit.[7] The introduction of *jus soli* at birth for the second generation of immigrants clearly illustrates that German legislation has moved towards a more inclusive and a more liberal model of citizenship. It should also be acknowledged that, before the reform in 1999, German citizenship laws counted among the most restrictive in Europe. On the other hand, *jus soli* at birth has been limited by the requirement to renounce one's second citizenship at the age of 23. This law concerns dual citizens who obtained one citizenship on the basis of descent (*jus sanguinis*) in another country and German citizenship on the basis of *jus soli* at birth.

The modes of *jus soli* citizenship acquisition after birth, more specifically residence-based and family transfer, have also undergone significant changes since the late 1980s.[8] The most substantial legal reform, introduced in 2000, decreased the residence period requirement from 15 to eight years. However, the new law introduced some limitations: namely, since 2000 only legal, long-term residents can naturalize in Germany. The reform also introduced additional naturalization conditions: a language test on the B1 level,[9] an oath to the constitution (*Grundgesetz*) and a declaration of loyalty to the German state.

The new Immigration Law introduced a 30-hour integration course that teaches the German political system, Basic Law, democratic principles, German history and culture.[10] The law stipulates that integration courses are recommended for immigrants who have a poor knowledge of the German language, are unemployed and receive social help (not only financial but also support in acquiring qualifications) or require to be integrated and therefore were recommended by civil authorities to attend an integration course.[11] Immigrants who have already been educated in Germany (school or university level), do not demand to be integrated any more or have a very good knowledge of German are exempt.[12] According to the law, late repatriates and their families are, like other immigrants, also required to take part in integration courses.

The law provides negative and positive sanctions. A positive sanction is that a person who successfully passes the test can naturalize after seven, not eight, years.[13] Negative sanctions, according to the federal office in Bremen,[14] have not been specified yet (the federal authorities are still waiting for detailed instructions). The federal offices were informed that the integration test would be introduced in Germany on 1 September 2008. There would be 310 questions formulated and the list would be available on the Internet. The courses would be financed by the federal authorities but the participants would be required to pay a symbolic fee of €30, which could be waived for a participant in a difficult financial situation. Participation in the course would be mandatory for some groups of immigrants who want to naturalize (see AufenthG, §44a).

The evaluation of the German integration test is problematic (Palmowski, 2008). Some German regions (Ländern), namely Hessen, Lower Saxony and Baden-Württemberg, introduced their integration tests as early as 2006 and early 2007. These tests were rather critically received by the German media and criticized for being too difficult, even for native Germans. The Baden-Württemberg test was also criticized for discriminating against Muslims; for example, one of the questions read: 'A woman should not be allowed to show herself in public or to travel without being accompanied by a man from her family. What is your opinion about this?' This and other similar questions were met with criticism in the local and national media in Germany.

At this stage it is still impossible to fully assess the German integration test: as already noted, the negative sanctions have not yet been specified. It can be argued, however, that to some extent integration politics is conducted in Germany with illiberal measures (Joppke, 2007), for instance, by introducing a mandatory participation requirement in the integration courses. This is particularly problematic given the fact that integration courses are, in the intention of the lawmakers, supposed to educate foreigners about liberal and democratic values being a foundation of German democracy. Moreover, the formulation of this law leaves a lot of space for discretionary practices. What does it mean, for example, that a person requires to be integrated? What kind of criteria should be employed in order to decide on this? How will these practices vary among civil servants? These questions will continue to remain unanswered for some time.

Family-transfers regulate citizenship acquisition within a family, which concerns both spouses and children. For spouses the requirements are one year's residence in Germany prior to marriage and two years of marriage duration. The other criteria stipulated in §8 of the Citizenship Law (StAG) must also be met; that is, possession of a recognized residence title (either a long-term residence permit or a settlement permit), language test and oath to the constitution. In these respects the criteria for family-transfers became similar to the basic residence-based mode of citizenship acquisition. The law regarding family-transfer was amended on 1 January 2000 and 1 August 2001, extending the applicability of family-transfer to registered homosexual partnerships.[15] National citizenship can also be transferred from a spouse who naturalized in Germany to his/her spouse who also wants to acquire German citizenship.[16]

Transfer of citizenship to a child applies to minors whose parents were not nationals of that state at the time of a child's birth or when his/her nationality was unclear. In Germany, until 1 July 1998, nationality was acquired *ex lege* by a child legitimized by a German national.[17] Since 1 July 1998 a child born after 1 July 1993 can acquire nationality by declaration if his/her father is a German national and her/his mother is a foreign national, paternity is acknowledged or determined, a child has been a legal habitual resident in Germany for three years and applies for German citizenship before reaching the age of 23.

German citizenship law also provided a separate naturalization path for persons born of foreign parents but raised as children in Germany. This naturalization procedure was applicable from July 1993 until December 1999, stipulating that, if no other circumstances applied, a young person between the age of 16 and 23 could acquire German citizenship after eight years of legal residence in Germany on condition that she/he had attended a German school for six years (four of which must have been at a school of general education).[18]

In conclusion, the outcome of the reform regulating residence-based acquisitions and family-transfers is difficult to assess. On the one hand, the length of residence required for naturalization was significantly shortened (from 15 to eight years). However, the new law introduced additional conditions for naturalization, including a language test, an oath to the constitution, a declaration of loyalty and an integration test. The latter is particularly problematic given its discretionary and coercive character. On the other hand, the late repatriates were subjected to the same rules as other immigrants, which is a strong indicator of de-ethnicization.

Affinity-based modes of citizenship acquisition (reacquisition and affinity) concern persons who either used to be citizens of a given state or maintain a cultural or a linguistic link with that state. German law allows its former citizens to reacquire German citizenship if they lost it between 1933 and 1945, even if they continue to reside abroad.[19] The descendants of former German citizens can be naturalized upon application. Since the early 1990s, however, a person born after 1 January 1975 can acquire German citizenship only if one of his/her parents was already a German citizen. Previously, it was sufficient if an applicant had a grandparent with German citizenship. Alternatively, those applicants (or their parents) who were residing on 1 September 1939 in the Polish territories and acquired the first or the second category of the *Deutsche Volks Liste* (DVL) can still apply for German citizenship.[20]

In German law, cultural entitlement to citizenship (affinity-based mode) was defined first by 'belonging' to the German nation and second by a post-war fate (anti-German persecution). The legal category of repatriate (*Aussiedler*) was created in the Act on Displaced Persons, *Bundesvertriebenengesetz* (BVFG) in 1953, stipulating in Article 1 that 'a German citizen is a person who belongs to the German nation and who repatriates from the territories belonging now to foreign administration in the East: Gdańsk, Poland, Lithuania, Latvia, Estonia, Soviet Union, Czech Republic, Hungary, Romania, Bulgaria, Yugoslavia, Albania'. Article 6 of BVFG read that belonging to the German nation can be certified by origin, language, upbringing and culture.

In 1992 the category of repatriate was replaced in the law by 'late-repatriate' (*Spätaussiedler*) and the applicability of the discrimination clause (post-war fate) was limited to the former territories of the Soviet Union. The German authorities decided that the newly democratized Central European States no longer posed any threat to the security of ethnic Germans living in those states. The reformed law, aiming at limiting repatriation, stipulated that only those born before 1 January 1993 could apply for a repatriation visa. According to the reformed law, repatriation was limited to 225,000 repatriates per year. Repatriates and their families were also required to pass a language test. Since 2005, repatriates and their families cannot obtain German citizenship unless they pass the German language test.

Reforms of the legislation that regulates affinity-based citizenship acquisition clearly diminished the role of ethnic entitlement to German citizenship. The reformed law not only limited the entitlement to the status of a repatriate but also introduced additional naturalization requirements. These legislative changes have in effect contributed to de-ethnicization of German citizenship.

Since the late 1980s the legislation regulating possession of dual citizenship has undergone some important changes (Martin and Hailbronner, 2003; Kreuzer, 2003; Wiedemann, 2003).[21] Even though dual citizenship is still considered an exception in German legislation, it has become more and more tolerated. The current law stipulates that dual citizenship is tolerable in the following circumstances; (i) if renunciation of the prior citizenship results in 'particularly difficult conditions' (i.e. the other state does not allow citizenship renunciation, the person concerned would be subject to humiliation, her civic rights would be violated or her economic property would be endangered) or (ii) reciprocity (if the other EU state allows its citizens to obtain German citizenship. These countries are: Greece, the United Kingdom, Ireland, Portugal, Sweden, Finland, France, Belgium, Italy, Hungary, Poland, Slovakia, Malta and Cyprus).

In the light of the German citizenship law (StAG), the tolerance of dual citizenship for the first generation became relatively high. With respect to the second generation, the entitlements are already different: children of immigrants born in Germany should choose between the German and the other citizenship upon reaching the age of 23. Otherwise, if they do not submit their declaration, German citizenship is automatically withdrawn. Children of repatriates born in Germany as well as children born to parents holding different citizenships[22] can, however, keep both their citizenships for their lifetime.

In German law there were no radical changes introduced concerning the loss of national citizenship. The law from 1999 specifies four situations in which German citizenship can be lost: first, upon acquiring another citizenship (unless that person asks for permission to keep the German citizenship;[23] second, upon application (but only if that person would not be stateless afterwards); third, upon reaching the age of 23 and not resigning from another citizenship of which that person is in possession; fourth, due to voluntary military service in another country (unless there is an international agreement between these two states regulating that issue). In the last case, a person can be exempted from military service in Germany, or, if the service in another country was shorter, would only need to stay in the army long enough to make up the difference). Finally, German law stipulates that public service employees, or persons having an official relationship with public law functions, may not be released from German citizenship. Persons subject to compulsory military service can be released from German citizenship only upon consent from the Federal Ministry of Defence.

The last provision to evaluate is quasi- or fuzzy citizenship, this being a partial citizenship status granted predominantly to extraterritorial co-ethnics. Article 116 of the German Basic Law, as well as the Act on Displaced Persons of 1956 and 1992, introduce the categories of 'German without a German citizenship' and 'ethnic national' (*Volkszugehörige*).[24] Article 116 in the Basic Law stipulates that a German is a person who possesses German citizenship or who has been expelled but belongs to the German nation (or his/her spouse or ancestors do) or who has lived in the territories that belonged to Germany on 31 December 1937 (Gdansk, Poland, Baltic States, CSSR, Czech Republic, Hungary, Romania, Bulgaria, Yugoslavia, Albania).

Ethnic Germans who want to acquire German citizenship have to fulfil certain criteria: they need to present evidence of their ethnic German origin and upbringing and also demonstrate a good knowledge of German language and culture. In contrast to Hungary or Poland, the German authorities regarded quasi-citizenship as a temporary status and at the same time the first step towards obtaining German citizenship. Therefore, this ambiguous status was not proliferated in Germany.

In conclusion, since the late 1980s German national citizenship law has become less ethnic and more liberal (see Table 4.1). This means that naturalization requirements are no longer of an ethnic, inscriptive nature, but are, rather, socio-political. The new requirements are: respect for the legal and political order, no threat to security, knowledge of the language and integration into German society.

The law regulating *jus sanguinis* at birth citizenship acquisition has not undergone any radical changes. However, it has been slightly de-ethnicized by limiting its applicability to the third generation of Germans born and residing permanently abroad. The introduction of *jus soli* at birth in 1999 liberalized the German citizenship law significantly. On the other hand, the outcome of residence-based acquisition reform is biased: the reform liberalized the law, but at the same time it introduced illiberal elements into the naturalization procedure, for instance a mandatory integration test. Moreover, the new law regulating integration tests leaves a lot of space for discretionary practices. The introduction of additional naturalization requirements has also led to de-liberalization of family-transfers. On the other hand, affinity-based modes of citizenship acquisition and the quasi-citizenship status have been radically de-ethnicized by diminishing the privileged status of ethnic Germans (late repatriates). The acquisition of a dual citizenship status has become more liberal; however, only a limited tolerance of the status was introduced. Finally, the law regulating the loss of national citizenship has not undergone any substantial changes.

Table 4.1 Tendencies observed in German law since the late 1980s

Mode of citizenship acquisition and loss	Tendency observed in German law (late 1980s–2007)
Jus sanguinis at birth	No radical changes, weak de-ethnicization
Jus soli at birth	Liberalization, strong
Residence-based acquisition	Mixed: liberalization (length of residence), de-liberalization (civic integration)
Family-transfer	De-liberalization
Affinity-based acquisition	De-ethnicization
Dual citizenship	Liberalization
Loss of citizenship	No radical changes
Quasi-citizenship	De-ethnicization

Source: Own compilation.

Since the late 1980s a strong tendency towards liberalization and de-ethnicization of national citizenship has been observed in Germany. The citizenship law that emerged after the reforms bears hardly any traces of an ethnic citizenship model and is much more liberal (see Figure 4.1). On the other hand, some of the new liberal laws are executed with slightly illiberal measures, for example the law regulating the implementation of the integration test. This law also leaves a lot of space for discretionary practices.

Hungary: return to ethnicity

In Hungary the major changes in citizenship legislation took place in 1993, a few years after the fall of communism (Figure 4.2). The reform introduced radical changes, though not necessarily liberalizing Hungarian law.

The current law from 1993 regulating *jus sanguinis* at birth acquisition stipulates that children can acquire Hungarian citizenship if their

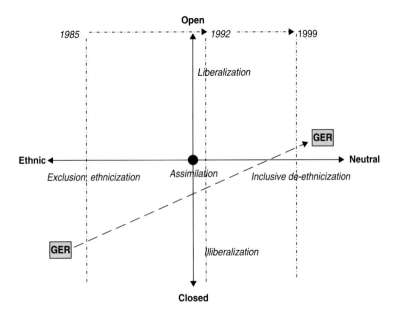

Figure 4.1   Evolution of German citizenship
Source: Own illustration.

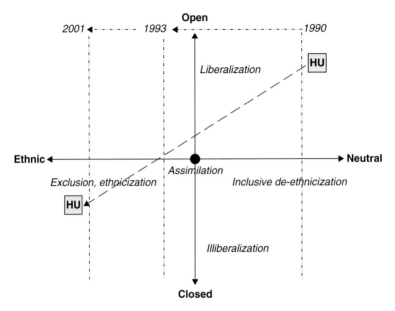

Figure 4.2 Evolution of Hungarian citizenship
Source: Own compilation.

parents are Hungarian citizens.[25] If only one parent is a Hungarian citizen, Hungarian citizenship can be awarded retroactively in the case of marriage, acknowledgement of paternity or determination of paternity (if a child is born out of wedlock). Current Hungarian law does not differ in these respects from the prior law. According to the law from 1957, both men and women can transfer Hungarian citizenship to their children. For persons born before 1957 to a Hungarian mother and a foreign father, a special application procedure was introduced. These persons can acquire Hungarian citizenship by sending a written statement to the president.[26]

The citizenship law from 1957, contrary to the current law, spelled out criteria for *jus soli* at birth citizenship acquisition. It stipulated that anyone who is not declared to be a citizen of another country but was born on the territory of Hungary should be regarded as a Hungarian citizen. However, the citizenship law enacted in 1993 does not mention that *jus soli* at birth is one of the basic principles of Hungarian citizenship acquisition, although it is permitted as an exception in the case of foundlings.[27] The cancellation of the *jus soli* at birth principle is only a provisional de-liberalization. In the light of the law from 1957, the principle applied only in the case of children whose nationality was not specified. Hence, the old and the current laws have the same effect.

Regarding residence-based acquisition, Hungarian citizenship law from 1957 stipulated that the only condition for naturalization is three years of legal habitual residence in Hungary.[28] In 1993 naturalization requirements became more restrictive. A person is entitled to naturalization only after eight years of legal habitual residence in Hungary (a long-term residence permit). Additional conditions were also introduced. An applicant must never have been subject to criminal proceedings in Hungary; she must have sufficient financial means and a place to live in Hungary and must pass in Hungarian a test examining the knowledge of 'constitutional basics'. Disabled persons, holders of a degree from an educational institution in Hungarian and persons older than 65 are exempt from the exam.

However, it needs to be stressed that Hungarian citizenship can be acquired by third-country nationals after not eight, but *de facto* 15 years. This is due to the fact that the reformed law grants a long-term residence permit only after five years of limited residence permit in Hungary. The years needed to obtain a long-term residence permit are in turn not counted towards naturalization. Finally, it is also possible to acquire Hungarian citizenship by Presidential decision in a shorter time and without fulfilling all additional conditions, if that is justified as being in Hungarian interests.

Hungarian law also provides a separate naturalization path for persons who have been raised on Hungarian territory. However, due to the fact that these persons were born to foreign parents, they could not acquire Hungarian citizenship by descent. Hungarian law stipulates that those minors who have been legal habitual residents for at least five years can acquire Hungarian citizenship by sending a written statement to the president (there is no application procedure). The statement must be made before reaching the age of 19.[29]

As regards family-transfers, the law regulating spousal transfer changed substantially in 1993.[30] According to the law from 1957, the only condition was three years of marriage duration and no residence requirement. Since 1993, family-transfer has been regulated similarly to the other naturalization modes, with the following requirements: three years of residence in Hungary, three years of marriage duration and completion of all the other additional naturalization conditions (knowledge of the constitution, etc.).

Hungarian law from 1957 did not require legal habitual residence from children adopted by Hungarian citizens, or children who were automatically given Hungarian citizenship if their parents did not have it.[31] The new law from 1993 introduced a period of three years' legal habitual residence for children who naturalized with their parents. They were also required to fulfil additional naturalization requirements. Children adopted by Hungarian citizens were exempt only from the residence requirement. Hungarian law also allows citizenship transfer from a child to a parent if a parent does not have Hungarian citizenship. The law from 1957 did not require any residence period in these cases, but the law from 1993 introduced a three years' residence requirement.

In 1993 no radical changes were introduced with respect to the reacquisition procedure, which had already been in force since 1957. Hungarian law since 1993 stipulates that a former Hungarian citizen can be renationalized by request if she has never been subject to criminal proceedings in Hungary and has sufficient financial means and a place to live in Hungary, and her acquisition of Hungarian citizenship does not affect the interests of Hungary.[32] Those whose citizenship was withdrawn by the acts 1947/X, 1948/XXVI, 1948/LX or 1957/V, or by the governmental decrees 7970/1946, 10515/1947 or 12200/1947, or who lost their citizenship between 15 September 1947 and May 1990 can reacquire their Hungarian citizenship by sending a written statement to the President (there is no application procedure). In 2001 an amendment was introduced stipulating that only those who never posed a threat to Hungarian security could reacquire Hungarian citizenship. However, in 2003 this amendment was cancelled.

Concerning affinity-based acquisitions, the law from 1957 stipulated that a person can apply for Hungarian citizenship if her ancestors were Hungarian citizens. According to the law from 1993, it is sufficient to prove that the ancestors were of Hungarian ethnicity and not necessarily Hungarian citizenship. Hungarian law from 1993 stipulates that those who declare themselves to be Hungarian nationals, who have ancestors with Hungarian citizenship and who reside in Hungary can be naturalized without fulfilling the habitual residence condition. However, the amendment from 2005 introduced a one year long residence requirement.

The law from 1947 allowed dual citizenship. However, bilateral treaties with other socialist countries aimed at avoiding it.[33] For instance, those who acquired dual citizenship due to their parents' different citizenships had to choose one. Otherwise, citizenship of these persons was determined on the basis of their place of residence. The law allowed the state authorities to deprive someone of their Hungarian citizenship if that person acted against national interest or was disloyal. In these respects, acquisition of a West European state's citizenship could have been also interpreted as an act of disloyalty towards Hungary. In consequence, dual citizenship was practically not allowed in communist Hungary.

In the 1990s the bilateral treaties were abolished. The new law on citizenship stipulated that 'no-one can be arbitrarily deprived of his or her citizenship or of the right to choose her or his citizenship'. It is interpreted as *de facto* (though not explicitly *de jure*) toleration of dual citizenship for Hungarian citizens who also possess another citizenship. In this respect Hungarian law allows dual citizenship for one category of persons: Hungarian citizens living abroad and being also in possession of another citizenship (dual citizenship by naturalization abroad). Other cases of dual citizenship are regulated by bilateral agreements on dual citizenship toleration between Hungary and the other EU states (the reciprocity principle). In the light of the Hungarian law, these cases are regarded as exceptions.

In 2003 the World Federation of Hungarians started collecting signatures for a referendum in which Hungarian citizens were supposed to decide whether ethnic Hungarians living abroad and not holding Hungarian citizenship should obtain it (Kovacs, 2006; Kiss and Zahoran, 2007). As a result of this bottom-up initiative a national referendum was scheduled on 5 December 2004. The question was as follows:

> Do you think Parliament should pass a law allowing Hungarian citizenship with preferential naturalisation to be granted to those, at their request, who claim to have Hungarian nationality, do not live in Hungary and are not Hungarian citizens, and who prove their Hungarian nationality by means of Hungarian identity card

issued pursuant to Article 19 of Act LXII/2001 or in another way to be determined by the law which is to be passed? (Kovacs, 2006)

The aim of the initiative was to grant ethnic Hungarians living abroad as citizens of other states the second, Hungarian citizenship. The initiators wanted first to draw on a descent principle (*jus sanguinis*) and grant Hungarian citizenship to the offspring of persons who were in possession of Hungarian citizenship before 1920, that is, right before the borders shifted (Kovacs, 2006). The initiators rejected that option because before 1920 many non-ethnic Hungarians, for instance Serbs, Slovaks and Croats, had been holders of Hungarian citizenship. As a consequence they opted for ethnic criteria based on self-declared identity, language and culture.

The issue also polarized political parties. The right-wing, conservative parties supported the initiative, while the social democrats and liberals were against it. The latter group advocated ignoring the referendum and not taking part in it. Indeed, the turnout in the referendum was not sufficient to recognize the referendum as valid (37.49 per cent). Opinion was also much divided: 51.57 per cent of voters supported the idea of de-territorialized dual citizenship, while the other half were against it.

If the turnout had been positive, a population of ten million Hungarian citizens would have enlarged to 12.5 or even 15 million (the number of ethnic Hungarians in the neighbouring states only and in all other countries) (Kiss and Zahoran, 2007). As Janos Kis, an opponent of the idea, argued, the majority of Hungarians were not ready to take a risk that would have changed Hungarian democracy so thoroughly (Kovacs, 2006); that is, the external Hungarian citizens would have obtained passive and active voting rights, allowing them to make decisions concerning a state in which they neither resided nor paid taxes (Bauböck, 2005b and 2007a). Finally, a positive outcome of the referendum would have profoundly ethnicized the status of dual citizenship in Hungary. In conclusion, the outcome of the referendum showed that Hungarian society was not ready to further ethnicize its national citizenship.

The last two provisions to discuss are the loss of citizenship and quasi-citizenship. Major changes concerning the loss of Hungarian citizenship were introduced in 1993. According to the law from 1957, it was possible to deprive someone of Hungarian citizenship because of disloyalty towards the Hungarian state or a serious crime.[34] In contrast, the new citizenship law from 1993 stipulated that no one can arbitrarily be deprived of his/her citizenship or the right to choose his/her citizenship. Any Hungarian citizen can renounce his/her citizenship through a written statement sent to the President, if he does not reside in Hungary, or has acquired or will acquire another citizenship, or is not subject to any criminal proceedings in Hungary and has no tax obligations or public debts. Hungarian citizenship can be reacquired within a year if the other citizenship was not granted. Hungarian citizenship can be withdrawn if the information presented by an applicant was false. In that case, however, citizenship cannot be withdrawn if a person has possessed it for at least ten years.

Quasi-citizenship was introduced in 2001. The Act on Hungarians Living Abroad, commonly called a Status Law, created a special, partial citizenship status for ethnic Hungarians residing in the neighbouring states.[35] According to the law, a quasi-citizen is a person who (i) is not a Hungarian citizen, (ii) declares himself to be of Hungarian nationality and speaks fluent Hungarian, (iii) is registered as a Hungarian national in the country of residence, (iv) belongs to organizations of Hungarian nationals, (v) is registered in the church as a Hungarian national, or (vi) does not live in Hungary (has neither a residence permit or a refugee status) but is a resident of one of these countries: Croatia, Romania, Serbia, Montenegro, Slovakia, Slovenia and Ukraine. An application shall be rejected if a person has been deported from Hungary or has an entry ban. The status, once acquired, extends also to a spouse and children if they are not Hungarian nationals. The status is certified with a special document called a Hungarian card, valid for five years, or without limit for children under 18 and persons over 60.

The first version of the Status Law, which entered into force on 1 January 2002, was already modified in 2003 due to the Romanian government's and the European Commission's critical opinions (Ieda *et al.*, 2004). In the first version of the law, holders of the Hungarian card were permitted to enter and reside in Hungary under very favourable conditions. In the amended version these provisions were cancelled. For instance, the first version of the Status Law stipulated that holders of the Hungarian Card could apply for financial help to cover the costs of establishing eligibility for work in Hungary. The amendment abolished the preferential treatment of the Hungarian

Card holders *vis-à-vis* other foreign workers and stipulated that the persons in question were subject to the same requirements as other foreigners. However, preferential healthcare provisions were retained in the amended version, stipulating that the holders of the Hungarian card should have their healthcare costs covered by the Hungarian state, even though they do not pay taxes in Hungary (Fowler, 2004).

The most generous provisions granted to the ethnic Hungarians were in education (Fowler, 2004). The amended version of the Status Law has even expanded the scope of rights. In the light of the Status Law from 2001, holders of the Hungarian Card who were educated in the Hungarian language before coming to Hungary received the same rights as Hungarian students. Teachers of the Hungarian language abroad, holding the Hungarian Card, were granted the same privileges as teachers working in Hungary.[36] The amended version of the Status Law from 2003 extended the circle of potential beneficiaries. It stipulated that all students holding a Hungarian Card are entitled to financial support and other students' privileges, whether they had been educated in Hungarian or in another language before coming to Hungary. The privileges were also extended to all teachers holding the Hungarian Card and also to those who teach subjects other than the Hungarian language.

During the analysed time-period, Hungarian national citizenship law has in general become more ethnic and less liberal (with the exception of the law regulating loss of national citizenship) (Table 4.2). On the one hand, that tendency was a consequence

Table 4.2 Tendencies observed in Hungarian law since the late 1980s

Mode of citizenship acquisition and loss	Tendency observed in Hungarian law (late 1980s–2006)
Jus sanguinis at birth	No major changes
Jus soli at birth	No major changes
Residence-based acquisition	De-liberalization
Family-transfer	De-liberalization
Affinity-based acquisitions	Ethnicization
Loss of citizenship	Liberalization
Dual citizenship (*de facto*, not *de jure*)	Ethnicization of the practice
Quasi-citizenship	Ethnicization

Source: Own compilation.

of a reawakened interest and concern with the Hungarian ethnic Diaspora abroad (prohibited during the communist period). On the other hand, it was the opening of the borders. The modes of citizenship acquisition at birth (*jus soli* and *jus sanguinis* at birth) did not undergo any substantial changes. Residence-based citizenship acquisition and family-transfer were made less liberal by introducing new restrictions for immigrants who want to naturalize in Hungary. Affinity-based acquisitions and quasi-citizenship became more ethnic. As already noted, quasi-citizenship is by definition ethnic, and can vary only with respect to the degree of ethnicization.

Dual citizenship, on the other hand, can take different forms: ethnic, non-ethnic, liberal or illiberal. In communist Hungary, on the one hand, the law tolerated dual citizenship, but on the other hand the bilateral treaties with other communist states aimed at avoiding it. Moreover, the acquisition of a West European state's national citizenship (as the second national citizenship) was interpreted as disloyalty and resulted in arbitrary withdrawal of Hungarian citizenship. Due to that negative legal heritage, the law introduced in democratic Hungary specified only one mode of national citizenship loss: voluntary abdication of the person concerned. That law contributed to the *de facto*, though not *de jure*, tolerance of dual citizenship in Hungary. Due to the legal interpretation, it is predominantly Hungarian emigrants who are entitled to the status. In consequence it can be argued that, in the *de jure* dimension, dual citizenship continues to be avoided in Hungary. However, given the *de facto* interpretation of the laws, dual citizenship is basically tolerated in the case of one group of persons: Hungarian emigrants. This gives the dual citizenship practice in Hungary (not law in this case) a slight ethnic character, which privileges persons of Hungarian origin *vis-à-vis* immigrants who might want to naturalize in Hungary and keep their first national citizenship.

Another issue is the interpretation of national citizenship law in the communist states. For instance, legal analysis showed that the law regulating residence-based acquisitions and family-transfers was more liberal than the current law. Does this mean that the communist authorities were more liberal or open towards immigrants than their democratic successors? Certainly not. The communist authorities had full powers to deny or deprive someone of national citizenship. Moreover, the text of the law is insufficient if there is no rule of law in a state. Does this mean that the analysis of communist countries' laws does not make sense at all? No, it certainly makes sense and is necessary. It should not be forgotten that the communist law constituted a 'point of reference' for the legislation enacted after democratization. What is particularly important here is that the analysis of the communist law requires embedding its interpretation in the political context. Hungary under communism was closed for immigration, as it is understood in the West European context. Hence, due to the political context it was unnecessary to construct very restrictive laws. On the other hand, a pure analysis of political context cannot replace legal analysis because it would basically fail to explain the legal process. Laws do not emerge in a vacuum or in total ignorance of the existing laws; quite the contrary – lawmaking is a cumulative process.

Poland: kinship ties that matter

It is a phenomenon of Polish citizenship law that the legal act regulating national citizenship has not been changed since 1962 (Górny, 2009). However, in 2006 a new act was written, which yet awaits parliamentary discussion. In general, the direction of changes in Polish citizenship legislation has been similar in many respects to Hungary (Figure 4.3).

The Polish Act on Nationality stipulates that a child acquires Polish citizenship at birth if at least one of the parents is a Polish citizen, regardless of whether a child has been born on Polish territory or abroad.[37] If parents wish to choose other citizenship for their child, they should do so within three months after their child's birth. These rules have not been changed since 1962. *Jus sanguinis* has also been the only mode of automatic citizenship acquisition at birth envisaged by Polish law. *Jus soli* at birth was never introduced in Poland, and the new project of nationality law does not include it as a general principle, except for foundlings and the stateless.

Residence-based citizenship acquisition has undergone some important changes. Before 1997, the only *de jure* condition for acquiring Polish citizenship was legal habitual residence in Poland for five years.[38] The Act on Polish Nationality from 1962 also stipulated that acquisition of Polish citizenship could be conditional on renunciation of the prior citizenship. Polish citizenship could also be

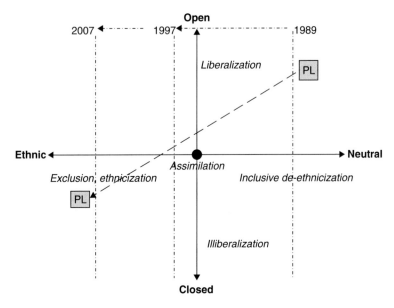

Figure 4.3   Evolution of Polish citizenship
Source: Own compilation.

acquired in a shorter period of time upon Presidential decision. The amendment from 1997 has identified only two types of residence titles eligible for naturalization; an unlimited residence permit in the case of EU citizens and a long-term/unlimited residence permit in the case of non-EU citizens.[39]

The Foreigners' Law from 2003 specified new conditions concerning the acquisition of an unlimited residence permit.[40] In the light of the law, third-country nationals can obtain an unlimited residence permit in Poland if they have resided in Poland for at least ten years without interruption.[41] It means that after ten years of residence in Poland (with a renewable limited residence period, issued for two years maximum) a person concerned has to reside in the state for another five years in order to be eligible for naturalization. Refugees and persons married to Polish citizens constitute an exception: refugees are entitled to obtain an unlimited residence permit after five years of limited residence in Poland, and persons married to Polish citizens after only two years. Although we find a similar practice in

Hungary, it cannot be argued that this is a widespread practice in Europe. In Germany, for instance, the years needed to acquire a long-term residence permit are counted towards naturalization as well.

Moreover, a bill of the new Nationality Act from 2006 proposed more radical changes.[42] It introduced a five-year-long permanent residence requirement for EU citizens who want to naturalize in Poland and a seven-year-long permanent residence requirement for non-EU residents. The bill also introduces additional requirements: an applicant needs to have sufficient means to provide for his/her living (an apartment and a permanent job) and must pass a language test. Persons who attended Polish schools abroad can be exempted from the language test. In conclusion, it can be argued that residence-based citizenship acquisition has been de-liberalized in Poland since the late 1980s, concerning mostly the length of residence required in order to obtain a permanent resident permit and Polish citizenship.

Regarding spousal transfer, the Act on Polish Nationality from 1962 stipulates that Polish citizenship can be transferred to a spouse within three months after marriage[43] and upon a submitted application. In the amendment from 1999, the entitlement was changed to three years of marriage duration and a minimum of six months' legal residency in Poland. The bill from 2006 introduces new requirements: two years' residence in Poland and three years of marriage duration for EU citizens and stateless persons, and five years' residence and three years of marriage duration for non-EU residents.[44] In addition, all applicants need to have sufficient means to provide for their living and pass a language test.

The Act on Polish Nationality from 1962 stipulates that citizenship can be transferred automatically to a child once his/her parent acquires Polish citizenship, upon the condition that the second parent agrees to it.[45] If a child is over 16 years old, she/he should take this decision on his/her own. In the amended version of the law from 1999, one reads that Polish nationality can be extended to children, unless they reside in Poland. In sum, the analysis illustrates that the law regulating family-transfers has also been de-liberalized.

In the light of Polish law, reacquisition of citizenship concerns two categories of persons: first, those who lost it due to a marriage to a foreigner and, second, those who were deprived of it for historical or political reasons.[46] The Act on Polish Nationality from 1997 stipulates that a former Polish citizen can reacquire her citizenship once her marriage to a foreigner is terminated. Before 1997 the procedure was available only to women.

The Act on Polish Nationality has provided since 1962 an opportunity for those persons who can prove their Polish origin to repatriate; not necessarily by having possessed Polish citizenship in the past, but rather by proving that they belong to the Polish nation. The bill of the new citizenship law from 2006 stipulates more clearly the conditions under which a person is eligible to have Polish nationality recognized.[47] A person can reacquire Polish citizenship if this was lost before 4 June 1989 based on (i) Article 11 of the 20 January 1920 Act on Citizenship of the Polish State, (ii) Article 11 or 12 of the 8 January 1951 Act on Polish Citizenship, (iii) Article 13, 14 or 15 of the 15 February 1962 Act on Polish Nationality in the version of the Act that was current at the moment of the loss of citizenship. Polish citizenship shall not be reacquired by persons who (i) voluntarily entered the military service of a state fighting against the anti-German coalition during the World War II; (ii) accepted a public post in a state fighting against the anti-German coalition between 1 September 1939 and 8 May 1945; (iii) are a threat to the national security or public order in Poland; or (iv) act against Polish vital interests.

Affinity-based citizenship acquisition concerns persons of Polish nationality willing to repatriate to Poland. Repatriation was regulated by the Act on Polish Nationality from 1962 until 2000, when a separate Repatriation Act was introduced. The Repatriation Act applies to persons of Polish nationality who were not eligible to repatriate to Poland during the repatriation programs between the late 1940s and early 1950s. It applies only to the former Polish eastern territories from 1939. The countries included in the repatriation program are: Armenia, Azerbaijan, Georgia, Kazakhstan, Kyrgyz Republic, Tadzykistan, Turkmenistan, Uzbekistan and the Asiatic part of Russia. Persons of Polish nationality from other territories can apply for a repatriation visa if they were subject to religious, national or political persecution. A person is eligible to acquire Polish citizenship if she is able to certify that at least one parent, one grandparent or two great-grandparents were Polish nationals or Polish citizens. An applicant also needs to confirm her Polish origin with knowledge of Polish traditions or the Polish language.

The direction of legal changes after 1989 shows that Polish national citizenship legislation continued to be drafted in a kin-state tradition. However, the repatriation legislation that was in force during the communist period allowed former Polish citizens living in the former territories of Poland to repatriate. On the other hand, the law introduced after 1989 changed the territorial applicability of the repatriation program by including the whole territory of the former Soviet Union *with the exception* of the former Polish territories. As a consequence, the population entitled to repatriation only had an indirect, ethnic link to the Polish state, which in effect also gave a more ethnic character to the new law.

The Act on Polish Nationality from 1962 clearly forbids dual citizenship.[48] It stipulates that 'a Polish citizen, in the light of Polish law, cannot be simultaneously regarded as a citizen of another state.' In Article 8 one reads that the 'Acquisition of Polish citizenship may be conditional upon presenting a certificate of the loss or renunciation of the foreign citizenship' and Article 13 stipulates that 'a Polish citizen can acquire a foreign citizenship only after consent of a due institution. Acquisition of a foreign citizenship results in the loss of Polish citizenship.' In 2001, Article 13 was amended in the following manner: 'A Polish citizen loses Polish citizenship upon his/her application, having received consent from the President of the Polish Republic to renounce his/her citizenship.'

The current law tolerates *de facto* dual citizenship, given the biased meaning of Article 2: 'A Polish citizen, in the light of the Polish law, cannot be simultaneously regarded as a citizen of another state.' The article is interpreted in the following way (Górny, 2009): a dual citizen (Polish plus other), when in Poland, is treated as a Polish citizen. Hence, the *de facto* tolerance of dual citizenship has its roots in two legal acts: one forbidding the arbitrary loss of citizenship and the other stipulating that a dual Polish citizen during his/her stay in Poland will be regarded only as a Polish citizen. However, this approach is not specifically Polish, but a common practice of all the countries tolerating dual citizenship.

Another important aspect of the law is the fact that it targets only one category of persons potentially interested in dual citizenship: Polish citizens living permanently abroad (dual citizenship as an effect of naturalization abroad). This current law is not concerned with immigrants who would also be interested in keeping their original citizenship and naturalizing in Poland. These cases are regulated by bilateral agreements on dual citizenship toleration between

Poland and the other EU states (the reciprocity rule). In the light of the Polish law, these cases are exceptions. In these respects, dual citizenship law in Poland only has an extraterritorial dimension.

The bill from 2006 introduces *de jure* toleration of dual citizenship, though maintaining the extraterritorial applicability of the law. Article 3 stipulates that 'a Polish citizen who possesses a citizenship of another state, has exactly the same rights and duties as a person who possesses only Polish citizenship.' The new bill differentiates between the level of toleration of dual citizenship for the first and the second generation. While there are basically no obstacles to acquiring dual citizenship for the first generation, the second generation is expected to choose one citizenship only.[49] Article 3 reads that a child whose parents (one Polish, one of another nationality) chose a foreign citizenship for their child within one year after his birth shall not acquire the second, Polish citizenship.

Polish law regulating loss of citizenship has become more liberal in the analysed time-period.[50] The law enacted during the communist period stipulated that a Polish citizen can acquire foreign citizenship only after consent of a due institution. The acquisition of a foreign citizenship resulted in the loss of Polish citizenship. Article 15 outlined the conditions under which a person could be deprived of Polish citizenship: first, disloyalty towards the Polish People's Republic (PRL); second, engagement in activities against the interest of the PRL; third, illegal departure from Poland after 9 May 1945; fourth, refusal to return to Poland after a plea by the state's organ; fifth, refusal to serve in the Polish army; and, sixth, a sentence abroad for a crime that is also punishable by Polish law. In the new version of the law, Article 15 was cancelled. Since 2001 loss of citizenship is regulated only by Article 13, which reads that a Polish citizen loses Polish citizenship upon his/her application, having received consent from the President of the Polish Republic to renounce his/her citizenship. The applicant needs to certify that she/he will not become stateless after renouncing Polish citizenship.

In Poland there were two different bills on partial, quasi-citizenship, one debated in 1999 and then rejected, and the second one debated and introduced in 2007.[51] The bill from 1999 defined a fuzzy citizen as a person who is neither a Polish citizen, nor a permanent resident in Poland, but who is an ex-Polish citizen by virtue of emigration or post-1945 border changes, or who is a descendent of such ex-citizens, or who has no connection to Polish citizenship but is 'attached to Polish nationality'. In order to apply for the status, a person needs to present evidence of Polish nationality or origin, for example, the Polish identity card, certificate of birth, marriage, school attendance, military service, evidence of deportation or imprisonment, or other documents officially confirming Polish nationality or Polish citizenship. If there are no documents certifying nationality, an applicant can also refer to membership in the Polish organizations or active involvement in the 'struggle for the Polish cause'. Finally, the status also extends to an applicant's spouse and children, if they are of different nationality.

Concerning border crossing, the bill of the Polish Card provided its holders with a 'national visa' allowing multiple border crossings and exemption from possession of a minimum amount of money upon border crossing. The holders of Polish Cards enjoy an unlimited residence right and an access to healthcare services on the same terms as Polish citizens, regardless of whether or not the persons in question are taxpayers in Poland. The bill did not specify whether the holders of the Polish Card are entitled to a work permit in Poland, but it stipulated that they have free access to public schools in Poland. The bill did not grant voting rights.

In the legal act from 2007, a 'Foreign Pole' category was introduced. A Foreign Pole is a person who can certify his Polish origin but does not have Polish citizenship, lives abroad and does not intend to repatriate to Poland (repatriation is a different legal procedure in Polish law). The law introduced the following conditions: an applicant must have at least one parent or one grandparent, or two great-grandparents, who were Polish nationals or Polish citizens. Additionally, an applicant should be able to prove his link to Poland by at least a basic knowledge of the Polish language or by cultivating Polish traditions and customs. Polish origin can be certified by the following documents: Polish ID, school, church or military certificates indicating nationality of a person, or documents from deportation or imprisonment. In the justification of the law, its authors proposed that cultivation of Polish traditions and customs should be the most important condition for being recognized as a Polish national.

In conclusion, the law from 2007 expanded the scope of privileges offered by the bill from 1999 by introducing the right to employment und unlimited residence in Poland. Otherwise, the law maintained all the privileges previously offered by the bill. However, in contrast to the first bill, the current law introduced a limited validity of ten years for the Polish Card. As already noted, the very introduction of quasi-citizenship is an indicator of ethnicization. Furthermore, in Polish law the entitlement has been strongly based on a declarative ethnic identity.

In the analysed time period, Polish national citizenship law became more ethnic and less liberal (see Table 4.3). In these respects the tendency observed in Poland was very similar to the legal developments in Hungary: the collapse of the communist regime and the establishment of democracy in Poland allowed a discussion on the ethnic Poles abroad to begin, and also the adaption of national legislation to a new political context. In effect, residence-based citizenship acquisition and family-transfer became less liberal by introducing longer residence periods and additional requirements. On the other hand, new modes or statuses of national citizenship were introduced; that is, affinity-based acquisition and quasi-citizenship, which clearly ethnicized Polish citizenship. Only the law regulating the loss of citizenship was liberalized. As in Hungary, the arbitrary withdrawal clause was replaced by a voluntary renunciation principle. Dual citizenship continued to be *de jure* forbidden. However, the principle of voluntary renunciation opened a possibility for *de facto* tolerance of dual citizenship. The group that profited from it were the Polish emigrants living abroad who were in possession of another national citizenship.

The Polish case also tackles the issue of discretionary practices (Górny, 2009). Discretionary practices emerge when the law is not

Table 4.3   Tendencies observed in Polish law since the late 1980s

Mode of citizenship acquisition and loss	Tendency observed in Polish law (late 1980s–2007)
Jus sanguinis at birth	No change since 1962
Jus soli at birth	Absent
Residence-based acquisition	De-liberalization
Family-transfer	De-liberalization
Affinity-based acquisition	Ethnicization
Dual citizenship (*de facto*, not *de jure*)	Ethnicization of the practice
Loss of citizenship	Liberalization
Quasi-citizenship	Ethnicization

Source: Own compilation

clearly formulated. This leaves space for wide interpretations concerning, for instance, naturalization requirements. The literature on citizenship recognizes discretionary practices as a negative phenomenon (Bauböck, 2005c). In practice, it means that each civil servant can require different criteria to be met by a person wanting to naturalize.

The communist period was also not free from discretionary practices. This implies that the analysis of the law itself does not provide us with a full picture of citizenship acquisition and loss under communism. However, that does not diminish the value of legal analysis itself. Rather, it has to be acknowledged that imprecise formulations could have led to different interpretations. In these respects the analysis of discretionary practices can be seen as a subsequent step of the legal analysis. In other words, legal analysis cannot be supplemented by empirical research on discretionary practices. However, research on discretionary practices is impossible without the foundation – legal analysis.

Finally, the interpretation of national citizenship law in communist Poland, as also in Hungary, should acknowledge the political context itself. Namely, liberal naturalization requirements do not automatically imply that communist Poland was open for immigration. Rather, they imply that the authoritarian rule was so strong that it was unnecessary to construct restrictive law – the political system often functioned in parallel to the laws controlling immigration and emigration. However, the Nationality Law from 1962 was not repealed in democratic Poland; on the contrary, after the introduction of a few amendments, the law is in force to this day. This example illustrates that, although the national citizenship laws of the communist states should be interpreted with care, they should not be disregarded, because they laid the foundations for new laws.

Conclusions

Comparing the evolution of national citizenship legislation in Germany, Hungary and Poland, one can see that Hungary and Poland have developed in exactly the opposite direction to Germany: German law has undergone a shift from the ethnic to the republican model, while Hungary and Poland have shifted from the *de jure* relatively liberal model to the ethno-republican eclectic combination (see Table 4.4). In these respects one can observe a very strong legal convergence

Table 4.4 Comparison of German, Hungarian and Polish tendencies in the selected modes of citizenship acquisition and loss

Mode of citizen-ship acquisition and loss	Tendency observed in German law	Tendency observed in Hungarian law	Tendency observed in Polish law	Compared	
				Germany; Hungary; Poland	Poland; Hungary
Jus sanguinis at birth	No radical changes, weak de-ethnicization	No major changes	No change since 1962		CONVERGENCE
Jus soli at birth	Liberalization, strong	No major changes	Absent		
Residence-based acquisition	Mixed: partly liberalization, partly de-liberalization	De-liberalization	De-liberalization	CONVERGENCE DE-LIBERALIZATION	CONVERGENCE; DE-LIBERALIZATION
Family-transfer	De-liberalization	De-liberalization	De-liberalization	CONVERGENCE De-liberalization	CONVERGENCE; De-liberalization
Affinity-based acquisition	De-ethnicization	Ethnicization	Ethnicization		CONVERGENCE, ETHNICIZATION
Dual citizenship	Liberalization	Ethnicization[52]	Ethnicization[53]		CONVERGENCE; ETHNICIZATION
Loss of citizenship	No radical changes	Liberalization	Liberalization		CONVERGENCE; LIBERALIZATION
Quasi-citizenship	De-ethnicization	Ethnicization	Ethnicization		CONVERGENCE; ETHNICIZATION

Source: Own compilation.

between Hungary and Poland, and a divergence between Germany, on the one hand, and Hungary and Poland, on the other.

As already noted in this chapter, the national citizenship legislation enacted in Hungary and Poland during the communist period needs to be 'handled with care'. The fact that the laws were not privileging external co-ethnics, or did not spell out very restrictive naturalization criteria for immigrants, does not mean that communist Hungary and Poland were countries open for immigration. On the contrary, these states had full control over emigration and immigration.[54] Concerning the external co-ethnics, Hungary and Poland could not undertake any initiatives, because the Soviet Union would not allow it for ideological and political reasons. As a consequence, although Hungarian and Polish citizenship laws were *de jure* quite liberal, the *de facto* practice was far from it. It could, therefore, be argued that Hungarian and Polish national citizenship evolved from non-ethnic and *de facto* non-liberal practices towards an ethnic law with republican elements.

The findings show that no liberal convergence of national citizenship laws took place. Rather, comparing Germany, Hungary and Poland, one can observe more divergence than convergence. The only two instances of convergence concerned residence-based acquisitions and family-transfers. The analysis showed that the German, Hungarian and Polish laws regulating these two modes of citizenship acquisition became similar over time. What is interesting is that these similar standards were reached through the process of liberalization of laws in Germany and de-liberalization in Hungary and Poland. In Germany the residence requirement has been decreased from 15 to eight years and new, additional conditions have been introduced: language and integration tests and an oath of loyalty to the constitution. In Hungary, the citizenship law in force until 1993 specified only one condition for naturalization: three years of legal habitual residence in Hungary. The new law (and its further amendments) extended the period of necessary residence from three to eight years, also introducing additional requirements: sufficient means to live in Hungary, and examinations on constitutional basics requiring *de facto* a good knowledge of the Hungarian language. Polish law has also introduced more restrictive naturalization requirements by introducing additional naturalization criteria similar to those in Germany and Hungary.

Similar developments have been observed among the other EU member states (Bauböck *et al.*, 2006). In the early 2000s many states have introduced a language test or are currently debating it, for example Germany, Poland (a bill), Hungary, Austria (1999), France, the United Kingdom, Finland and the Netherlands. More and more Western European states have also introduced an integration test (Joppke, 2007). Furthermore, requirements concerning the length of residence have become relatively similar in Europe; they now vary from five to ten years, for instance ten years in Austria and Italy, seven years in Belgium, and five years in the United Kingdom, Spain and France (Bauböck *et al.*, 2006).

In Germany, Hungary and Poland family-transfers were legally incorporated into the category of residence-based citizenship acquisitions. As a consequence, naturalization requirements in family-transfers and residence-based acquisitions became very similar, given the length of residence required for naturalization and additional requirements such as a language test. In Germany the current requirements are one year of residence and two years of marriage duration, a specific residence title (permanent residency) and a language test. In Hungary the requirements have changed from three years of marriage duration to three years of residence and marriage duration, a language test and sufficient financial means. In Poland the law enacted during the communist period only required an application to be submitted three months after marriage. In 1999 the law changed the entitlement to three years of marriage duration and six months of residency.

The Polish and Hungarian laws have converged almost entirely. Those modes of citizenship acquisition that concern immigrants' naturalization paths (residence-based acquisitions and family-transfers) became more restrictive (they were de-liberalized). On the other hand, the special statuses, or modes of citizenship acquisition, concerning co-ethnics living abroad (reacquisition, cultural acquisitions and quasi-citizenship) became more ethnic. Dual citizenship status was not *de jure* introduced in Poland and Hungary; rather, we can speak of tolerance of a dual citizenship practice for one selected group: Polish and Hungarian emigrants living abroad and being in possession of another state's citizenship. Only the laws regulating the loss of citizenship were liberalized in Hungary and Poland.

5
Explaining Convergence and Divergence of National Citizenship Legislation: A Comparative Analysis of Parliamentary Debates

Citizenship reforms in Germany, Hungary and Poland: an introduction

The previous chapter analysed how the German, Hungarian and Polish national citizenship laws changed between the late 1980s and 2007. Contrary to the popular 'liberal convergence' thesis, national citizenship legislation of these countries has not, in general, become more liberal. Rather, it has been established that the legislation regulating migrants' naturalizations became more similar but not more liberal. On the other hand, citizenship laws dealing with external Diasporas abroad (cultural acquisitions) have diverged; namely, they became more ethnic in Poland and Hungary and less ethnic in Germany. The goal of this chapter is, therefore, to explain *why* citizenship legislation developed in these particular directions. In order to answer this question, the chapter analyses parliamentary (plenary) debates in Germany, Hungary and Poland.

Germany: an immigration state?

After World War II Germany became an immigration state, but the dominant political discourse denied it until the 1990s (Shaw, 2007). In fact, the composition of German society changed significantly in the post-war decades. It is estimated that at the end of the 1990s there were 3.5 million repatriates, 7.3 million former guest-workers and their family members (including their offspring already born in Germany) and 1.4 million refugees residing in Germany (Bade and Oltmer, 2003). Their legal status has been defined not only by different laws but also by different normative principles (Elrick *et al.*, 2006).

After World War II the borders of Germany shifted, leaving a few million ethnic Germans abroad. For the German post-war governments it was a duty to bring these people back home (Bade and Oltmer, 2003). Article 116 in the Basic Law (*Grundgesetz*) stipulates that a German is a person who possesses German citizenship, or who has been expelled but belongs to the German nation (or his/her spouse or ancestors do), or who was living in the territories that belonged to Germany on 31 December 1937 (Gdansk, Poland, Baltic States, CSSR, Czech Republic, Hungary, Romania, Bulgaria, Yugoslavia, Albania). The Act on Displaced Persons, *Bundesvertriebenengesetz* (BVFG), introduced in 1953, stipulates in Article 6 that belonging to the German nation can be certified by origin, language, upbringing and culture. This wide, ethnic definition of German citizenship opened the possibility of immigration to those ethnic Germans who (for various reasons) did not possess German citizenship (Rock and Wolff, 2002).[1]

The first wave of repatriates, coming mostly from Poland, integrated well into the political system. Repatriates became members of political parties and other important public institutions; for instance, in 1959 they constituted 18 per cent of all members of parliament (Levy, 2002).[2] By the late 1950s, repatriates amounted to one-fifth of the German population. Although the first wave of repatriates declared German to be their mother tongue, they were not automatically accepted by the natives. Repatriates were very poor (having lost their entire property), which caused social hostilities, and often had different cultural customs from the native population. With the Aid Law (*Soforthilfegesetz*) from 1948 and the Burden Act (*Lastenausgleichgesetz*) from 1952, German governments improved the financial situation of repatriates, which contributed positively to repatriates' integration into German society. Eventually, in 1960, a social survey established that repatriates could no longer be distinguished as a separate group: the distinction between natives and repatriates had disappeared from German society (Levy, 2002).

The situation changed at the beginning of the 1990s. Poland and other countries in Central Europe successfully democratized. For that reason the German government changed the entitlement to repatriation, stipulating that only ethnic Germans suffering from discrimination or persecution in their countries of residence should be entitled to repatriation. The collapse of the Soviet Union and the newly emerged successor states' permissive attitude towards emigration made it possible for thousands of ethnic Germans to repatriate. The late-repatriates differed substantially from the first wave: their knowledge of German was very poor, because the Soviet Union did not allow them to use German in public, and they were often very poorly educated, which was often also a result of ethnic discrimination in the Soviet Union (Heinrich, 2002). In the 1990s the German economy began to slow down and the national budget was additionally heavily burdened by the costs of reunification. The difficult economic situation and the large inflow of immigrants (late-repatriates and refugees) led to social unrest, hostility towards foreigners and increased popularity of radical right movements. In these circumstances it was very difficult for late-repatriates to find their place in German society and the labour market. In addition, German governments began to cut down repatriates' special social benefits (Klekowski von Koppenfels, 2002).

As a consequence, in the early 1990s the notion of German citizenship was challenged in a bottom-up way. On the one hand, the repatriation programme started to lose its social legitimacy because German society began to perceive repatriates as foreigners, mostly due to their poor knowledge of the German language. On the other hand, the second generation of guest-workers, born and socialized in Germany, still had the status of foreigners in Germany (Blotevogel *et al.*, 1993; Hedwig, 1996; Klopp, 2002). The first legislative change came in 1992. Faced with social unrest and financial problems, the ruling right-wing coalition (CDU/CSU) and the opposition (SPD) signed the *Asylkompromiss*[3] in 1992, aiming at limiting the inflow of refugees into Germany, which had reached 400,000 by 1992 (Faist, 2007). The Asylum Compromise also advocated changes in the constitutional provisions on asylum. As an addition to the new asylum regulations, the document also introduced changes to the law regulating repatriation of ethnic Germans. The *Asylkompromiss* stipulated that the number of repatriates would be reduced to a predefined quota for each year. Furthermore, financial help for repatriates became restricted. By setting limits on repatriation, *Asylkompromiss* was the first significant step towards de-ethnicization of German citizenship, and at the same time the beginning of a new phase (Ette, 2003; Faist *et al.*, 2004).

In the 1990s the opposition, the SPD and the Greens, began to advocate the introduction of a more liberal citizenship law and, more specifically, a law stipulating a much shorter residence time required for naturalization, lower fees and tolerance of dual citizenship. The CDU/CSU objected to the changes proposed by the opposition, as did the FDP, who were unable to agree with a more open definition of German citizenship. In the early 1990s, however, the naturalization entitlements concerning the second generation of immigrants were slightly liberalized. A child born before 1 January 1993 to a foreign mother and a German father could apply retroactively for German citizenship.[4] An applicant had to fulfil the following conditions: acknowledgement of paternity, uninterrupted residence in Germany for three years and submission of the application before reaching the age of 23.

In parallel to the plenary debates, a public debate took place in the German media. As a result of these processes, the reforms proposed by the opposition parties were met with considerable support from German society.[5] During that period the discourse on immigration changed significantly. It was no longer questioned that Germany is an immigration state, and immigration itself began to be perceived as a contribution to the German economy and culture.

Having won the elections in 1998, the coalition of SPD and the Greens proposed an entirely new law on national citizenship, which was intended to replace the old law dating from 1913 (Faist, 2007). The major achievement of the new law was shortening the residence period requirement from 15 to eight years. The initial bill also aimed at reforming dual citizenship status by allowing it for the *jus soli* dual citizens (concerning the second or third generation of immigrants born in Germany)[6] as well as naturalized dual citizens. The latter provision was dropped from the bill after the CDU referendum initiative in Hessen against dual citizenship,[7] while the first was modified. The FDP proposed, at first, to replace full tolerance of dual citizenship for the *jus soli* citizens with an *Optionsmodell*, according to which dual citizens (born to two foreign parents in Germany) should choose one citizenship only upon reaching the age of 23.

The CDU/CSU voted unanimously against the whole of the new law, arguing that, even though the two parties supported shortening of the residence requirements, they disapproved of the *Optionsmodell*. In their opinion *Optionsmodell* was nothing other than a first step towards a full tolerance of dual citizenship. The new law was passed in 1999 due to the sufficient support of the SPD, the Greens, the PDS and half of the FPD.

The new immigration law, implemented in 2005, followed the direction of the legislation enacted since the beginning of the 1990s. First of all, the new law decreased the importance of ethnicity and, second, it adapted more closely to the needs of the German market. The law stipulated, for instance, that repatriates must meet the same naturalization requirements as the other categories of foreigners, such as a certificate of adequate language proficiency. On the other hand, residence permits became more accessible for a highly qualified labour force (a follow-up of the Green Card 2000 initiative, granting residence permits to highly qualified third-country nationals); at the same time, access of unqualified third-country nationals to the German market was restricted.

In the last 15 years German citizenship and immigration laws have ceased to draw on ethnic principles and have instead acknowledged the needs of the liberal market economy (Faist, 2007). The collective meaning of German citizenship itself has also been redefined in the process of parliamentary and public debates (Miller-Idriss, 2006; Coenders and Scheepers, 2008). An ethnic, assimilation-oriented model has been replaced by a more republican, integration-oriented model.

Hungarian citizenship legislation after 1989: the diaspora question

After the fall of communism the Hungarian parliament drafted a new citizenship law, which was aimed at respecting democratic values as well as establishing some formal links with the Hungarian diaspora abroad. As a result, Hungary, which was no longer constrained by the Soviet Union, re-linked national citizenship with ethnicity (Ieda *et al.*, 2004).

After World War I, Hungary lost two-thirds of its territory and thus one-third of its population. Although Poland and Germany also lost territory after World War II, their territorial losses were not as large as those of Hungary (Kovacs and Tóth, 2007). Moreover, Poland and Germany initiated long-term repatriation programmes after the war, helping the ethnic population to return to their homeland. In Hungary no similar, long-term initiative was undertaken, which led to a situation where almost three million ethnic Hungarians were left outside the borders of Hungary. During the communist period it was also forbidden to raise the issue of the external Diaspora in Hungary. However, after the fall of communism, the issue of external co-ethnics found itself high on the public agenda.

In Hungary, parliamentary debates on national citizenship law reform began in the early 1990s. The need to compensate ethnic Hungarians living abroad was stressed from the beginning. It was argued that persons who had been persecuted by the totalitarian regime could individually seek to reacquire their citizenship, while the Diaspora's status should be regulated collectively.

With regard to the status of foreigners in Hungary, naturalization requirements enshrined in the new citizenship law from 1993 became more restrictive in terms of both the length of required residence and additional criteria. However, in Hungary this issue did not lead to a polarization of the political scene as it did in Germany. The issues that polarized political parties very deeply were quasi-citizenship (the Status Law) and dual citizenship (Kovacs, 2006; Kiss and Zahoran, 2007).

In 1998 the right-wing government of Viktor Orban came to power. The major right-wing political party, FIDESZ, declaring itself to represent the interests of the Hungarian diaspora abroad, proposed the Status Law (Fowler, 2004; Kiss and Zahoran, 2007), granting partial citizenship status to ethnic Hungarians living abroad.[8] The opposition parties, as well as a significant part of Hungarian society, were against granting the external co-ethnics wide privileges or fully-fledged national citizenship. The Status Law found majority support in parliament, to the disapproval of the European Commission and Hungary's neighbouring states. The Venice Commission, established in order to examine the Status Law and its international consequences, recommended the introduction of changes limiting provisions offered to the external co-ethnics (Ieda *et al.*, 2004). Following Romania's protests, the law was passed after incorporation of the changes; however, it continued to be perceived as revisionist by the Romanian government.

In 2003 the World Federation of Hungarians, an organization not well integrated into Hungarian politics (Kovacs, 2006), began collecting signatures in order to organize a referendum in Hungary on the creation of a trans-border, de-territorialized dual citizenship (no residence requirements for its holders), granted to all external co-ethnics. The first reaction of all political parties in Hungary was cautious; however, after some time, the main right-wing parties (FIDESZ and MDP) and the president of Hungary declared their support for the referendum. The social democrats and liberals objected, and the Hungarian public was divided on the issue. In the debate preceding the referendum, social democrats mainly pointed out the high welfare costs of the new law. Their agitation against participating in the referendum resulted in an insufficient turnout, and the referendum was not binding. The turnout of the referendum was indeed not sufficient: 63.33 per cent of the eligible voters did not cast their votes. Among those who did vote, 51.57 per cent were in favour and 48.43 per cent against. These results point to the following conclusions: not only political parties, but also Hungarian citizens, are deeply polarized on this issue. However, it should not be forgotten that many opponents of extending Hungarian citizenship to external co-ethnics decided not to cast their votes at all.

The legal initiatives undertaken in Hungary over the last 15 years were clearly concentrating on external co-ethnics, and to a much lesser extent on immigrants. Hence, after the reopening of ethnic issues in the post-communist period, the problem of the external Diaspora remained, for a long time, high on the public and political agenda.

Polish citizenship legislation after 1989: old law, new priorities

In Poland, as in Hungary, the reforms of national citizenship law were only initiated after 1989. However, despite quite a few attempts, the complex reform of the legislation regulating national citizenship acquisition and loss was only partly completed by early 2008.

At the beginning of the democratization period, the citizenship law from 1962 was still in force. Political parties agreed that the law, enacted during the communist period, needed to be replaced by a new citizenship act reflecting democratic principles and human rights. In the first half of the 1990s, the left-wing, social democratic governments[9] only introduced a number of the most urgent amendments, concerning, for instance, gender equality. A complex reform of the national citizenship law was not on the social democrats' agenda. First, national citizenship was a sensitive issue to deal with for a political party that was founded to a large extent by politicians formerly belonging to the communist party. Second, actors pushing for a reform of the national citizenship law were mostly Poles living permanently abroad. Poland, being a sending state, has not attracted many immigrants who could also be interested in citizenship reform. Only the right-wing parties were interested in reforming the national citizenship law, or more specifically the legal status of the ethnic diaspora abroad. Having won in the elections in 1997, the right-wing coalition AWS came up with a legal initiative.

The most intensive phase of the debate on national citizenship law reform took place in the late 1990s and early 2000s. The right-wing coalition prepared proposals for three new legal acts, which were to replace the old law from 1962. These were a proposed new citizenship law, a separate act regulating repatriation and a proposed quasi-citizenship law (the Polish Card). Only one of the projects was ratified by the parliament in 2000, namely the Repatriation Act. The Polish Card was ratified in 2007 at the initiative of Jarosław Kaczynski's right-wing government. In 1999 the proposal of the Polish Card was rejected due to its weak substance and concerns about its reception by the EU.[10]

By early 2008 the Polish parliament had still not ratified a new national citizenship act. Work on national citizenship law reform, initiated by the right-wing government in the years 1999–2001, was not continued by the social democrats who took over in 2001. The major controversy in the debates concerned dual citizenship and how it should be regulated in Polish law. The next right-wing government, in office from 2005 to 2007, ratified the Polish Card one month before the election in 2007. Although that government resumed commission-work on a new national citizenship law, no proposal regarding the law entered plenary debates.

In sum, the legislative changes introduced after 1989 show that Polish political actors were more occupied with the Polish Diasporas abroad than immigrants living in Poland. The fall of communism allowed a revival of an ethnically defined national identity in Poland. On the other hand, the unfinished legislative process regarding a new citizenship law shows that no consensus or clear majority on important issues concerning naturalizations or dual citizenship has yet emerged in Poland.

Plenary debates in Germany, Hungary and Poland – major topics

Table 5.1 shows which modes of national citizenship acquisition and loss were most intensively debated in Germany, Hungary and Poland (in percentages).

The major difference between Germany, on the one hand, and Hungary and Poland, on the other, is that in Germany the most debated aspects of the national citizenship legislation concerned naturalization of immigrants, whereas in Hungary and Poland they concerned the ethnic Diasporas abroad. In Germany the following topics received the most attention: dual citizenship (36 per cent of all the discussed components of national citizenship law), residence-based acquisitions (22 per cent) and *jus soli* at birth (17 per cent). In Hungary and Poland these were: quasi-citizenship (45 per cent in Hungary, 32 per cent in Poland) but also cultural acquisitions (28 per cent in Poland, 10 per cent in Hungary). On that basis it can already

Table 5.1 A comparison of the debated modes of citizenship acquisition and loss in Germany, Hungary and Poland

	Germany	Hungary	Poland
1	Dual citizenship (36%)	Quasi-citizenship (45%)	Qusi-citizenship (32%)
2	Residence-based acquisition (22%)	Dual citizenship (19%)	Cultural affinity acquisition (28%)
3	*Jus soli* at birth (17%)	Loss of citizenship (10%)	Dual citizenship (15%)
4	Cultural affinity acquisition (9%)	Cultural affinity acquisition (10%)	Reacquisition by a former national (10%)
5	Socialization-based acquisition (5%)	Residence-based acquisition (7%)	Loss of citizenship (5%)
6	*Jus sanguinis* at birth (4%)	*Jus sanguinis* at birth (2%)	Residence-based acquisition (4%)
7	Transfer to a child (3%)	Reacquisition by a former national (4%)	*Jus sanguinis* at birth (2%)
8	Spousal transfer (1%)	Spousal transfer (2%)	Spousal transfer (2%)
9	Reacquisition by a former national (1%)	*Jus soli* at birth (1%)	Transfer to a child (1%)
10	Loss of citizenship (1%)	Transfer to a parent (1%)	*Jus soli* at birth (1%)

Note: Total numbers: Germany, 339; Hungary, 280; Poland, 382.

Source: Own compilation.

be noted that the German reform focused on integration of immigrants, whereas the Hungarian and Polish reforms aimed at regulating the status of the ethnic Diasporas abroad.

Dual citizenship received a lot of attention in all the three states under study (36 per cent in Germany, 19 per cent in Hungary, 15 per cent in Poland). However, the context in which it was debated, as well as its implications, differed among these countries. In Germany dual citizenship was debated in the framework of integration of immigrants into a receiving state (in this case Germany), while in Hungary and Poland the framework was integration of emigrants and ethnic diasporas with a sending state (in this case Hungary and Poland). The difference between dual citizenship for expatriates and immigrants was conducted on the sub-codes level. The sub-chapter presenting justificatory strategies devotes more attention to this problem, which is only briefly mentioned here.

Actors

Plenary debates in Germany, Hungary and Poland were dominated by political parties. It was only in Poland that experts representing the interior ministry were also invited to take part in the plenary sessions.[11] The analysis covers a period of over 15 years; hence it also includes those parties that no longer exist or that merged with another party under a new name. This was particularly the case in Poland, where the right wing of the political scene was characterized by very high fluctuation.

The number of statements given by different parties should be viewed with caution. A low number of statements does not imply that a given party had no interest in national citizenship legislation reform. Rather, in each state the speech-time is assigned proportionally to the number of seats that a party has won in parliament. The authors of a bill, or a ruling coalition, are usually entitled to speak first and are granted more time. As a result, a low number of statements can be an effect of structural factors and not necessarily low interest in a given bill. Tables 5.2 to 5.4 present aggregate positions of political parties in Germany, Hungary and Poland measured on the liberalization–de-liberalization and ethnicization–de-ethnicization scales.

The Social Democratic Party (SPD), the Greens (*die Grünen*), the Party of Democratic Socialism (PDS) and the Left (*die Linke*)

Table 5.2 Statements of political parties in Germany

Party		Liberalization:Deliberalization	De-ethnicization:Ethnicization
SPD	No. of statements	52:4	12:3
	in per cent	93:7	80:20
BÜNDNIS 90/DIE GRÜNEN	No. of statements	32:2	5:0
	in per cent	94:6	100:0
PDS	No. of statements	13:0	4:1
	in per cent	100:0	80:20
CDU/CSU	No. of statements	21:77	0:10
	in per cent	21:79	0:100
FDP	No. of statements	14:15	1:2
	in per cent	48:52	33:67
DIE LINKE	No. of statements	2:0	0:0
	in per cent	100:0	
Unaffiliated	No. of statements	0:0	1:0
	in per cent	–	100:0
All statements	No. of statements	136:98	24:17
	in per cent	58:42	59:41

Source: Own compilation.

Table 5.3 Statements of political parties in Hungary

Coalition/Party		Liberalization:Deliberalization	De-ethnicization:Ethnicization
A021 Fidesz	No. of statements	18:2	3:35
	in per cent	90:10	8:92
A022 MSZP	No. of statements	4:10	13:12
	in per cent	29:71	52:48
A023 FKGP	No. of statements	2:1	0:5
	in per cent	67:33	0:100
A024 SZDSZ	No. of statements	3:6	11:2
	in per cent	33:67	85:15
A025 MDF	No. of statements	6:2	0:8
	in per cent	75:25	0:100
A026 MIEP	No. of statements	0:0	0:5
	in per cent	–	0:100
A027 KDNP	No. of statements	6:3	0:3
	in per cent	67:33	0:100
Unaffiliated	No. of statements	6:0	0:0
	in per cent	100:0	–
All statements	No. of statements	53:36	37:118
	in per cent	60:40	24:76

Source: Own compilation.

Table 5.4 Statements of political parties in Poland

Coalition/Party		Liberalization:Deliberalization	De-ethnicization:Ethnicization
A0201 UW	No. of statements	18:1	7:21
	in per cent	95:5	25:75
A0202 AWS	No. of statements	32:2	7:78
	in per cent	94:6	8:92
A0203 Ruch Odbudowy Polski	No. of statements	3:0	0:0
	in per cent	100:0	–
A0204 SLD	No. of statements	6:3	30:12
	in per cent	67:33	71:29
A0206 Ruch Odbudowy Polski	No. of statements	1:3	0:1
	in per cent	25:75	0:100
A0207 PSL	No. of statements	1:6	4:12
	in per cent	14:86	25:75
A0209 PIS	No. of statements	0:0	1:9
	in per cent	–	10:90
A0210 Stronnictwo Konserwatywno-Ludowe	No. of statements	0:0	6:0
	in per cent	–	100:0
A0211 PO	No. of statements	0:0	4:8
	in per cent	–	33:67
A0212 Samoobrona	No. of statements	0:0	1:4
	in per cent	–	20:80
A0213 LPR	No. of statements	0:1	1:3
	in per cent	0:100	25:75
A0214 Unia Pracy	No. of statements	0:0	0:2
	in per cent	–	0:100
A0205 Unaffiliated	No. of statements	1:7	1:9
	in per cent	13:88	10:90
Experts	No. of statements	6:3	8:14
	in per cent	67:33	36:64
All statements	No. of statements	69:26	71:180
	in per cent	73:27	28:72

Source: Own compilation.

supported liberalization and de-ethnicization of national citizenship legislation.[12] On the other hand, the Christian Democratic Union/ Christian Social Union (CDU/CSU) and the Free Democratic Party (FDP) were advocating for more de-liberalization and ethnicization. The German debate shows, first, that the right-wing parties are reluctant to ease immigrants' access to German citizenship. Second, they prefer an ethnic conception of citizenship, which grants ethnic co-nationals living abroad privileged access to German citizenship. On the other hand, the left-wing parties in Germany are in favour of an inclusive national citizenship. They strongly support immigrants' territorial, residence-based entitlement to citizenship and disapprove of the preferential treatment of the co-ethnics.

In Hungary, the right-wing and conservative parties (Fidesz, FKGP, MDF, MIEP and KDNP)[13] were strongly in favour of national citizenship ethnicization, but also relatively in favour of liberalization. The left wing party (MSZP) as well as the liberal party (SZDSZ) were strongly against ethnicization and in favour of liberalization (SZDSZ) or divided between liberalization and de-liberalization (MSZP). The analysis showed that the right-wing parties' statements in favour of liberalization were not connected with naturalization of immigrants, but with liberalization of the law regulating national citizenship loss (introduction of the voluntary renunciation principle and cancelling of arbitrary withdrawal). On the other hand, the left-wing parties' statements were indeed connected with naturalization of immigrants.[14] However, the low number of statements dealing with liberalization/de-liberalization of citizenship indicates that these issues were not of high importance for the Hungarian parliamentarians.

In the Polish parliamentary debate the right-wing and conservative parties[15] (AWS, PIS, ROP or LPR) were all strongly in favour of ethnicization. In contrast to the major right-wing parties (AWS, PIS), the social democrats (SLD) advocated clearly for de-ethnicization of national citizenship. Social democrats did not really take any position with respect to liberalization/de-liberalization of national citizenship (there were only two statements; one for, one against). Only the liberals, UW, and the right-wing AWS gave a substantial number of statements in favour of liberalization (12 and 16). As in Hungary, the statements of the AWS and UW mostly concerned the law regulating loss of national citizenship. In Poland the reform of the law dealing with national citizenship loss was perceived as part of the de-communization strategy, which featured high on the right-wing parties' agenda.[16]

As a consequence, the right-wing parties, both conservative (AWS, PIS) and liberal (UW, PO), were in favour of the ethnic model, while the social democrats were against it. The dimension of liberalization/de-liberalization of citizenship was not very prominent in the Polish debate, which is illustrated by the small number of statements.

In sum, the findings confirm that both party cleavages, left–right and TAN–GAL (traditional/authoritarian/nationalist versus green/alternative/libertarian) (Hooghe *et al.*, 2002), do play a role in national citizenship policy. Not only the left-wing parties were against the ethnic model of national citizenship and in favour of liberalization; the 'GAL' parties in Germany, Hungary and Poland shared the same opinion. The 'TAN' parties were in favour of ethnicization and, in Germany, also in favour of de-liberalization (CDU/CSU). On the other hand, the 'TAN' parties in Hungary and Poland were in favour of liberalization. However, this does not automatically imply that the Hungarian and Polish conservative parties advocated for less restrictive naturalization requirements. A closer analysis showed that in Poland and Hungary these parties were more concerned with liberalization of the law regulating national citizenship loss than residence-based acquisitions. Interestingly, experts from the ministry of the interior advocated more de-liberalization in that area.

Argumentative strategies

Most of the statements were accompanied by justifications. The parliamentarians would give their reasons for holding a positive or a negative opinion on a discussed legal proposal. In the coding procedure the justifications were coded as a separate category 'D'. A justification (or justifications) accompanying each statement was simply written down during the coding. When all the debates had been coded, the justifications were clustered into a few thematic groups. This clustered data is presented in the tables below.

In the German parliamentary debates 'integration', followed by 'national unity and identity' and 'practices and relations in other states', was the most frequent justification. In Hungary it was 'national unity and identity', followed by the 'EU law', 'economic factors' and 'practices in the other states'. Poland reflected a slightly different pattern: the most frequent justification was 'economic factors', followed by 'national unity and identity', 'compensatory practices', 'practices in other states' and 'EU law'. Table 5.5 presents more detailed information for each country.

The next three sub-chapters concentrate separately on Germany, Hungary and Poland and discuss the arguments that were used in the parliamentary debates in these countries. In other words, this analysis presents *how* the various modes of national citizenship acquisition and loss, as well as statuses, were debated, and *which* actors used the respective justifications. The modes and statuses are as follows: (i) *jus sanguinis* at birth; (ii) *jus soli* at birth; (iii) residence, family-transfers and socialization-based acquisitions; (iv) cultural acquisitions and quasi-citizenship; (v) dual citizenship; and (vi) loss of citizenship.

Germany – from ethnic exclusion to civic inclusion

According to the *jus sanguinis* at birth principle, citizenship is inherited automatically at birth from parent(s), without fulfilling

Table 5.5   Top ten justifications per country

	Germany	Hungary	Poland
1	Integration (23%)	National unity and identity (22%)	Economic factors (18%)
2	National unity and identity (12%)	EU law (14%)	National unity and identity (17%)
3	Practices and relations in other states (11%)	Economic factors (14%)	Compensatory practices (16%)
4	Ties with a receiving state (11%)	Practices and relations in other states (10%)	Practices and relations in other states (11%)
5	Interests (10%)	Rights (8%)	EU law (9%)
6	Ideologies and principles (8%)	Compensatory practices (8%)	National law and legal traditions (8%)
7	Economic factors (7%)	Ties with a sending state (8%)	Rights (6%)
8	Rights (7%)	Ties with a receiving state (6%)	Communist heritage (6%)
9	Ties with a sending state (5%)	Integration (6%)	Crime (5%)
10	EU law (4%)	Importance of citizenship (5%)	Integration (5%)

Note: Total numbers of justifications: Germany, 343; Hungary, 344; Poland, 493.

Source: Own compilation.

any additional requirements. In Germany, as well as in Hungary and Poland, this principle has long been acknowledged as a dominant citizenship acquisition principle. Contrary to expectations, in Germany a privileged status of *jus sanguinis* at birth was not defended predominantly in the name of national or ethnic identity. The CDU/CSU parliamentarians most often defended the special status of *jus sanguinis* at birth principle by referring to 'practices in other states'. They attempted to show that in other, mostly European, states *jus sanguinis* at birth is a dominant citizenship acquisition mode, and hence there is nothing unusual or wrong with German law. The critics (the SPD, the Greens and the PDS (later the Left)), would also refer to 'practices in other states' in order to show that it is actually more common in Europe to combine the *jus soli* and the *jus sanguinis* principles. They would also stress that the dominance of *jus sanguinis* is an anachronism:

> In most European states such as Sweden, Italy and the Netherlands, national citizenship combines the territoriality and blood principle. Especially the British and French law represents this tradition. The German blood principle is really an exceptional anachronism in the European context, i.e. from the Wilhelminian times. (The Greens, 9 February 1995)[17]

The SPD and the Greens also argued that the dominance of the *jus sanguinis* principle hinders integration and weakens ties with receiving states. Albeit sporadically, the Greens even referred to the Nazi context:

> Also in the Weimar Republic citizenship acquisition was free from the national component. That has fundamentally changed in the Third Reich. [...] The German nation was open only for the native ethnic Germans. Foreigners were brought to the Third Reich as slaves or displaced; the Jews were deprived of citizenship and exterminated in gas chambers. The purification of the German blood was the prime goal of the state. (The Greens, 12 May 1989)[18]

The principle of *jus soli* at birth implies that a person born in a territory of a given state is entitled to automatically acquire national citizenship of that state, regardless of whether or not the parents of that person were citizens of that state. The principle was introduced in Germany by the reform in the late 1990s. However, the debate on *jus soli* at birth had begun much earlier. Since the late 1980s the German political elites had been disputing whether Germany had become an immigration state and whether the introduction of the *jus soli* at birth was necessary. In 1989 one of the CDU/CSU parliamentarians argued: 'The Federal Republic of Germany was, in the opinion of the previous governments and the current one, no immigration state and cannot be one. We are not an immigration state and we cannot become one!' (The CDU/CSU, 12 May 1989).[19] This statement proved to be very important for the whole German parliamentary debate on national citizenship. It was also quite frequently referred to as a negative example by those who did indeed perceive Germany as an immigration state (*Deutschland ist ein Einwanderungsland*).

The parties in favour of the *jus soli* at birth principle (the SPD, the Greens and the Left) referred to the following arguments: 'ties with a receiving state', 'integration' and 'practices in other states'. They argued that the second generation of immigrants, already born in Germany, are not foreigners and should not be treated as such. In their view, automatic naturalization is an essential part of an integration process because a person cannot be fully integrated into a society without being its citizen. In order to make their argument stronger, they referred to legal practices in the other European states where the *jus soli* at birth principle coexists with the *jus sanguinis* principle.

The opponents of the *jus soli* at birth, the CDU/CSU, justified their position mainly with two kinds of argument: 'integration' and, to a lesser extent, 'practices in other states'. In their opinion, it would be irresponsible to grant the second generation automatic access to German citizenship without being certain that these persons are well enough integrated. The CDU/CSU claimed, rather, that foreigners should choose German citizenship consciously and not be granted it automatically. In their view, naturalization should be the last step in the integration process:

> Whether you want it or not: there are people who have lived here since one or two generations and are not willing to integrate. These people will not be integrated once they receive the German passport. I am therefore saying: the grant of a passport does not lead to integration. I believe it is the final stage of the integration process. (27 March 1998, CDU/CSU)[20]

Residence and socialization-based acquisitions are non-automatic modes of national citizenship acquisition after birth. As well as residence requirements, there are usually other additional conditions to be fulfilled by an applicant, that is, a language test. In 1989 the Greens were already strongly advocating liberalization in this area:

> When will you finally come to understand that a vivid, democratic common existence in our society cannot be based on the ethno-national awareness but only upon the principle that the people who live here permanently enjoy the same rights and, having accepted that common foundation, pursue different political, cultural, economic and social interest? (The Greens, 20 May 1989)[21]

In Germany, citizenship reform had a mixed outcome. On the one hand the residence requirement was shortened (from 15 to 8 years), but on the other hand additional requirements were introduced. The German political parties had very diverse opinions regarding residence, family-transfers and socialization-based naturalizations. 'Integration' was a frequent justification used both in favour of and against liberalization. Fast and easy naturalization was a precondition for a successful 'integration' for the social democrats and the Greens, while for the CDU/CSU the preconditions for 'integration' were good knowledge of the language, respect for the German constitution (*Grundgesetz*) and no security threat.

The proponents of liberalization of residence-based acquisition (SPD, the Greens, the PDS and the Left) often referred to 'ties with a receiving state', 'integration' and 'rights'. The CDU/CSU and the FDP, in comparison, referred to 'integration' and, to a limited extent, 'rights'. The SPD and the Greens argued that quicker naturalization strengthens ties with a receiving state. They also claimed that a facilitated naturalization is a democratic and universal right of long-term residents. The CDU/CSU also referred to 'rights' in their discourse, but they wanted to show that immigrants naturalized too quickly could threaten German democracy.

> What we want most of all is a real integration. This is why we want to shorten the required residence period. We want more entitlement for naturalization. But knowledge of the language shall be the precondition for naturalization so that we understand each other.

We want the foreigners to respect Article 3 of the Constitution: men and women are equal. (CDU/CSU, 27 March 1998)[22]

In the initial phase of the debate (the early 1990s) the language test did not enjoy widespread support. The Greens, the PDS and later the Left were against it. The Greens changed their position after they entered a coalition with the SPD in 1998. The PDS and the Left doubted whether the introduction of a language test would really foster integration. Instead they proposed to introduce voluntary and cost-free language education:

> [...] stricter naturalization requirements are introduced, that should not be overseen. The main point is that [an applicant] needs to know the language sufficiently. I am asking you, what is sufficient? Who decides what is sufficient? Also those who are themselves to blame either for being unemployed or for finding themselves in a difficult social situation will not be naturalized. (PDS, 19 March 1999)[23]

In the mid-2000s the Greens attempted to liberalize the law further. However, the idea of shortening the residence-requirement period from eight to four years was met with strong criticism by the CDU/CSU and the FDP. They were afraid that naturalization after only four years of residence could lead not only to language disintegration in Germany but also to a regression of religious freedom or women's rights. The CDU/CSU also did not support the idea of granting refugees residence-based entitlement to citizenship.

Culture-based citizenship acquisition is based on an ethnocultural entitlement to national citizenship. In practice it means that a foreigner who can prove an ethnocultural unity with a state of which he or she wants to become a citizen can undergo a facilitated naturalization.[24] A reacquisition is a slightly similar procedure, allowing a person who was deprived of national citizenship against his/her will to reacquire it. Culture-based acquisition, on the other hand, concerns persons who have never held citizenship of the state of which they want to become citizens.

In Germany it was the shift of borders in 1945 and a *jus sanguinis*-based definition of national citizenship enshrined in the law from 1913 that gave rise to many culture-based citizenship acquisitions.

The German post-war law was constructed with the aim of providing external nationals with a return option consisting of a facilitated naturalization. This policy direction was challenged at the beginning of the 1990s: the SPD and the Greens wanted to change the law, and the CDU/CSU objected at first. Eventually, the Asylum Compromise from 1992[25] introduced yearly quotas of repatriation and other limitations. In the parliamentary discussions the defenders of the policy, the CDU/CSU and the FDP, argued that it was Germany's duty to compensate for the historical hardships of the ethnic Germans living abroad.

> Though the financial situation is still difficult, we want the victims of the Nazi regime, to whom the expelled also belong, be compensated during their life-time. (FDP, 5 December 1992)[26]

The arguments used in favour of a privileged treatment of the co-ethnics were not drawing on references to national unity or identity. Rather, the SPD, the Greens and the PDS were justifying their position predominantly by 'national unity and identity' and secondly by 'economic factors'. They argued that repatriation takes place at the expense of German reunification. Above all, the social democrats and the Greens claimed that repatriates do not share German identity; they neither know modern German culture nor speak the language well. In the view of these parties, modern German identity had ceased to correspond with the old law. Some more radical parliamentarians from the PDS even argued that the law was ethnically discriminatory:

> A late repatriate is supposed to be a German because he complies with the criteria of being part of the German people. A person being part of the German people is somebody who has committed himself to German national identity, insofar as this commitment is confirmed by certain characteristics such as descent, language, education, and culture. To my mind, this definition stands for an ethnic exclusion and privileges certain parts of the population with foreign citizenship and residence in another state. (PDS, 5 December 1992)[27]

In the late 1990s the red–green coalition came up with a legislation proposal introducing a limited tolerance for dual citizenship. The

CDU/CSU was against it, but one-third of the FDP parliamentarians supported the opposition's proposal. The proponents of dual citizenship referred most frequently to the following justifications: 'practices in other states', 'interests' and 'integration'. The authors of the bill, the SPD and the Greens, frequently pointed out positive experiences of the other European states with dual citizenship. They would also show that the problems related to dual citizenship are usually exaggerated.

> The over-dramatization of the issue of dual citizenship in Germany is evidenced by the positive experience of other states. Let us look at France, Great Britain and the Netherlands. Let us take an example of the popular Queen Beatrix. She holds not only one, not two, not three but four citizenships: Dutch, German, British and Canadian; listen and wonder. (Erwin Marschewski, CDU/CSU: that is really desirable!) No Dutch, Mr. Marschewski, has ever questioned the loyalty of Queen Beatrix towards the Netherlands.' (SPD, 19 March 1999)[28]

In the view of the SPD and the Greens, introduction of dual citizenship also meets the interests of both immigrants and political parties; immigrants obtain the right to be politically represented, and political parties the right to represent them. Apart from obtaining active and passive political rights, naturalization was also claimed to expand immigrants' social and cultural rights. Integration played a smaller, though still a significant, role. The SPD parliamentarians argued that introduction of dual citizenship would foster integration of immigrants because they would no longer need to make a choice between citizenship of a sending and a receiving state (in this case Germany).

The opponents of dual citizenship, the CDU/CSU and two-thirds of the FDP, referred to 'integration', 'importance of citizenship' and 'practices in the other states'. They claimed that integration would actually suffer if dual citizenship were introduced in Germany. In their view, dual citizenship weakens ties with a receiving state and leads to loyalty problems and crime;

> The new law that you plan to introduce forces us to permanently keep those people that do not fit to our society and that have done everything to locate themselves at the margins of our society. (Sebastian Edathy, SPD: I find it much worse that we need to

keep you permanently!) Ladies and gentlemen, I have said: crime is also an issue that we need to take into consideration. (CDU/CSU, 19 March 1999)[29]

According to the critics, dual citizenship also challenges the importance of national citizenship: 'The German passport is not just any document, but it rather presupposes a conscious recognition of the German state' (FDP, 19 March 1999).[30] Importance of citizenship was one of the reasons why the *Optionsmodell*, offering a limited tolerance of the *jus soli* dual citizenship (in the case of children born in Germany to two foreign parents), did not win the CDU/CSU's approval. The *Optionsmodell* stipulated that these persons can keep dual citizenship until reaching maturity. At that time they are obliged to choose one citizenship only. The CDU/CSU voted against this, claiming that the *Optionsmodell* would lead to *de facto* wide tolerance of dual citizenship in the future. In the FDP the opinions were divided: some 30 per cent of the FDP parliamentarians were in favour of the *Optionsmodell*.

The PDS was also critical, but, in contrast to the CDU/CSU, argued that the *Optionsmodell* does not provide enough tolerance for dual citizenship. Nonetheless, the PDS voted in favour of the new law, seeing it as a small step in the right direction. The PDS was the only party to bring attention to the discriminatory nature of the *Optionsmodell*. The new law stipulated that the second generation of immigrants had to choose one out of their two citizenships, while repatriates' children could keep both citizenships forever.

In Germany loss of citizenship was only debated in the context of dual citizenship. The dominant argument was that immigrants applying for German citizenship should renounce the citizenship of a sending state.

Table 5.6 summarizes the findings for Germany by presenting arguments that led to the legal changes. The analysis showed that in Germany the ethnic model of national citizenship is in retreat. The reforms were conducted in the spirit of an inclusive, republican understanding of national citizenship, which is open to incorporate those immigrants who are ready to integrate linguistically into German society, respect German law and the values of a liberal, European democracy, and do not have a criminal record. Modern German identity has, at the same time, undergone a substantial change. The political parties agreed that the links established during

Table 5.6   Summary of arguments used in the parliamentary debate in Germany

Mode of citizenship acquisition and loss	Tendency observed in German law	Arguments that fostered the legal change
Jus sanguinis at birth	No radical changes	
Jus soli at birth	Liberalization, strong	1. Ties with a receiving state 2. Integration 3. Practices in the other states
Residence-based acquisition and family-transfer	Mixed: partly liberalization, partly de-liberalization 'Republicanization'	1. Integration 2. Ties with a receiving state
Affinity-based acquisition and quasi-citizenship	De-ethnicization	1. National unity and identity 2. Economic factors
Dual citizenship	Liberalization	1. Practices in the other states 2. Interests
Loss of citizenship	No radical changes	

Source: Own compilation.

residence in Germany have a stronger collective-identity-building potential than an ethnic origin. The debate has also shown that, although all the German political parties agreed on fostering immigrants' integration into German society, their understanding of the process is very different. The SDP, the Greens, the PDS and the Left perceived naturalization as part of the integration process, while for the CDU/CSU and the FDP naturalization was a final step and reward in the integration process.

Hungary – a difficult legacy of the Trianon Treaty

The discussion on *jus sanguinis* at birth in Hungary was dominated by arguments referring to either the residence-based or the ethnic identity-based entitlement. The dominance of the latter principle has been challenged by the social democrats (SZDSZ) and defended by the right-wing parties (KDNP):

> Hungarian citizenship – as in continental legal systems and according to our legal traditions – is attributed on the basis of the principle of jus sanguinis or descent. (KDNP, 2 March 1993)[31]

The right-wing parties were not willing to diminish the role of an ethnic origin in national citizenship acquisition. On the other hand, the social democrats argued that ties with a receiving state are more important than a national identity or legal tradition, which in Hungary envisaged a dominant role of the *jus sanguinis* principle. The social democrats also suggested the introduction of limited heritability of the *jus sanguinis* at birth principle. In their opinion native Hungarians, after residing abroad for three generations or more, should cease to inherit Hungarian citizenship. This idea has been supported by a few right-wing Fidesz parliamentarians:

> Hungarian citizenship should be easily awarded to those who have real ties with this country. Unfortunately, the bill that is under discussion here does not serve this goal. In contrast, it strengthens the current practice which makes it possible for Hungarian emigrants to inherit Hungarian citizenship through many generations, even to those descendants who do not have any ties with the country and who, eventually, do not speak Hungarian. It is certainly appropriate that children of Hungarians living abroad acquire Hungarian citizenship if they have some relations with their motherland. However, it is unjustified that those who do not claim such rights and are citizens of another country are automatically entitled to Hungarian citizenship and to the responsibility towards the Hungarian state. (Fidesz, 4 May 1993)[32]

The *jus soli* at birth principle was only briefly mentioned in the Hungarian parliamentary debates. Under the new law the applicability of this principle was limited to stateless persons and foundlings. In general, there was widespread agreement among the parliamentarians that Hungary does not need a second mode of automatic citizenship acquisition at birth.

Residence- and socialization-based acquisitions were more intensively debated. The most frequent justifications, both against and in favour of liberalization in that area, revolved around 'integration', 'practices in the other states' and 'economic factors'. In this debate quite a large group of social democrats and liberals (MSZP, SZDSZ) were in favour of a more restrictive law, especially concerning language integration and the required length of residence.

Arguments in favour of liberalization in this area drew most often on 'integration', by pointing to the fact that more demanding naturalization criteria can hinder integration. The Hungarian right-wing, conservative parties (Fidesz, MIEP) also frequently referred to liberal naturalization practices in other states, mostly in the neighbouring and the old EU member states. They would also point to economic profits, arguing that migrants' work is very valuable for the Hungarian market. However, what the conservative, right-wing parties most often meant were ethnic Hungarians living abroad, and not a wide category of all naturalizing immigrants. In these respects the discussion on residence-based naturalization in Hungary was very much context-dependent.

The opponents, recruited mostly from the social democratic and liberal parties, claimed that a longer period of residence and language requirements would lead to a better integration of foreigners.

> In order to avoid the devaluation of the institution of citizenship, this bill imposes stricter conditions upon those who would like to acquire citizenship. These new conditions are similar to or the same as existing European rules. According to these new rules, a person applying for citizenship is required to live in the territory of Hungary for a given period of time, to have a clean criminal record and to integrate into Hungarian society. As the current law lays it down, before acquiring Hungarian citizenship, the applicant should reside in Hungary as an immigrant for at least three years. This rule – the period of three years – fits neither our circumstances nor current European practice any longer. This period is too short for the prospective Hungarian citizen to adapt, to accept the conditions of and integrate into our society. (2 March 1993, government, social-democrats, MSZP)[33]

The opponents were also in favour of introducing further restrictions to the law regulating spousal transfers. Their argument was that a more restrictive law in that area would correspond better with European standards and help to prevent potential misuses in the future. Given the economic factors, the social democrats and liberals perceived immigration as a threat to the Hungarian market.

In the debates on cultural acquisitions, including quasi-citizenship, a deep polarization of the political scene was observed. The majority of the left-wing parliamentarians (MSZP and SZPSZ) were against ethnicization of national citizenship, while the right-wing parties (mostly FIDESZ) were advocating strongly for it. The polarization of the debate was to a large extent caused by the contradiction between the two conflicting principles. The first principle stipulated that democratic Hungary should support ethnic Hungarians in the countries of their residence. According to the second principle, Hungary is obliged to bring the co-ethnics back to Hungary.

Parliamentarians who were in favour of an ethnically-defined citizenship referred most of all to 'national unity and identity', 'economic factors' and 'conformity with the EU and international law'. The opponents of ethnicization drew mostly on economic factors and lack of conformity with EU law. The right-wing parties argued that it is a matter of responsibility to support a facilitated naturalization of those ethnic Hungarians who want to settle in Hungary. Their naturalization should be quick and require no period of residence. In the right-wing parties' view, Hungary should pursue an 'open door' policy, showing solidarity with the external co-ethnics:

> The Government, proposing the Status Law, faces the legacy of the twentieth century in which borders divide the once united body of Hungarians. We cannot change the borders, but we can surmount or bridge the divide. The Status Law is a confrontation with the fact that these borders are mental. The majority of people from the motherland have been afraid of expressing that they form one community with those parts of the nation who live beyond borders. And where there is fear, there is no freedom. The Fidesz-MPP believes that we, Hungarians, within or beyond borders are free at last; free to stand for cooperation with those who declare themselves to belong to us. Hungarian communities remain living beyond borders, but national solidarity cannot have limits any longer. (Fidesz, 19 April 2001)[34]

The discussion on the Status Law (Hungarian quasi-citizenship) was particularly intensive and polarized. The left-wing parties (MSZP, SZPSZ) objected to the Status Law, arguing that it did not comply with EU and international law and that it would lead to ethnic discrimination. They also feared that the Status Law would lead to an oversupply of labour, which would lower the wages in Hungary:

> The most critical or problematic point is that these workers – as in the majority of neighbouring countries where standards of living and wages are significantly lower than in Hungary – often offer to

do jobs at a lower price than do Hungarian workers, which unfortunately can have a wage-decreasing effect. This is a very serious problem which we have to face. At the meeting of our committee we already expressed that we have to build in guarantees in the law that can ensure that Hungarians from neighbouring countries receive wages that are at least as high as Hungarian workers usually get in a given industry and a given job. (Parliamentary Committee for Employment, 19 April 2001)[35]

The Hungarian social democrats were also concerned with the international repercussions of the law. They pointed to the fact that neighbouring states (mostly Romania) might see the Status Law as revisionist.

The right-wing parties, on the other hand, were arguing that the Status Law offers an incentive to 'stay at home' instead of 'leaving home' (i.e. the state of residence). In their opinion, the Status Law facilitated only temporary settlement of the external co-ethnics, who, after some limited time of working or studying in Hungary, would go back to their countries of residence. As well as identity- or compensation-based arguments, the right-wing parties also pointed towards positive economic effects, and argued that by allowing legal employment of the external co-ethnics the Status Law would solve the problem of underemployment in Hungary. The right-wing parties also referred to similar laws enacted in the old and the new EU member states, in order to show that the Status Law was in conformity with so-called 'European practices'. They would also claim that the Status Law was, in fact, in line with the important EU and international legal norms (the Council of Europe's Framework Convention for the Protection of National Minorities, the European Card for Regional or Minority Languages, the UN Minority Rights Declaration) as well as bilateral treaties with the neighbouring countries and the EU *acquis*. In sum, it could be observed that the issue of ethnic diaspora abroad generated a lot of controversies and eventually resulted in two different approaches to the issue. The implemented approach clearly fosters an ethnic model of national citizenship.

The debate on dual citizenship also generated a heated and politically polarized debate, with the right-wing parties (FIDESZ, KDNP, FKGP) supporting the introduction of dual citizenship and the left-wing parties (MSZP, SZDSZ) being against it. In contrast to Germany, in Hungary the group interested in acquiring the second, Hungarian, citizenship were co-ethnics living abroad, not immigrants living in Hungary. The Hungarian right-wing parties justified their position predominantly with 'practices in other states', 'ties with Hungary' and 'economic factors'.

> Thus, granting Hungarian citizenship based on preferential naturalization is not against the regulations and principles of the European Union. Almost all member states of the European Union acknowledge and apply the institution of dual citizenship. One could make a long list of the similarities and differences between the practices of EU member states, like that of Germany, Portugal, Greece, Spain, Italy, France, the Scandinavian countries or the UK, but also Estonia and Latvia. [...] So if you look a bit closer [...] Slovakia acknowledges and applies the institution of dual citizenship. [...] Moreover, in Romania, no law forbids dual citizenship. A foreign citizen can relatively easily acquire Romanian citizenship as well; it is enough for that person to prove his or her Romanian ancestry of whatever kind. (Fidesz, 17 November 2004)[36]

The opponents referred mostly to 'ties with a receiving state', 'economic factors' and to a lesser extent 'practices in the other states'. The debate often revolved around two opposite statements: 'keep the ethnic Hungarians at home' and 'give them incentive to leave home (country of residence)'. The left-wing parties argued that the introduction of dual citizenship would encourage ethnic Hungarians to leave their countries of residence, for instance Romania, and come to Hungary, which would imply high costs for the Hungarian welfare system and lead to oversupply of labour in the Hungarian market.

> Based on their dual citizenship, those who – as foreign citizens – needed a working permit in Hungary until now, in order to work, will be able to get jobs of any kind without permission – as Hungarian citizens. We believe that this can lead to serious pressures on the labour market, especially in the Eastern and Northern regions that are close to the border. This particularly effects younger generations. Newcomers can crowd out those who are employed now. Every 100,000 newcomers bring an increase

in expenses of unemployment-benefits by 50 billion forint. (The Hungarian government, 17 November 2004)[37]

The left-wing parties were stressing that, by decoupling social benefits from permanent residence, all the external Hungarian citizens, who do not contribute to the welfare system, would nonetheless be entitled to profit from it. The left-wing parties were not questioning the Hungarian-ness of the external co-ethnics, but rather, given the sensitivity of the issue, they decided to build support for their position. They focused mainly on economic arguments, which they assumed to be more appealing to the voters. The right-wing parties were claiming the reverse, namely, that the introduction of dual citizenship would provide ethnic Hungarians with an incentive to stay in their countries of residence and visit Hungary only on a short-term basis.

In the discussion on the loss of citizenship, arguments in favour of liberalizing the law were clearly dominant. The citizenship law enacted during the communist period stipulated that an arbitrary withdrawal of Hungarian citizenship was possible, if a person acted against the vital interests of the Hungarian state. In democratic Hungary an arbitrary withdrawal of national citizenship was cancelled and replaced by a voluntary renunciation rule. Not surprisingly, the arguments used by the parliamentarians revolved around universal rights, communist heritage and EU law.

Table 5.7 summarizes the findings from the Hungarian parliamentary debate. In the debate two different types of arguments collided. On the one hand, the discussion on naturalization of immigrants revolved around a strong integration imperative and national market protectionism. In these discussions references to the practices of other states, mostly EU member states, were very frequent. The Hungarian parliamentarians aimed to show that an introduction of stricter naturalization requirements was not wrong, but, rather, corresponded with the criteria that the other EU member states had already introduced. On the other hand, the debate on culture-based acquisitions revolved mostly around arguments of national unity and identity, turning Hungarian citizenship into an extraterritorial, ethnicity-based phenomenon. In general, the arguments used in the Hungarian debate indicate that immigration of foreigners was approached with caution or fear, justified by practices in the other EU states. The drive towards extending national citizenship

Table 5.7 Summary of arguments used in the parliamentary debate in Hungary

Mode of citizenship acquisition and loss	Tendency observed in Hungarian law	Arguments that fostered the legal change
Jus sanguinis at birth	No major changes	
Jus soli at birth	Strong de-liberalization (principle cancelled)	No substantial debate
Residence-based acquisition and family-transfer	De-liberalization	1. Integration 2. Practices in the other states 3. Economic factors
Affinity-based acquisition and quasi-citizenship	Ethnicization	1. National unity and identity 2. EU law (conformity) 3. Economic factors
Dual citizenship	Ethnicization	1. Ties with a receiving state 2. Economic factors 3. Practices in the other states
Loss of citizenship	Liberalization	1. Rights 2. Communist heritage

Source: Own compilation.

to the external co-ethnics (as dual or quasi-citizenship) shows that ethnicity was recognized as a more legitimate entitlement for naturalization than permanent residence. Finally, the discussion on the loss of national citizenship revealed a slightly different tendency: loss of citizenship was the only mode that was clearly liberalized in Hungarian law. The arguments fostering liberalization revolved around communist heritage (de-communization) as well as universal and EU rights.

Poland – 'A mother will have enough bread for all the children'[38] – a victory of the ethnic model

In the Polish parliamentary debate on national citizenship the *jus sanguinis* and the *jus soli* at birth principles were neither contested nor widely debated. There was consent among the parliamentarians that *jus sanguinis* is the basic principle for automatic citizenship acquisition. The arguments in favour of maintaining a special status of the *jus sanguinis* at birth were in the majority, pointing out the importance of national citizenship but also national law and legal traditions. Legal path-dependency, understood as continuation of the legal traditions established in the 1920s, was also presented as something positive.

The *jus soli* at birth principle generated no contention; all the statements given in the parliament were in favour of the principle, referring mostly to rights, national law or legal traditions. Although the Polish parliamentarians did claim that the *jus soli* principle is important, they all regarded it as a supplementary principle only:

> *Jus soli* should still remain a supplementary principle. It is to prevent, as it has been until now, the case of statelessness among children. (7 June 2000)[39]

They argued, for instance, that the first democratic law on Polish national citizenship had already introduced *jus soli* at birth as a supplementary principle of citizenship acquisition. Apart from legal path-dependency, justifications referring to rights or universal standards were also prominent. Parliamentarians argued that *jus soli* at birth prevents statelessness by granting Polish citizenship to stateless persons' children.

Residence-based acquisitions, though not intensively debated, generated more controversies among the parliamentarians. Naturalization of immigrants was a new topic in the Polish parliament. Parliamentarians were strongly oriented towards 'practices in other states' as well as 'the EU law' in the discussions. Interestingly, 'practices in other states' were mostly mentioned by parliamentarians who advocated a stricter law in this area. Other arguments drew on economic factors or the threat of crime. Arguments in favour of liberalization were less frequent, referring also to 'practices in other states', 'EU law', 'rights' or 'ties with a receiving state'. In these discussions the European Convention on Nationality from 1997 played quite an important role. Parliamentarians who were in favour of liberalization of residence-based acquisition referred to the ECN as a document spelling out the legitimate, modern European standards:

> Poland, as a member of the Council of Europe, is going to ratify the European Convention on Nationality in the near future and

this legal act precedes the ratification. [The Convention] includes rules which are recognized now as standard. (UW, 3 July 2000)[40]

In the discussions on spousal transfer and socialization-based acquisitions, arguments referring to 'universal rights' or 'ties with a receiving state' were used in support of liberalizing the law. On the other hand, those who were in favour of a stricter law in this area referred to the threat of crime or potential misuses of a liberal law.

As already mentioned, Poland has had very little experience with immigration; however, many parliamentarians believed that Poland will have to prepare for this situation when it becomes an attractive, receiving EU state. They believed that immigration will cause various integration, financial and security problems. When dealing with a new problem, Polish parliamentarians frequently consulted legal practices in other states:

[According to the new legal act] a foreigner can be granted Polish citizenship upon his own application, under the condition that he has been a permanent resident in Poland for at least 5 years. In the Senate there were voices advocating a shortening of this period, but eventually in the voting the time period was even extended. [Our reasons were the following:] in the other European states' laws the time period required for naturalization usually comprises of 5 years. There were also fears of foreigners naturalising too quickly. (UW, 22 September 1999)[41]

'Concerning language criteria: they are now being introduced in various countries. We will also think about it during our work on the new citizenship law and the reform of the foreigners' law.' (expert from the Ministry of Interior, 23 May 2006)[42]

Cultural acquisitions were debated very intensively in the Polish parliament. The debated proposal introduced three new modes of culture-based citizenship acquisition: reacquisition, repatriation and quasi-citizenship.[43] Concerning the reacquisition procedure, the vast majority of parliamentarians agreed that only those persons who had lost Polish citizenship against their will during the communist period should be entitled to reacquire it. Only a very few social democrats and liberals (SLD and the UW) suggested that reacquisition should also be open to persons who had emigrated for economic reasons.

Repatriation law generated more disagreement. In the first phase of the debate (the late 1990s) some circles of social democrats and liberals disapproved of the whole policy, arguing that it was too expensive and introduced unnecessary ethnic privileges that violated the principle of solidarity in the welfare system. Furthermore, there were also voices that questioned the 'Polish-ness' of repatriates and warned that repatriation could open the door to organized crime from the former Soviet Union.

The repatriation law was eventually passed in parliament, albeit in a modified, narrower form. The law only allowed repatriation from the Asiatic republics of the former Soviet Union and not from the former Polish territories in the east. The major argument behind this was to compensate Poles from the regions of the Soviet Union that had never been covered by any repatriation programme, in contrast to the contemporary territories of Belarus or Ukraine (repatriation programme 1945–1962). A few years later, in the 2000s, the right-wing party PIS unsuccessfully attempted to modify the law by changing its applicability from the former Asiatic republics to the whole territory of the former Soviet Union. The project met with disapproval, mostly due to financial considerations.

The proposal of the Polish Card (quasi-citizenship) was first met with strong criticism in 2000/2001, mostly concerning its legal quality. The SLD widely criticized the project. However, in 2006, one month before the new elections, the right-wing government of the PIS passed the Polish Card. It maintained a wide definition of the status and even extended the scope of privileges offered to the holders of the Card, for instance, by granting them the right to reside and to work legally in Poland.

Cultural acquisitions were justified by 'compensatory practices', 'economic factors' and 'national unity and identity'. On the other hand, the critics referred to 'economic factors', 'compensatory practices', 'national unity or identity'. Concerning the reacquisition procedure, the most frequent theme in the proponents' discourse was the suffering of the ethnic Poles in the former Soviet Union:

> The next matter is citizenship reacquisition. Our goal was to return Polish citizenship to those, for whom the loss of citizenship was an injustice or a result of persecution. [...] After fierce discussions in the commission, it was decided that those persons who left Poland due to economic reasons only, which can be proved by the

respected documents, should not be concerned by the new law. (expert from the Ministry of Interior, 3 July 2000)[44]

The vast majority of parliamentarians argued that the offspring of the persecuted persons should be given a chance to repatriate, as they were raised in the Polish culture and language. The parliamentarians knew, however, that the reality presents itself differently. Most of the ethnic Poles, who had already successfully undergone the national recognition procedure, could not speak the language of their Polish great-grandparents or grandparents. As a result, the advocates of repatriation defended the policy by saying that the Soviet system, not the ethnic Poles, was to blame, as it had prohibited the cultivation of minority languages. It is, therefore, the duty of a Polish state to reintegrate the repatriates into the Polish culture and language.

10 years after the establishment of the independent Polish Republic it is high time to call in that part of the Polish nation. The part, which for so many years suffered injustice, harm, isolation. As many parliamentarians stressed in the former debate, we often only verbally assure these Poles about love, gratefulness and compassion. Metaphorically speaking: Mother having five children will not say that she does not have enough bread. She may give smaller portions but there will be bread for all the children. Especially those who sacrificed their lives and were deported to Kazakhstan. (AWS, 22 September 1999)[45]

The proponents of repatriation admitted that the law would imply high costs for the Polish budget, but in their opinion the parliament should not be too ungenerous. Rather, they believed that Poland would profit economically from repatriation because young repatriates would contribute with their social capital.

Among social democrats and liberals there were, however, more sceptical voices, who argued that those who had experienced persecution personally should be given priority to repatriate, but not their offspring. Moreover, in order to prevent potential abuses, the SLD advocated a more careful security check of all the applicants. Economic factors played the most important role in their argumentation. Social democrats pointed to the fact that some suggested elements of the proposal, such as an employment guarantee, could not be met given high unemployment and financial difficulties in Poland.

They also raised concerns about the sustainability of the Polish welfare system, which, in their opinion, would be heavily burdened by the repatriation programme:

> It seems that in this project the central state authorities are held responsible for providing employment, apartments, recognition of the pensions and education acquired abroad. We do not know today if the budget of the Polish state will be able to meet all these commitments. As the experience of Germany shows, mass flow of repatriation is a serious financial burden also for the central budget. In the last decade, 1989/1998, the number of repatriates in Germany increased by 2 millions and the federal government was spending approximately one billion DM on repatriation program yearly. (UW, 22 September 1999)[46]

The debate on dual citizenship was also very controversial. In Poland, as in Hungary, it was the ethnic Poles abroad who were most interested in the introduction of dual citizenship. In the late 1990s the right-wing coalition block, AWS, prepared a proposal for the citizenship law, which was debated in 1999/2000. Although all the political parties in the parliament agreed that there was a need to replace the old law from 1962 with a new one, controversy surrounded some of the proposed legal changes, such as dual citizenship, preventing them from reaching a compromise. Parties whose members (in the majority) objected to dual citizenship were the SLD, the PSL, the UW and the ROP.

In the initial phase of the debate it became clear that a very wide *de jure* tolerance of dual citizenship could be in conflict with the Polish constitution and, more precisely, the principle of citizens' equality. In order to prevent a legal conflict, the following had already been proposed during the commission's work: a dual citizen (i.e. Polish–German), when in Poland, should be treated as a Polish citizen only. As a result, this formulation of the law had already been debated during the plenary sessions of the parliament. The proponents of dual citizenship were stressing the importance of citizenship, saying that the formulation of the law guaranteed respect for Polish citizenship and the constitution.

> Some controversies and disagreements were generated by Article 4, which stipulates that: "a Polish citizen cannot be simultaneously

regarded by the Polish authorities as a citizen of another state."
In my view, the reading of the article is good and logical. It is a
liberal arrangement, which does not forbid a Polish citizen pos-
sessing citizenship of another state, but requires clearly from that
citizen to subordinate to the Polish law only when staying on the
Polish territory. (SLD, 3 July 2000)[47]

The right-wing AWS would often argue that dual citizenship was
in conformity with Polish national law and legal traditions. They
referred, for instance, to the pre-World War II laws or conventions
that already tolerated dual citizenship. Finally, according to AWS,
the new law would only legalize the current *status quo*, that is, *de
facto* toleration of dual citizenship in Poland. The AWS also frequently referred to 'practices in other states' in order to show that
approximately half of the EU member states have already introduced
dual citizenship. This argument was meant to convince other parliamentarians that dual citizenship is a common and legitimate legal
phenomenon, which could also be introduced in Poland.

  According to the social democrats, dual citizenship remains in
conflict with the basic notion of citizenship and its unity and hence
should remain an exception, not a rule. The social democrats claimed
that if the Poles abroad continued pushing for dual citizenship they
probably did not fully understand the importance of national citizenship. National law also played an important role in their rhetoric.
References to the former and current Polish law were meant to show
that *de jure* toleration of dual citizenship is *not* in the Polish legal
tradition. Finally, other states' practices, and more specifically limited toleration of dual citizenship, were also a frequent justification.

> [...] In less than a half of these states [EU member states] dual citi-
> zenship is in force, whilst in the second half – single citizenship
> only. States which introduce multiple citizenship are usually post-
> colonial or immigration states, like Australia, USA, France or UK.
> It is also important that our nearest Western neighbour, Germany,
> but also the Scandinavian States, tolerate one citizenship only.
> Despite all these controversies, I am convinced that dual citizen-
> ship is not in the Polish interest. (3 July 2000, SLD)[48]

Loss of citizenship was debated predominantly in the context of
the communist period. The old citizenship law stipulated that a

person who acted against the political interests of the Polish state could be deprived of national citizenship by the state authorities. It was therefore important for the drafters of the new law to introduce a voluntary renunciation clause. The amended law stipulates that Polish citizenship can be renounced only upon an application from the person concerned. In the analysed parliamentary debates there were only arguments in favour of a voluntary citizenship loss, justified by 'rights', 'communist heritage', 'EU law' and 'practices in other states'.

In the course of the right-wing coalitions' reforms in 2001 and 2007, the right-wing parties' ethnic vision of national citizenship was introduced. The new laws were not free from controversies: the left-wing SLD, fostering a republican model of citizenship in Poland, objected to all the changes leading to the law's ethnicization. A deep discrepancy regarding a general vision of Polish citizenship prevented them from reaching a compromise in the debate on the nationality act. In general, Polish citizenship became more open to ethnic nationals living abroad and more closed *vis-à-vis* non-ethnic immigrants. Given the co-ethnics policy, two factors had a particular influence: national/ethnic identity and a need to compensate the co-ethnics living abroad for historical injustice. Reform of residence- and socialization-based acquisition was strongly influenced by practices in other states. The only liberalized mode was the loss of citizenship. The arguments used in the discussion revolved around communist heritage, universal and EU rights, and practices in other states. Table 5.8 summarizes the findings.

Empirical findings – synthesis

Tables 5.9 to 5.11 summarize the findings for each state under study by presenting all argumentative strategies used for each mode of national citizenship acquisition and loss. They show how the various modes of national citizenship acquisition and loss were debated in each state, that is, the share of arguments for and against ethnicization and de-ethnicization and liberalization and de-liberalization. The headings of the tables should be interpreted as either de-ethnicization or liberalization (first column) and either ethnicization or de-liberalization (second column), depending on which dimension (liberalization or ethnicization) applies to the given mode of

Table 5.8 Summary of arguments used in the Polish parliamentary debate

Mode of citizenship acquisition and loss	Tendency observed in Polish law	Arguments that fostered the legal change
Jus sanguinis at birth	No major changes	
Jus soli at birth	Does not exist (except for otherwise stateless children)	
Residence-based acquisition and family-transfer	De-liberalization	1. Practices in the other states
Affinity-based acquisition and quasi-citizenship	Ethnicization	1. Compensatory practice 2. National unity and identity 3. Economic factors
Dual citizenship	Ethnicization	1. Practices in the other states 2. Importance of citizenship 3. National law and legal tradition
Loss of citizenship	Liberalization	1. Rights 2. Communist heritage 3. EU law 4. Practices in other states

Source: Own compilation.

citizenship acquisition or loss. The statements are presented by means of the following scale:

1–2 statements: *
3–5 statements: **
6–8 statements: ***
9–11 statements: ****
12–14 statements: *****
15 statements or more: ******

Divergence concerned *jus soli* at birth, cultural acquisition, quasi-citizenship and dual citizenship. Convergent development was observed foremost in residence- and socialization-based citizenship

Table 5.9 Argumentative strategies per each mode of national citizenship acquisition and loss: Germany

Topoi	De-ethnicization / Liberalization	Ethnicization / De-liberalization
Jus sanguinis		
Practices in the other states	*	**
Integration	*	*
National unity and identity	*	*
Ties with a receiving state	*	*
Jus soli at birth		
Integration	****	***
Ties with a receiving state	*	*
Residence- and socialization-based acquisition, family transfers		
Integration	*****	******
Rights	***	*
Ties with a receiving state	***	
Cultural acquisitions and quasi cit.		
National unity and identity	****	*
Compensatory practices	*	***
Economic factors	***	
Dual citizenship		
Integration	**	******
Practices in the other states	****	***
Importance of citizenship	*	*****
Interests	****	**
Loss of citizenship		
ties with a receiving state	*	
All statements	Liberalization	Liberalization
No. of statements	136	98
In per cent	58	42
	De-ethnicization	De-ethnicization
No. of statements	24	17
In per cent	59	41

Source: Own compilation.

acquisitions, family-transfer and loss of citizenship. The following paragraphs present the arguments used in the parliamentary discourse that led to the legislative changes in each state.

The *jus soli* at birth principle was introduced only in Germany. Its introduction was legitimized by a need to foster integration of immigrants (the most frequently coded argument in the German debate)

Table 5.10 Argumentative strategies per each mode of national citizenship acquisition and loss: Hungary

Topoi	De-ethnicization / Liberalization	Ethnicization / De-liberalization
Jus sanguinis		
Ties with a receiving state	**	
National law and legal tradition		**
Importance of citizenship	*	
Jus soli at birth		
EU law	*	
Residence- and socialization-based acquisition, family transfers		
Integration	***	***
Practices in the other states	**	**
Economic factors	*	*
Cultural acquisitions and quasi cit.		
National unity and identity		******
Economic factors	*****	*****
EU law	**	*****
Dual citizenship		
Ties with a receiving state	****	**
Economic factors	****	**
Practices in the other states	**	***
Loss of citizenship		
Rights	**	
Communist heritage	**	
EU law	*	*
All statements	Liberalization	Liberalization
No. of statements	53	36
In per cent	60	40
	De-ethnicization	De-ethnicization
No. of statements	37	118
In per cent	24	76

Source: Own compilation.

and strengthen their ties with a receiving state. These arguments indicate that the immigration experience played a decisive role in this reform. These findings also confirm Weil and Hansen's thesis (Hansen and Weil, 2001), according to which receiving states change their national citizenship laws under pressure to integrate large numbers of long-term immigrants.

Table 5.11 Argumentative strategies per each mode of national citizenship acquisition and loss: Poland

Topoi	De-ethnicization / Liberalization	Ethnicization / De-liberalization
Jus sanguinis		
Importance of citizenship		**
National law&legal traditions		**
Ties with a receiving state	*	
Jus soli at birth		
Rights	*	
National law and legal traditions	*	
Residence- and socialization-based acquisition, family transfers		
Practices in the other states	*	**
EU law	*	
Economic factors		*
Rights	*	
Ties with a receiving state	*	
Crime	*	*
Cultural acquisitions and quasi cit.		
Compensatory practices	**	******
Economic factors	******	******
National unity and identity	***	******
Dual citizenship		
Importance of citizenship	***	*****
National law and legal traditions	**	***
Practices in the other states	***	**
Loss of citizenship		
Rights	**	
Communist heritage	**	
EU law	**	
Practices in the other states		
All statements	Liberalization	Liberalization
No. of statements	69	26
In per cent	73	27
	De-ethnicization	De-ethnicization
No. of statements	71	180
In per cent	28	72

Source: Own compilation.

The second case of divergence concerned cultural citizenship acquisitions and the status of quasi-citizenship. Germany introduced significant limitations in that area, while Hungary and Poland expanded. In Hungary and Poland national citizenship law enacted during the communist period was severely de-ethnicized due to pressure from the communist authorities. After the fall of communism, Hungary and Poland began to tailor their national citizenship laws freely, re-ethnicizing them. In these respects, the development of the Hungarian and Polish national citizenship laws in the 1990s was similar to the legal changes that took place in Germany after World War II. In Hungary and Poland the arguments in favour of culture-based citizenship acquisition and quasi-citizenship were justified with arguments revolving foremost around compensatory practices, national unity and identity. These findings indicate that experience with communism played an important role; Hungary and Poland were strongly motivated by a willingness to compensate their co-ethnics for the hardships and discrimination that they had experienced under the communist regimes. From their perspective it was part of general de-communization politics.

The German parliamentarians decided to diminish the privileged status of external compatriots, which they justified by economic factors (high costs of the law) as well as national unity and identity. In their opinion German national identity had changed and the late repatriates, despite their German ethnic origin, could not automatically become an integral part of it.

The laws regulating dual citizenship status also developed in divergent directions. In Germany the legal changes followed a receiving state's pattern (immigrant-oriented), while in Hungary and Poland they followed a sending state's pattern (emigrant-oriented). In addition, in each state, dual citizenship status was perceived as a challenge to the existing laws and traditional understanding of national citizenship. For that reason each state also referred frequently to legal practices in other states. However, the decisive factor here explaining the direction of legal change was immigration or emigration experience.

Convergence concerned foremost the laws regulating residence- and socialization-based citizenship acquisitions and family-transfer. Concerning the first three modes, Germany acted again as a receiving state, referring most often to the need for integration of immigrants, strengthening their ties with a receiving state as well as respecting their human rights. Hungary and Poland, on the other hand, also acknowledged the need to integrate immigrants, but, in order to develop a concrete strategy, they intensively observed other states' legal practices in that area.

Parliamentary debates on national citizenship legislation – conclusions

The hypotheses tested in this book attempted to explain convergence and divergence of national citizenship legislation in Germany, Hungary and Poland. The two factors responsible for divergent tendencies among the three states were specific migration experience (emigration or immigration) and experience with a communist regime, which led to awakening of ethnic issues after the fall of the system. Convergence of national citizenship legislation was explained here by horizontal diffusion of European norms and standards.

Divergence 1: redressing past wrongs
- *Divergence of national citizenship legislation is caused by legislative practices aiming to redress past wrongs.*

Divergence 2: post-war migration experience
- *Divergence of national citizenship legislation can be explained by migration experience: sending states are concerned with inclusion of external Diasporas, while receiving states are concerned with inclusion of immigrants (long-term permanent residents).*

Convergence: horizontal norm diffusion
- *Horizontal diffusion of international and EU norms leads to convergence of national citizenship legislation in the EU member states.*

In the literature there are two prominent approaches explaining divergence of national citizenship legislation, the first drawing on historical path-dependency (Brubaker, 1992) and the second on post-war migration experience (Weil, 2001). According to Brubaker, national citizenship legislation diverges due to different conceptions of nationhood: states with ethnic conception of nationhood will also have an ethnic citizenship legislation, while states with civic conception of nationhood will have a civic citizenship legislation. Conception of nationhood and citizenship legislation are closely bound up with each other; therefore it is impossible that states with different conceptions of nationhood would develop a similar citizenship legislation. According to Brubaker, conception of nationhood does not evolve over time, but remains stable.

In the light of this approach, national citizenship legislation of Germany, Hungary and Poland should develop according to the same pattern, given the fact that these states share an ethnic conception of nationhood. As a consequence, national citizenship legislation of these states should also reflect ethnic principles. The empirical findings of this book challenged Brubaker's thesis. First, national citizenship legislation of these three states diverged: the German citizenship legislation became less ethnic, and the Polish and Hungarian more ethnic. Apparently, in the German case, ethnic nationhood tradition ceased to inform national citizenship legislation. Concerning the Hungarian and the Polish case, the discourse analysis conducted in this chapter demonstrated that ethnic citizenship legislation does not have to be explained by ethnic conception of nationhood as such, but can be explained by a need to redress past wrongs. Poland and Hungary ethnicized their national citizenship legislation in order to compensate their co-ethnics for the persecution and hardships that they experienced after the borders shifted. The arguments that fostered the introduction of quasi-citizenship legislation or repatriation law in Poland clearly illustrate that pattern. The debates on national citizenship reacquisition also show that ethnicity as such was not sufficient to reacquire Polish or Hungarian citizenship; emigrants who had left these two states voluntarily during the communist period, mostly for financial reasons, were approached differently by the parliamentarians than emigrants who had been forced to leave Poland or Hungary for political reasons.

According to the second approach, divergence in citizenship legislation can be explained by post-war migration experience (Weil, 2001). This hypothesis was based on the assumption that migration is said to have an impact on national citizenship legislation. As a consequence, it is claimed, receiving states are concerned with integration of immigrants, and sending states with inclusion of Diasporas. This hypothesis was confirmed by the empirical analysis presented in this book. Germany, one of the largest receiving states in post-war Europe, reformed its national citizenship legislation with the aim of integrating the large number of long-term immigrants. German citizenship law decreased the period of residence required for naturalization from 15 to 8 years and introduced a new territoriality-based principle of citizenship acquisition – *jus soli* at birth. The most frequent arguments in favour of the changes were 'integration' and 'ties with a receiving state'. On the other hand, the Hungarian and Polish citizenship legislation reforms strengthened the link with the Diasporas abroad, not only with the co-ethnics who found themselves abroad due to shifting borders but also with emigrants. In the light of the reformed Hungarian and Polish legislation, emigrants became the only group entitled to possession of dual citizenship. The co-ethnics, on the other hand, acquired a partial citizenship status, allowing them to reside and work legally in their kin-states.

The literature also offers two hypotheses explaining legal convergence. According to the first one, national citizenship legislation converges due to the impact of top-down Europeanization (Checkel, 1999, 2001). The second hypothesis explains convergence by parallel path-dependencies (Hansen and Weil, 2001). The first hypothesis was not confirmed by the empirical findings of this book. First, there is no *de facto* top-down Europeanization of national citizenship. The competences of the European institutions are too weak to foster legal convergence in a top-down manner. Second, contrary to expectations, the old EU member state, Germany, proved to be less concerned with the standards advocated by the European institutions than the two new member states. While Polish and Hungarian parliamentarians oriented themselves quite frequently towards the European Convention on Nationality from 1997, the German parliamentarians ignored it entirely in the plenary debates.

The second hypothesis explaining legal convergence, namely, parallel path-dependencies (Hansen and Weil, 2001), was also challenged by the empirical findings of this book. According to Hansen and Weil, convergence of national citizenship legislation is caused by domestic factors only. The authors argued that horizontal observation or coordination does not take place between European states. Rather, convergence takes place if states face similar problems and challenges in their domestic politics. However, the empirical analysis of this book demonstrated that legal convergence is indeed brought about by horizontal norm diffusion. Convergence also took place despite the fact that Germany, on the one hand, and Hungary and Poland, on the other, have very different domestic experience with immigration. Furthermore, the level of domestic politicization did not play a decisive role.

6
Towards Convergence: Horizontal Europeanization of National Citizenship Legislation

Introduction

The previous chapter presented the findings from analyses of parliamentary debates in Germany, Hungary and Poland. Among other things, it was established that Europeanization, particularly horizontal, played quite a prominent role in the reforms of the national citizenship laws in the countries under study. This was contrary to the existing contributions to this research field (for instance Checkel, 1999, 2001; Vink, 2001). This chapter sheds more light on the problem and at the same time tests the most recent hypotheses put forward in this book.

In this chapter Europeanization will be defined broadly as a domestic adaptation to European regional integration (Graziano and Vink, 2007). A broad definition of Europeanization aims to cover both vertical and horizontal integration processes. This is in response to the goals of the new research agenda on Europeanization (Graziano and Vink, 2007), which aspires to break with the orthodox conceptualization of Europeanization as a top-down transposition of legal norms (Sedelmeier and Schimmelfennig, 2002; Sedelmeier, 2005). The new research agenda stresses that adaptation to European regional integration does not have to be limited to top-down processes. The research scope should, rather, include direct (implementation of European integration) (Caporaso *et al.*, 2001) as well as indirect effects (horizontal effects of European integrations). Furthermore, the diversity of empirical inferences should also be extended to include, for instance, an analysis of the domestic discourses. As Graziano and Vink (2007) noted: 'Effects of Europeanization can be indirect, the so-called horizontal effects may be seen as indirect Europeanization where domestic changes are the result not so much of top-down imposition from Brussels but rather of increased policy competition between countries as a result of growing exchange of information [...]'.

This book operationalizes the mechanism of Europeanization according to (i) the nature of the norms' transposition and (ii) the dimensions of the decisive actors' communication. The first classification distinguishes positive, negative and framing integration (Knill and Lehmkuhl, 1999; Vink, 2001). The second distinguishes horizontal and vertical Europeanization (Koopmans and Erbe, 2003). Positive integration concerns the implementation of European directives or regulations and examines the variety in implementation of directives among the member states. However, there is no binding EU legislation on national citizenship, which means that the EU cannot exercise any influence on member states' legislation concerning national citizenship.

Negative integration is a consequence of a common market's emergence and hence concerns de-regulatory practices. The rulings of the European Court of Justice play an important role regarding national citizenship. By supporting the principle of free movement of people the ECJ can, in some respects, constrain the member states' restrictive policies. The ECJ's activities affecting national citizenships can only be indirect. They concern provisions of national citizenship law that, for instance, violate the basic principles of the common market. Finally, framing integration takes place when the actions of decisive actors are informed by objectives or norms that can be attributed to the EU (Knill and Lehmkuhl, 1999).

A vertical link can be established between actors from the European and the national level, given the second dimension, while a horizontal link takes place between actors from different member states. Positive and negative integration functions only in the vertical dimension, as opposed to framing integration, which functions in both. This is possible due to the fact that national actors can act as informed by the norms originating in their view directly from the European level or indirectly from the other EU member states.

After examination of the parliamentary debates on national citizenship law reforms in Germany, Hungary and Poland, it was established that horizontal Europeanization, manifested by references to other states' national citizenship laws, was, first, more intensive than vertical Europeanization. Secondly, it was clearly dominant in some modes of national citizenship acquisition or statuses (i.e. dual citizenship).

Convergence: horizontal norm diffusion
- *Horizontal diffusion of international and EU norms leads to convergence of national citizenship legislation in the EU member states.*

This chapter begins by presenting legal aspects of the Europeanization of national citizenship. In the next step it deals with empirical evidence from vertical and horizontal Europeanization. Finally, the chapter briefly presents communication channels that allowed the parliaments in the countries under study to obtain information about legal practices in the other, mostly EU, states.

Vertical Europeanization of national citizenship legislation in the EU member states: a legal perspective

Vertical Europeanization manifests itself through positive and negative integration mechanisms. There are no measures (regulations or directives) concerning national citizenship that the EU would have at its disposal. As a consequence, the EU legal acts have only a limited and indirect influence on the national citizenship of the member states. Article 17 (1) EC, introduced in 1992 by the Treaty of Maastricht on the European Union, stipulates that '1. Citizenship of the Union is hereby established. Every person holding the nationality of a Member State shall be a citizen of the Union.' On the other hand, the Declaration no. 2 on nationality of a Member State, attached to the Maastricht Treaty, provides the following information: 'The Conference declares that, wherever in the Treaty establishing the European Community reference is made to nationals of the member states, the question whether an individual possesses the nationality of a member state shall be settled solely by reference to the national law of the member state concerned.' These two quotations illustrate that the emergence of EU citizenship has not created new competences for the EU regarding national citizenship (Bauböck, 2007b; Bellamy, 2008; Maas, 2008). Rather, it is stated clearly that the member states themselves decide on issues concerning national citizenship. As Vink rightly noted: 'European citizenship clearly confers some rights on people, be they national citizens, Union citizens or third-country nationals, but for the moment at least, these entitlements confirm rather than undermine the vigour of national citizenship' (Vink, 2005, p. 158).

The most active institution in the field of national citizenship has been the Council of Europe. It has produced the three most important documents in that area: the Convention on the Reduction of Cases of Multiple Nationality and Military from 1963, the Second Protocol to 1963 Convention, and the European Convention on Nationality from 1997 (Hailbronner, 2003). Article 1 (1) of the 1963 Convention stipulates that 'Nationals of the Contracting Parties who are fully of age and who acquire of their own free will, by means of naturalization, option or recovery, the nationality of another Party shall lose their former nationality. They shall not be authorized to retain their former nationality.' The Convention has been ratified by 13 states, and only ten states were bound by Chapter 1.

In the 1970s and 1980s the provisions of the Convention stipulating avoidance of dual citizenship were challenged by the introduction of gender equality in national citizenship law (Benhabib and Resnik, 2009). In the 1960s most of the European states would still apply different criteria concerning naturalization or dual citizenship acquisition by women and men. As a consequence of that process, the number of multiple nationality cases, resulting from the combination of *jus sanguinis* and *jus soli* principles in the maintained and acquired citizenship, has significantly increased. In 1993 the Second Protocol, which allowed exceptions to the main rule to be enshrined in the 1963 Convention, was therefore introduced (Hailbronner, 2003). The Protocol envisaged three exceptions: first, if a person acquires citizenship of another Contracting Party on whose territory he either was born and is resident, or has been ordinarily resident for a period of time beginning before the age of 18; second, if a person acquires the citizenship of his spouse; thirdly, if a minor whose parents are citizens of different Contracting Parties acquires the citizenship of one of his parents.

The next document, the European Convention on Nationality (ECN) from 1997, aimed at further liberalization of national citizenship law but remained neutral regarding dual citizenship. Articles 3–5 entail codification of customary international law regarding nationality, article 6 deals with rules of citizenship acquisition, and articles 7–8 provide an exhaustive list of grounds for loss of nationality. The ECN has been ratified by 16 states (12 EU/EEA member states), Iceland and Norway (the ratification took place in 2007/2008). Most states ratified the ECN without reservations; Austria was an exception, with 11 reservations.

Many states had to reform their citizenship law in order to adopt the ECN. It was particularly important that the ECN stipulated a precise and exhaustive list of conditions under which national citizenship could be lost. The grounds for acquisition were much less detailed. The grounds for national citizenship loss were the following: voluntary acquisition of another citizenship, acquisition of citizenship by means of fraud, voluntary foreign military service, activities violating vital interests of the State, lack of a genuine link because of permanent residence abroad, lack of fulfilment of the preconditions required for acquisition during childhood, adoption by foreigners, or renunciation if the person concerned also possessed another nationality. The ECN Article 6 (3) stipulated, concerning citizenship acquisition, that the residence period required for naturalization should not be longer than ten years (lawful and habitual residence) and that some groups, such as spouses, children of nationals, refugees, stateless persons, adopted children and under-aged residents, should have facilitated access to citizenship.

Finally, the European Court of Justice (ECJ) also contributes to the vertical Europeanization of national citizenship, though to a limited extent. The ECJ can only interfere in member states' national citizenship laws if these violate EU citizens' freedom of movement. The two interventions, Micheletti and Kaur cases[1] (Vink, 2001), have confirmed member states' exclusive competences within national citizenship law. However, this principle is only applicable as long as the national laws pay 'a due regard to Community laws' (Vink, 2001). The most recent cases reflect the same approach. In the cases C-192/05 Tas-Hagen and Tas and C-499/06 Nerkowska v. Social Security Institution,[2] the ECJ ruled that the persons concerned were entitled to social provisions (financial compensation which Poland and the Netherlands grant their civilian war-victims) despite the fact that they had taken up residence in another member-state. The ECJ justified the decisions, arguing that exercising the right of an EU citizen to freedom of movement should not hinder the rights that a person has as a citizen of an EU member state. The link with the state of citizenship also continues to be effective after taking residence in another state. In the Chen case, C-200/02,[3] the ECJ stated that it was not an abuse of EU rights to take advantage of Irish citizenship rules, as it is for the member states, and not for the EU, to decide whether to confer citizenship on a person. As a consequence, both the child born in Ireland and its Chinese mother were entitled to legal residence in the United Kingdom as well as all provisions associated with it. As a consequence, the rulings of the ECJ confirmed that it is up to the member states to define the rules of national citizenship acquisition and loss, but the application of the law should not be in conflict with the EU law regulating the free movement of people, which in fact is a very thin provision.

Vertical and horizontal Europeanization – empirical evidence

The empirical evidence from analysis of the parliamentary debates showed that in all three states under study, namely Germany, Hungary and Poland, horizontal Europeanization was more intensive than vertical. Horizontal Europeanization manifested itself first and foremost through references to legal practices in other states; the share of references to other states' practices was comparable in all the three states. However, vertical Europeanization was significantly more prominent in Hungary and Poland than in Germany. In Germany the significance of the EU and the Council of Europe's laws, or general legal principles, was basically very limited (see Chapter 5).

According to the most significant contribution to the analysis of horizontal norm diffusion in the area of national citizenship (Hansen and Weil, 2001), the liberal convergence of immigrants' status in West European states can be explained by two factors: first, large-scale immigration in the post-war period and, second, the need to integrate a large and often growing resident population of third-country nationals. As the authors themselves argued (Hansen and Weil, 2001, p. 19):

> [...] this convergence has resulted not from policy emulation or explicit harmonization – the decision of one nation to copy

another's nationality law or of several states to harmonize theirs – but 'parallel path-development'; the arrival at similar responses to a common imperative, namely the need to integrate large (and sometimes growing) populations of the third-country nationals.

This book takes a different stance on the issue. On the one hand, it acknowledges the fact that legal convergence emerges when states are faced with the same, or a similar, challenge. On the other hand, the analysis conducted in this book showed that other states' legal practices enjoyed high legitimacy among parliamentarians debating national citizenship's reforms. Although there was no explicit tendency towards harmonization, legal practices in the other states were taken into consideration in some aspects of national citizenship law. Moreover, practices in the other states enjoyed very high legitimacy.

In this book it is argued that horizontal Europeanization manifests itself through references to the other EU member states' legal practices. Chapter 3 provided a detailed presentation of methodology. This section will serve only as a reminder of the most important methodological aspects concerning operationalization of horizontal Europeanization. The coding scheme adopted in this book allowed the identification of different modes of national citizenship acquisition and loss (the dependent variable of this book) as well as justifications provided by parliamentarians. It was thereby possible to establish which modes of national citizenship acquisition and loss were affected by either vertical or horizontal Europeanization.

Only selected modes of national citizenship acquisition and loss were significantly[4] exposed to horizontal or vertical Europeanization. In Germany it was *jus sanguinis* (horizontal), *jus soli* at birth (horizontal) and dual citizenship (horizontal). In Hungary it was *jus soli* at birth (EU law), residence-based (horizontal) and cultural acquisitions (vertical) and dual citizenship (horizontal). In Poland it was residence-based acquisition (both), dual citizenship (horizontal) and the loss of national citizenship (both).

The divergent impact of vertical Europeanization in Germany, on the one hand, and Hungary and Poland, on the other, cannot be attributed to conditionality. First of all, in Poland and Hungary national citizenship law as such was not exposed to conditionality. The only exception was the Status Law in Hungary,[5] which was evaluated by the Venice Commission established in 2001 especially for that purpose. The Venice Commission examined the Hungarian Status Law in order to establish whether the law had an ethnically based discriminatory effect. As a result, the commission requested some changes that would diminish the privileged status of ethnic Hungarians versus other foreigners. The modifications were debated and approved in the Hungarian parliament. Nonetheless, even if we were to exclude the debate on the Status Law from the analysis, vertical Europeanization would still remain more prominent in Hungary and Poland than in Germany.

A parallel vertical impact can be attributed to the conventions produced by the Council of Europe. In Poland, in particular, the European Convention on Nationality (ECN) from 1997 became a relatively visible reference document in the process of drafting and debating the new law on national citizenship. Polish parliamentarians mostly referred to the ECN when justifying the reform of the law regulating national citizenship loss, thus prohibiting arbitrary withdrawal of citizenship. To a limited extent, Hungarian parliamentarians have also oriented themselves towards the standards enshrined in the ECN. Only in Germany was this not the case – the European Convention on Nationality from 1997 escaped the notice of German parliamentarians.

References to other states' legal practices

The results of this study confirm the findings of other contributors to the field, which established that vertical Europeanization of national citizenship is limited. However, that does not help to resolve the puzzle of why, in some aspects, national citizenship laws of the EU member states have become very similar (though not necessarily more liberal). What can be established, nevertheless, is that a weak, vertical Europeanization was not responsible for triggering convergence among the member states. Rather, this book has established that, in the modes of national citizenship that have converged, horizontal Europeanization was much more intensive. Figure 6.1 presents horizontal linkages between the three states: Germany, Hungary and Poland.

It can be seen that German legislation was very frequently referred to by Polish parliamentarians. In fact, among the Polish actors no other state received more references than Germany. For German

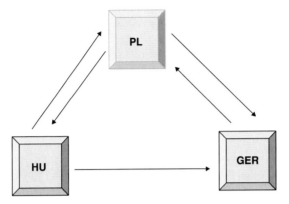

Figure 6.1   Horizontal network: Germany, Hungary and Poland
Source: Own presentation.

parliamentarians Polish national citizenship legislation was not an important reference point, while Hungarian national citizenship legislation was not referred to at all. Poland and Hungary referred to each other to a comparable, moderate extent. For Hungary, German national citizenship legislation was significant, although not the most important reference source.

The network analysis also provided information about other states to which Germany, Hungary and Poland referred in a positive or negative manner. The three countries under study (Germany, Hungary and Poland) were the 'active' members of the network, which means that these states were referring to each other and also to other states. The thickness of arrows indicates the number of references, both positive and negative (Figure 6.2).

Although the difference is not very large, Hungary and Poland referred more intensively than Germany to the legal practices in other states. When the three states are compared it can be observed that the old EU member states, mentioned intensively by the German, Hungarian and Polish parliamentarians, became the so-called 'trend-setters'. States that received the most references from all the three states were: Austria, the United Kingdom, France, Italy, the Scandinavian States, EU (general reference) and Spain.

The second factor that played a role was geographic proximity. That is to say, all the three states frequently referred to the neighbours.

(a)

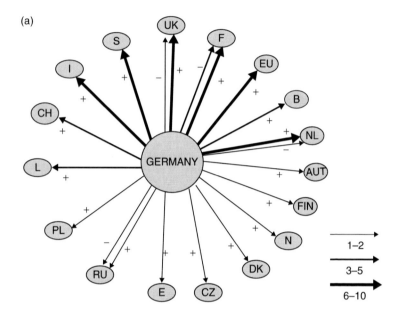

(b)

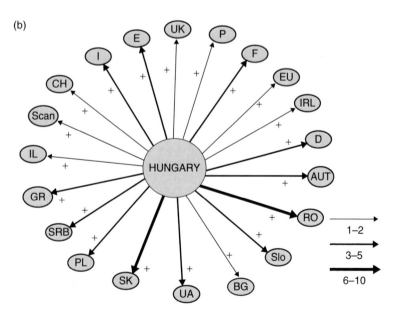

Figure 6.2   Continued

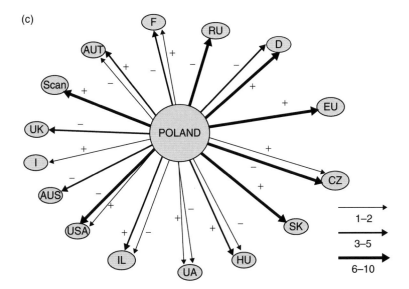

Figure 6.2 Network: (a) Germany, (b) Hungary and (c) Poland

Note: AUS – Australia, AUT – Austria, B – Belgium, BG – Bulgaria, CH – Switzerland, CZ – Czech Republic, D – Germany, DK – Denmark, E – Spain, EU – European Union, F – France, FIN – Finland, GR – Greece, HU – Hungary, I – Italy, IL – Israel, IRL – Ireland, L – Luxemburg, N – Norway, NL – the Netherlands , P – Portugal, PL – Poland, RO – Romania, RU – Russia, S – Sweden, Scan – Scandinavian States, SK – Slovakia, Slo – Slovenia, SRB – Serbia, UA – Ukraine, UK – United Kingdom, USA – Unites States of America
Source: Own presentation

Observation of neighbours was very intensive – in each state under study a neighbouring country received the most references. Germany was mostly oriented towards the legislation in the Netherlands; Poland was oriented towards Germany and Hungary towards Romania.

In contrast to Poland and Hungary, German parliamentarians referred less frequently to the legislation of the new member states. These new member states were Poland, the Czech Republic and the Baltic States (general category). Poland and Hungary, on the other hand, were very well informed about citizenship legislation in the whole group of the old EU member states. The unique feature of Poland was its references to more distant countries such as Russia, Israel, the United States and Australia.

As already noted, the negative references in Germany were very limited and concerned only to a limited extent the legislation in France, the United Kingdom and Russia. However, the negative references to these states constituted a very small percentage. The French and the British law were subject to criticism due to their dominant *jus soli* tradition, which German parliamentarians did not want to implement to the same extent. On the other hand, Russian citizenship law was criticized for not being democratic enough. In Poland the negative references were relatively frequent. Russian citizenship law received only negative evaluations from Polish parliamentarians, who found the law undemocratic and discriminatory. Russian citizenship law was also criticized for its 'zero tolerance' towards dual citizenship, which closed the possibility for ethnic Poles living in Russia to apply for Polish citizenship. As in Germany, Polish parliamentarians were not willing to follow the citizenship models of the traditional *jus soli* states such as France, the United Kingdom, the United States or Australia. Instead, German citizenship law enjoyed the highest legitimacy among Polish parliamentarians.

As already mentioned, not all of the modes of national citizenship acquisition and loss were influenced by horizontal Europeanization. Dual citizenship was impacted significantly by horizontal Europeanization in the three states under study, while residence-based acquisitions (regulating naturalization of immigrants) impacted on Hungary and Poland only. In the latter case the legal outcomes were convergent, but not in the case of dual citizenship.

Germany, Hungary and Poland introduced *de facto* tolerance of dual citizenship, which was nonetheless perceived as an exception. That means that the law does not openly allow dual citizenship but is, however, interpreted in a manner that allows exceptions from the rule (Hungary and Poland) or specifies the list of exceptions (Germany). In Germany and Poland the starting point was 'no tolerance', in Hungary *de jure* tolerance for dual citizenship (details of the legal provisions can be found in Chapter 4). The major difference is, however, the formulation of the law: in contrast to Germany, Hungarian and Polish law was constructed in such a way as to offer dual citizenship only for the external Diasporas abroad and not for immigrants.

Dual citizenship is, nonetheless, a relatively new legal issue; hence, none of the states under study have had experience of it. For decades possession of dual citizenship was forbidden in these states. It is only since the 1990s that *de facto* tolerance has begun to win support. In this situation the lawmakers experimented first with partial solutions to the problem, for instance 'exceptional' tolerance of dual citizenship. The ECN from 1997 provides rather general guidelines on how to regulate dual citizenship problems. These guidelines leave a lot of space in which to manoeuvre between a full *de jure* and partial–exceptional tolerance for dual citizenship. In Germany, Hungary and Poland it was observed that parliamentarians and lawmakers were seeking best policy practices among other member states. They carefully screened not only the laws themselves but also other states' concrete experiences. Finally, they took into consideration the existing legal standards in their countries in order to examine the misfit between an old and a new law.

The empirical evidence shows that the reformed laws regulating residence-based acquisitions in Hungary and Poland have come to resemble quite closely the laws introduced in the old EU member states. Chapter 4 contains a detailed comparative legal analysis, whereas the following will only present the general tendency. In Germany the residence requirement was decreased from 15 to 8 years, but new, additional conditions were introduced: a language test and an oath of loyalty to the constitution. The citizenship law in force in Hungary until 1993 spelled out only one condition for naturalization: three years of legal habitual residence in Hungary. The new law (and its further amendments) extended the period of necessary residence from three to eight years, introducing also additional requirements: sufficient means to live in Hungary and an exam on constitutional basics requiring *de facto* a good knowledge of Hungarian. The naturalization procedures in Poland were until 1997 subject to the law enacted during the communist period, which defined only one condition for naturalization: five years of legal habitual residence in Poland. The new project of citizenship law from 2006 introduced new conditions: five years of legal habitual residence for EU citizens, seven years for non-EU permanent settlement permit holders and ten years for non-EU residents who do not have a permanent settlement permit. The bill also spells out additional criteria: sufficient means to live in Poland (a permanent job and an apartment) and a language test.

The requirements concerning spouses have converged as well. In Germany the requirements are one year of residence and two years of marriage duration, as well as a specific residence title (permanent residency) and a language test (introduced in 2000). In Hungary the entitlement has changed from three years of marriage duration to three years of residence and marriage duration, as well as a language test and sufficient financial means. In Poland the old law only required an application to be submitted three months after the marriage. In 1999 the law changed the entitlement to three years of marriage duration and six months of residence, while the new bill proposes two years of residence and three years of marriage duration for EU citizens and five years of residence and three years of marriage duration for non-EU citizens.

While reforming the law regulating residence-based acquisitions, Hungary and Poland relied heavily on other states' experience in that area. Hungary and Poland have never experienced immigration as intensively as, for instance, most of the Western European states, such as France, Germany or Great Britain. During the communist period even internal migration between the states belonging to the soviet bloc was very limited. Moreover, due to economic and political reasons more people were emigrating from Hungary and Poland than immigrating from the other states. After the beginning of the 1990s economic emigration, especially from Poland, continued to be very intensive.

The communist citizenship laws in Hungary and Poland did not specify many naturalization requirements like language tests or economic conditions. In fact, they did not have to. The political system itself prevented free movement of persons, even within the soviet bloc. The reformed laws, enacted after the beginning of the 1990s, were clearly more restrictive. Why? As already argued, Poland and Hungary have never received many immigrants, either during the communist period or afterwards. Poland and Hungary have had no experience with immigration to an extent comparable with the old EU member states. Nonetheless, they adopted laws aiming to restrict a *de facto* non-existent demand for Polish and Hungarian citizenship among potential immigrants.[6] The West European states' practices in this area were not questioned. They enjoyed high legitimacy in both Hungary and Poland. As the parliamentarians themselves argued, they were convinced that in a few years' time their states would be faced with a similar demand for naturalization of immigrants as the traditional, West European receiving states. The parliamentarians believed that potential interest in Polish or Hungarian citizenship would be motivated by the desire to acquire EU citizenship. The introduction of more restrictive naturalization laws was therefore intended to prepare Poland and Hungary for the 'inevitable'.

Information channels

It is of importance who provides parliamentarians with information, if legal practices in other states play such an important role in areas where states have no or little experience. Whether information is gathered regularly or *ad hoc*, and the political orientation of the information-gathering institution, are also not without importance. A short questionnaire allows us to establish some of these facts.

According to the Information Office of the Internal Affairs Commission in the *Bundestag*, which, among other things, is responsible for national citizenship, the German parliamentarians working in that commission can obtain information about foreign national citizenship legislation from two types of sources. The first, and major, source is the German Ministry of the Interior. The second source of information is trips undertaken by German parliamentarians themselves in order to deepen their knowledge and talk to the people who are affected by a given law. The Ministry of the Interior gathers information on other states' national citizenship laws on a rather *ad hoc* basis, usually when the parliament discusses a proposed new law or amendment and needs information about practices in the other states. However, the ministry has run, for at least a decade, a database that can quickly be updated if necessary. For that reason, the Commission on Internal Affairs usually does not have long to wait for information or expertise requested from the Ministry of the Interior. Finally, personal trips by parliamentarians, although infrequent, constitute an additional source of information.

Unfortunately, it was impossible to obtain any information from the Hungarian parliamentary commissions dealing with national citizenship. However, the two Polish parliamentary commissions responsible for national citizenship and related issues provided some useful information. The Commission for Unity with the Polish Diaspora Abroad by the upper chamber (Senat) does not regularly provide its members with information on national citizenship laws in other countries. Only when the commission is involved in the preparation of new legislation do they turn to the Information and Documentation Office for the information on legislation in the other states. This compendium is then distributed among all the parliamentarians who sit in the upper chamber. In the lower chamber, Sejm, it is the Administration and Internal Affairs Commission that deals with national citizenship legislation. The commission also gathers the information about other states' legislation *ad hoc*. The commission traditionally turns to the Sejm Analysis Office for information and expertise during work on a new legal project. Since the late 1990s, all the parliamentarians sitting in the lower chamber can find specific information on the intranet (internal network). The commission is not obliged to ask for information or expertise; this is up to its members. Additionally, parliamentarians sometimes order information on their own from the Sejm Analysis Office or in any other institution (such as a think tank). This is, however, a rare practice in the national citizenship law area.

The Polish Interior Ministry also has an informative function, although solely in the latter phase of the legislative process, that is, when a bill is being discussed and not when it is being written. It is common practice for an expert from the ministry to take part in the hearing and give his opinion on the bill.

Unfortunately, it was impossible to obtain any information from the interior ministries in the countries under study. Hence the logic or incentives according to which information on other states' legislation is gathered could not be established. This part of the process is technocratic and absolutely not transparent in its nature. The subsequent part of the process, which took part in parliaments, was more transparent. On the one hand, information is gathered *ad hoc* by parliaments, but, on the other hand, these are specialized institutions that are responsible for providing legal expertise. Moreover, this practice is repeated whenever a new law or amendment is being prepared. However, on that basis it can be established that the parliaments do not 'copy' other states' legislation in a mechanical way; rather, they want to compare the laws, obtain a Europe-wide overview and learn from other states' practices.

Conclusions

In this chapter Europeanization has been widely defined as a domestic adaptation to European norms in order to cover both vertical and horizontal processes of norm adaptation. The results of this research challenge the existing findings, which claimed that there is no Europeanization of national citizenship policies in the EU member states (Checkel, 1999, 2001a; Vink, 2001). The studies conducted so far focused on the vertical mechanisms of norm transposition, which in the case of national citizenship policy were indeed very weak, if not non-existent. This research began with the assumption that weak implementation instruments and vague definition of the standards are unlikely to cause a widespread convergence of laws among the EU member states. In such cases Europeanization is more likely to take place in a horizontal dimension as a process of exchanging best practices. Horizontal Europeanization does not preclude an indirect impact of the EU norms, spreading not in a top-down manner but indirectly in the form of standards already 'processed' by the member states (Lavanex, 2007). Drawing on these assumptions, the following hypothesis has been tested:

Convergence: horizontal norm diffusion
- *Horizontal diffusion of international and EU norms leads to convergence of national citizenship legislation in the EU member states.*

The analysis of the empirical data (analysis of parliamentary debates in Germany, Hungary and Poland) showed that vertical Europeanization was not as intensive as horizontal, which in some modes of national citizenship acquisition was basically dominant. As a result, it can be argued that, in the absence of precisely defined EU norms and strong enforcement mechanisms, the EU member states orient themselves towards legal practices in the other EU states. Interestingly, the new member states, Hungary and Poland, were more oriented than Germany towards EU law. Moreover, this orientation towards EU law was mostly voluntary, because conditionality applied only to one aspect of national citizenship law in Hungary, namely the Status Law.

The analysis allowed the identification of the following two patterns: trend-setting by the old EU member states and the observation mode by the neighbours. The first pattern shows that the national citizenship legislation of the old EU member states became a reference model for Germany as well as for Hungary and Poland. Second, the three states under study frequently referred to their neighbours. In Germany these were other Western European states (mainly the Netherlands), and in Hungary and Poland the new member states as well. Polish parliamentarians referred most often to the German legislation, while the Hungarians referred to the Romanian law on national citizenship.

In the course of the analysis it has been established that Germany, Hungary and Poland frequently referred to legal practices in other states if they had little or no experience with a given policy area or law; for instance, dual citizenship in all three states, residence-based acquisitions in Hungary and Poland, and *jus soli* at birth in Germany.

Legal convergence was observed in the laws regulating residence-based acquisition, but not dual citizenship. Although all three states carefully screened other states' legal practices concerning dual citizenship, the outcome of the reforms was rather divergent. The only convergent aspect of the reforms was the fact that dual citizenship came to be *de facto* tolerated and regarded as an exception to the rule. Otherwise, the reforms in Germany made access to dual citizenship easier for immigrants, while the reforms in Hungary and Poland, in contrast, served the interests of emigrants. In these respects the states' particular experience with migration, either immigration or emigration, proved to be decisive. On the other hand, practices in the other states triggered, without doubt, convergence of residence-based acquisition and family-transfers. In Hungary and Poland, which adapted their legislation to the West European standards, practices in the other states were the major source of legitimacy informing the reforms.

The parliaments in Germany and Poland would gather information on other states' legal practices on a relatively *ad hoc* basis, that is, when they were engaged in preparation of a new law or a bill. However, they would rely on professional information-providing institutions, such as interior ministries or information services based in parliament. The goal of these consultations was to deepen their knowledge on other states' legal practices and learn from other states' experience. As a consequence, selected aspects of legislation in the states under study have converged with the legal practices in the other EU states. In the course of the process national citizenship laws in these countries have become more similar, though not more liberal. Hence, horizontal Europeanization, unlike vertical Europeanization, does not necessarily foster liberalization.

7
Conclusions

In a migratory world, and particularly in the European Union, national citizenship has become highly transnational. It has ceased to be exclusive or limited by boundaries of the nation states and instead has become portable, exchangeable, extraterritorial and multiple (Bauböck, 1994a, 1994b; Barry, 2006). In other words, citizens of the EU member states 'carry' their national citizenship rights with them when they take up residence in another state and cannot be deprived of their national citizenship against their will. Moreover, in most of the EU member states it has also become possible to acquire citizenship of another state without being forced to renounce the original one.

In the European Union two factors have been foremost in challenging the exclusivity of national citizenship and promoting its transnationalization: the establishment of European Union citizenship, and migration flows, both within the EU and from third countries. The possession of EU citizenship guarantees freedom of movement to its holders as well as protection against discrimination in the labour market of another EU member state. On the other hand, large-scale migration within the EU and from third countries has blurred the boundaries between the native and foreign populations. Immigrants in one country are at the same time emigrants from another state: they have links with both a receiving and a sending state and, thus, are exposed to the legislation of both states.

This book examined how the German, Hungarian and Polish national citizenship legislation has evolved in this 'new environment'. The analysis covered a period of almost 20 years, namely,

147

from the late 1980s to the present. The aim was to establish *how* and *why* national citizenship legislation has changed in these countries. The research questions posed in this book were:

1. What kind of tendency (convergence, divergence) can we observe if we compare national citizenship legislation in Germany, Hungary and Poland in the period 1985–2007?
2. How can we explain the legislative reforms in these states?

Liberal convergence was conceptualized in this book as a development of national legislation towards a common, predefined standard like 'liberal citizenship'. If the development takes place in an opposite direction, national citizenship becomes illiberal. Convergence, on the other hand, was conceptualized in this book as narrowing of differences between policies or laws over a given period of time. This implies that national citizenship legislation of two or more states becomes similar, though the direction of change may vary. For instance, a given legal standard, such as eight years' residence requirement for naturalizing immigrants, can be reached in the course of either liberalizing or de-liberalizing reforms.

National citizenship was defined in this research as a legal status that binds a person to a particular state under the domestic law and is regulated by specific provisions concerning acquisition and loss of this status (see Chapter 1). The dependent variable of this book was conceptualized as selected modes of national citizenship acquisition and loss as well as statuses:

- modes of citizenship acquisition at birth by '*jus sanguinis* at birth' or '*jus soli* at birth';
- modes of citizenship acquisition after birth: residence-based citizenship acquisition, family-based transfers, socialization-based or affinity-based acquisitions;
- modes of national citizenship loss;
- the status of dual citizenship and quasi-citizenship.

The goal of the book was not only to map the legislative changes in each state but also to explain their development, here conceptualized as convergence or divergence. The literature on the subject provides four major explanations for convergence and divergence of national citizenship law. According to Rogers Brubaker (1992), national citizenship legislation diverges due to different conceptions of nationhood. Namely, states with an ethnic conception of nationhood (such as Germany) will have an ethnic national citizenship legislation, while states with a civic conception of nationhood (such as France) will have a civic national citizenship legislation. All the three states selected for the analysis (Germany, Hungary and Poland) represent the ethnic conception of nationhood. However, contrary to expectations, the national citizenship legislation of Germany has been strongly de-ethnicized in recent years. On the other hand, the national citizenship legislation of Hungary and Poland became more ethnic over the analysed period; nonetheless, as the empirical analysis illustrated, that process was not triggered by the ethnic conception of nationhood but rather by a willingness to address and compensate past wrongs (Liebich, 2007). As a result, 'redressing past wrongs' was identified in this book as the first factor explaining legal divergence:

Hypothesis 1: Divergence of national citizenship legislation is caused by legislative practices aiming to redress past wrongs.

The second important approach in the literature (Weil, 2001; Joppke, 2001) attributes legal divergence to post-war migration experience. According to Weil, receiving states tend to be concerned with inclusion of immigrants, while sending states strive to maintain links with their external Diasporas. The empirical analysis conducted in this book confirmed this thesis. Germany, one of the largest receiving states in Europe, concentrated on including long-term immigrants by facilitating their access to national citizenship. Poland and Hungary, on the other hand, focused on strengthening the legal link with the Diasporas abroad. As a consequence, post-war migration experience was recognized as the second factor explaining legal divergence:

Hypothesis 2: Divergence of national citizenship legislation can be explained by migration experience: sending states are concerned with inclusion of external Diasporas, while receiving states are concerned with inclusion of immigrants (long-term permanent residents).

The literature also offers two approaches that explain legal convergence of national citizenship: top-down Europeanization and parallel path-dependencies. According to the first approach (Checkel,

1999, 2001; Vink, 2001, 2002), convergence of national citizenship legislation among the EU member states can be triggered by top-down pressure from the EU institutions. However, the EU institutions have no formal competences concerning national citizenship legislation of the member states. The existing norms are also not legally binding. Furthermore, the institution that has been particularly active in this area is the European Council, a pan-European institution. Not surprisingly, the existing empirical research observed no top-down Europeanization of national citizenship law. According to the second approach, national citizenship legislation converges because of domestic factors (Hansen and Weil, 2001). Legislative convergence occurs if different states face the same challenge and come up with the same solution, though without coordinating it with each other.

The empirical findings of this book challenged both of these approaches. First, it was demonstrated that national citizenship legislation has indeed undergone Europeanization. However, this process did not occur in a vertical, top-down dimension, but rather in a horizontal manner. Second, this book demonstrated that legislative convergence is brought about not by domestic factors but by horizontal exchange of best practices among states. As a consequence, this book identified horizontal norm exchange as a factor explaining legislative convergence:

> *Hypothesis 3: Horizontal diffusion of international and EU norms leads to convergence of national citizenship legislation in the EU member states.*

Vertical Europeanization was not as intensive as the horizontal dimension, which was particularly prominent concerning naturalization of immigrants and dual citizenship. As a result, in the absence of precisely defined EU norms and strong enforcement mechanisms, the EU member states oriented themselves towards legal practices in the other EU states. All the states intensively observed their neighbours in particular: German parliamentarians oriented themselves in most cases towards Dutch legislation, Polish parliamentarians towards German legislation, and Hungarians towards Romanian legislation. Second, the legislation of the old EU member states acquired a strong trend-setting role, among both old and new EU member states.

The analysis of national citizenship legislation and parliamentary debates allowed us to establish that states orient themselves much more frequently towards the legal practices in other states if they themselves have little or no experience with a given policy area or law: for instance, dual citizenship in Hungary, residence-based acquisition (naturalization of immigrants) in Poland, and *jus soli* at birth in Germany. In these modes of citizenship acquisition, horizontal Europeanization was particularly prominent. However, legal convergence was observed only in the legislation regulating residence-based acquisitions, but not dual citizenship. Although all the three states carefully screened other states' legal practices concerning dual citizenship, the outcome of the reforms was rather divergent. The only convergent aspect of the reforms was the fact that dual citizenship came to be *de facto* tolerated and regarded as an exception to the rule. Otherwise, the reforms in Germany made access to dual citizenship easier for immigrants, while the reforms in Hungary and Poland served the interests of emigrants.

Contribution to comparative citizenship and Europeanization studies

This book makes several, both theoretical and methodological, contributions to comparative citizenship research and to Europeanization studies. The case-selection of this study was quite innovative: this book compares three European kin-states, one representing the Western European states (Germany) and two representing the East Central European states (Hungary and Poland). Until now, comparative, empirical research has focused on either Western or Eastern European states, but rarely on both at the same time. This book fills the gap by analysing three states that represent the same type of statehood (ethnic kin-states) but that otherwise have had different political experiences in the post-war period. That case-selection made it possible to establish patterns of legislative convergence and divergence that are common to both West and East European states.

The legal analysis presented in this book was conducted in a systematic way, that is, by focusing on specific legal provisions of national citizenship acquisition and loss. The first comparative study to adopt such a systematic approach was not published until 2006 (Bauböck *et al.*, 2006). Previous studies would analyse changes in national citizenship legislation in a rather unsystematic way, referring very often to national citizenship legislation in a given state as one entity. That approach frequently led to overgeneralizations.

The empirical research conducted in this book was not limited to analysis of legal acts, which is still the dominant approach in this field. In order to explain causes of the legal reforms, a discourse analysis of parliamentary debates in Germany, Hungary and Poland was also conducted. Analysis of parliamentary debates made it possible to establish the incentives that motivated the lawmakers in each state to reform the law. Analysis of parliamentary debates constitutes a standard approach in comparative politics nowadays. However, these studies would rarely be conducted in a methodologically systematic way: in most cases the content of the debates would simply be summarized (Vink, 2001; Kovacs, 2006; Faist, 2007; Górny and Koryś, 2007). The application of the Atlas.ti software in this research allowed a sophisticated, theory-driven qualitative and quantitative discourse analysis. As a consequence, the presentation of empirical findings was more convenient for hypothesis-testing.

In a theoretical dimension, this book contributes to the currently very popular debate concerning liberal convergence of national citizenship legislation in Europe. According to this thesis, national citizenship legislation in the European states is becoming not only more similar but also more liberal with time (Hansen and Weil, 2001; Howard, 2005). On the other hand, the most recent publications have challenged this thesis (Bauböck *et al.*, 2006). The empirical analysis conducted in this book also confirmed the lack of liberal convergence among the analysed states. However, it was established that, although national citizenship legislation did not become more liberal overall, it converged towards similar standards in some aspects of national citizenship legislation. For instance, the empirical analysis demonstrated that Polish and Hungarian legislation regulating naturalization of immigrants was adapted to the Western European standards. However, that process was not an effect of liberal convergence: German legislation regulating naturalization of immigrants reached the current legal standard in the course of liberalization, while Hungary and Poland had to de-liberalize their laws in order to reach the same standard.

The major theoretical contribution of this book concerns identification of new factors accounting for convergence and divergence in national citizenship legislation. It was also established that proximate factors, rather than path-dependency, explain better the legislative reforms. The two factors identified as accounting for divergence were redressing past wrongs and post-war migration experience. On the other hand, legislative convergence was explained in this book by horizontal norm diffusion. The latter finding also contributes to the literature in Europeanization studies: it demonstrates that, in a horizontal dimension, Europeanization occurs even in policy areas that are exclusively within the competences of nation states. Horizontal Europeanization of national citizenship legislation was also stronger than vertical; however, that process led to convergent, but not more liberal, legislation.

The empirical findings of this study demonstrate that, although national citizenship legislation remains within the exclusive competences of the member states, its changes do not depend on domestic processes alone, contrary to what Hansen and Weil claimed (2001). Rather, as the three prominent cases of Western and Eastern Europe have demonstrated, the EU member states tailor their citizenship legislation as informed by the norms that are widely acknowledged in the EU as well as by other states' legal practices in that area. The Europeanization of national citizenship law could, therefore, be summarized 'in a nutshell' by four attributes: horizontal, indirect, voluntary and best practices-oriented.

Directions for further research

This book examined patterns and dynamics of convergence and divergence in national citizenship legislation in the three European kin-states: Germany, Hungary and Poland. Looking beyond these three cases, the question is whether the findings of this book might also apply to the other old and new EU member states. Arguably, the mechanisms of decision-making, as well as the type of Europeanization that accounts for legal convergence in this study, can be expected to operate also in the other EU member states. However, only an in-depth analysis of other cases would allow us to acquire a more nuanced account of whether national citizenship reforms across the whole EU will converge, and why. Namely, an examination of a larger number of cases would allow us not only to further test the research hypotheses put forward in this research but also to contribute to the examination of horizontal Europeanization mechanisms, which are still under-researched in comparative national citizenship studies.

Appendix

The coding

Tables A.1 to A.3 present a list of plenary debates, which were selected for the comparative analysis. The tables also give information about the content of the debates as well as legislative period during which they took place.

Table A.1   Plenary debates in the German parliament

Debate	Content	Legislative period
12.5.1989	Citizenship law reform, unsuccessful (Staatsangehörigkeitsgestetz, StAG)	1987–1990 (right-wing coalition)
5.12.1992	Reform of the law concerning expelled population (BVFG, Bundesvertriebenengesetz)	1990–1994 (right-wing coalition)
9.2.1995	StAG, national identity and citizenship, unsuccessful	1994–1998 (right-wing coalition)
8.2.1996	StAG, dual citizenship, naturalizations – residents and children	
27.3.1998	Immigrants and dual citizenship	
19.3.1999	StAG	
7.5.1999	StAG major reform, completed	1998–2002 (left-wing coalition)
29.6.2006	Naturalizations	2005– (right-wing coalition)
26.10.2006	StAG amendments, dual citizenship	2005– (grand coalition)

Source: Own compilation.

Table A.2   Plenary debates in the Hungarian parliament

Debate	Content	Legislative period
1.3.1993	Citizenship Act (*A magyar állampolgárságról szóló törvényjavaslat általános vitája*)	1990–1994 (centre)
4.5.1993	Citizenship Act (*A magyar állampolgárságról szóló törvényjavaslat részletes vitája*)	
1.6.1993	Citizenship Act (*Miniszteri válasz a magyar állampolgárságról szóló törvényjavaslat határozathozatala előtt*)	
19.4.2001_A and 8.5.2001_B	Debate on the Act on Hungarians living in neighbouring countries (*A szomszédos államokban élő magyarokról szóló törvényjavaslat általános vitája*)	1997–2001 (right-wing coalition)
17.11.2004	'New Nation-Politics at Home and Abroad' (*Politikai vita a Parlamentben 'Új magyar nemzetpolitika belföldön és külföldön' címmel*)	2001–2006 (left-wing coalition)
1.12.2004	General debate on a proposal for a Parliamentary Resolution on the 'nation citizenship' of Hungarians living in neighbouring countries and establishing a 'homeland' programme package (*A határon túli magyarok nemzetpolgárságáról és a szülőföld-programcsomag létrehozásáról szóló országgyűlési határozati javaslat általános vitája*)	
3.5.2005	Amendment of the Citizenship Act (1993/LV), (*A magyar állampolgárságról szóló 1993. évi LV. törvény módosításáról szóló törvényjavaslat általános vitája*)	
17.5.2005	Amendment of the Citizenship Act (1993/LV), (*A magyar állampolgárságról szóló 1993. évi LV. törvény módosításáról szóló törvényjavaslat részletes vitája*)	

Source: Own compilation.

Table A.3 Plenary debates in the Polish parliament

Debate	Content	Legislative period
22.9.1999	Repatriation (Ustawa o repatriacji)	1997–2001
3.7.2000	Citizenship law, dual citizenship (Ustawa o obywatelstwie polskim), unsuccessful	(right-wing coalition)
6.7.2000	Polish citizenship law (Ustawa o obywatelstie polskim), unsuccessful	
12.10.2000_A	Repatriation (Ustawa o repatriacji), successful	
12.10.2000_B	Reform of the Polish citizenship law (Ustawa o obywatelstwie polskim), unsuccessful	
19.6.2001	The Polish Card (Karta Polaka), unsuccessful	
27.8.2003	Repatriation (Ustawa o repatriacji), amendments, successful	2001–2005 (left-wing coalition)
23.5.2006	Immigrants, naturalizations (Ustawa o cudzoziemcach)	
5.9.2007	The Polish Card (Karta Polaka), successful	2005–2007 (right-wing coalition)

Source: Own compilation.

There are four family codes: actors (A), topics (B), types of statements (C) and justifications (D). The family code 'A' represents actors' characteristics, for instance; party affiliation, membership in parliamentary committees (if mentioned), ministries and so on.. The family code 'B' represents selected modes of citizenship acquisition, loss and statuses (dual and quasi-citizenship) that stand for the dependent variable. Most of the codes were adapted directly from the NATAC typology,[1] though some codes were slightly altered and some added.

The family codes 'B':

B.01 *Jus sanguinis* at birth
B.02 *Jus soli* at birth
B.03 Residence-based acquisition
B.04 Socialization-based acquisition
B.05 Spousal transfer
B.06 Transfer to a child

B.07   Transfer to a parent
B.08   Extension to a spouse of C2 nationality who acquires nationality of C1[2]
B.09   Reacquisition of the formal nationality
B.10   Acquisition based on specific nationality
B.11   Cultural affinity acquisition
B.12   Dual citizenship
B.13   Loss of citizenship
B.14   Quasi-citizenship[3]

Figure A.1 presents a snapshot from the 'Atlas.ti' software showing the family-code 'D.03 residence-based acquisition' and its sub-codes used in the analysis of the Polish parliamentary debates. The

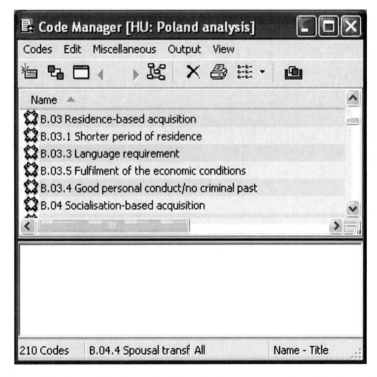

Figure A.1   A snapshot from the Atlas.ti software presenting a family- and sub-codes

Source: Own compilation.

Table A.4 Explanation of the 'D' codes

'D' codes	Explanation
D.01 National unity and identity	Ethnicity and blood-ties, national
D.02 Laws	solidarity and pride...
D.02.1 National law and legal traditions	Other states' citizenship law referred to positively or negatively
D.02.2 EU law	For example, negative impact on
D.02.3 International law	relations with state X
D.03 Practices and relations of other states	For example, high costs for a state's budget
D.03.1 A common practice in the other/EU states	HR, international rights
D.03.2 Relations with the other states	For example, Democracy, multiculturalism...
D.04 Economic factors	For example, Integration into a society
D.05 Rights	National citizenship has a legal
D.06 Ideologies and principles	value and importance
D.07 Integration and naturalization process	For example, Party's or immigrants' interests
D.08 Importance of citizenship	For example, 'Immigrants are
D.09 Ties with a sending state	criminals', criminalization
D.10 Ties with a receiving state	For example, A moral duty to
D.11 Interests	compensate ethnic Poles in
D.12 Crime	Kazakhstan who suffered and were
D.13 Communist heritage	deported under the communist
D.14 Compensatory practices	regime

Source: Own compilation.

sub-codes were not exactly similar in each state under study due to the fact that the debates had a slightly different specificity.

Codes 'C' represent types of statements; positive (for) or negative ones (against). The 'D' codes stand for justifications, which were organized into thematic clusters only after coding all debates. Some of the 'D' codes require a more detailed explanation. Table A.4 presents the 'D' codes with a short explanation.

When a statement was coded, namely; after all the adequate sub-codes were assigned, it was possible to assess this statement on the two-dimensional scale (liberalization – de-liberalization, ethnicization – de-ethnicization). For instance:

A late repatriate is supposed to be a German because he complies with the criteria of being part of the German people. A person being part of the German people is somebody who has committed himself to the German national identity, insofar as this commitment is confirmed by certain characteristics such as descent, language, education, and culture. To my mind, this definition stands for an ethnic exclusion and privileges certain parts of the population with foreign citizenship and residence in another state. (PDS, 1992.12.5)[4]

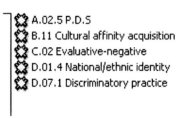

This statement is a critical voice concerning the privileged naturalization of the German co-ethnics. As a consequence it was classified as a statement in favour of national citizenship's de-ethnicization in the analysis. The same procedure was applied to each single statement.

Table of legislation

Germany

1914	Reichs- und Staatsangehörigkeitsgesetz (RuStAG), later Staatsangehörigkeitsgesetz (StAG)	Nationality Law
1949	Grundgesetz (GG)	Basic Law
1953	Bundesvertriebenengesetz (BVFG)	Federal Expellee Law
1955	Gesetz zur Regelung von Fragen der Staatsangehörigkeit (StAngRegG)	Law regulating citizenship issues
1965	Ausländergesetz (AuslG)	Foreigners Law
1990	Aussiedleraufnahmegesetz	Repatriates' Reception Law
1993	Kriegsfolgenbereinigungsgesetz	Law for the Settlement of Consequences of the War
2000	Verwaltungsvorschriften zum Staatsangehörigkeitsrecht (StAR-VWV)	Administrative Regulation on Citizenship Legislation
2005	Aufenthaltsgesetz	Residence Law
2005	Zuwanderungsgesetz	Immigration Act

Hungary

1957	évi V. törvény az állampolgárságról	Act V on Hungarian nationality
1993	évi LV. törvény a magyar állampolgárságról	Act XV on Hungarian citizenship
2001	évi LXII. törvény a szomszédos államokban élő magyarokról	Act LXII on Hungarians living in the neighbouring countries
2003	évi LVII. törvény a szomszédos államokban élő magyarokról szóló 2001. évi LXII. törvény módosításáról	Act LVII amending Act LXII of 2001 on Ethnic Hungarians living in neighbouring countries

Poland

1962	Ustawa o obywatelstwie polskim	Act on Polish Nationality
1997	Poprawka do Ustawy o obywatelstwie polskim	Amendment to the Act on Polish Nationality
1997	Konstytucja Rzeczpospolitej Polskiej	Constitution of the Republic of Poland
1999	Poprawka do Ustawy o obywatelstwie polskim	Amendment to the Act on Polish Nationality
2000	Ustawa o Repatriacji	Repatriation Act
2003	Poprawka do Ustawy o obywatelstwie polskim	Amendment to the Act on Polish Nationality
2003	Ustawa o cudzoziemcach	Foreigners' Law
2007	Ustawa o Karcie Polaka	Act on the Polish Card

EU Treaties:

- Treaty on European Union (1992) *Official Journal C 191 of 29 July 1992*

Council of Europe:

- Convention on Reduction of Cases of Multiple Nationality and Military Obligations in Cases of Multiple Nationality from 1963
- The Second Protocol to 1963 Convention and the European Convention on Nationality from 1997
- European Convention on Nationality (ECN) from 1997

European Court of Justice, Cases:

- Maria Vicente Micheletti and Others v. Delegacion del Gobierno en Cantabrie (C-369/90)
- Kaur case (C-192/99)
- Tas-Hagen and Tas (C-192/05)
- Nerkowska v. Social Security Institution (C-499/06)
- Chen case (C-200/02)

Summary of the legislative reforms in Germany, Hungary and Poland

Table A.5 National citizenship law in Germany – legal changes since 1985

Mode of acquisition of nationality	(Main) relevant article in law for this mode of acquisition	Brief description (criteria of eligibility, type of acquisition)	Changes since 1985
BIRTHRIGHT-BASED MODES OF ACQUISITION OF NATIONALITY AT BIRTH (AUTOMATIC OR NON-AUTOMATIC)			
***Jus sanguinis* at birth**			
Jus sanguinis at birth:	§4 para. 1 StAG; exception in §4 para. 4 StAG	Acquisition by descent: child of German parent; acknowledgement or determination of paternity required, if only the father is a German national; exception to acquisition by *jus sanguinis*: the child is born abroad after 31.12.1999 and has his/her permanent residence abroad, unless the child would suffer from statelessness, or the German parent notifies the child's birth to the German diplomatic representation	§4 para. 1 s. 2 amended on 1.7.1993 and 1.7.1998; exception in §4 para. 4 StAG introduced on 1.1.2000
***Jus soli* at birth**			
Jus soli at birth (except foundlings or persons with unclear nationality)	§4 para. 3 StAG	Acquisition by birth: child of foreign nationals, if born on German territory and if one parent has had his/her legal habitual residence in Germany for 8 years; furthermore, the parent must possess an unlimited residence permit, or he/she must be a national of another EU Member State enjoying freedom of movement, or he/she is a national of an EEA-State having equal status	introduced on 1.1.2000; amendments on 1.1.2005 resulting from the new German Immigration Act

Continued

Table A.5 Continued

Mode of acquisition of nationality	(Main) relevant article in law for this mode of acquisition	Brief description (criteria of eligibility, type of acquisition)	Changes since 1985
MODES OF ACQUISITION OF NATIONALITY AFTER BIRTH and DUAL CITIZENSHIP STATUS			
Residence-based acquisition (not targeted at any special group)	§§10 et seq. StAG	Acquisition by naturalization, entitlement: 8 years of legal habitual residence in Germany (before 2000: 15 years); furthermore, the applicant must possess an unlimited residence permit or a certain kind of limited residence permit, or he/she is a national of another EU Member State enjoying freedom of movement, or he/she is a national of an EEA-State having equal status; also conditions since 2000: language skills (B1 level), confession to the constitution and declaration of loyalty	introduced on 1.1.1991; entitlement since 1.7.1993; further amendments on 1.1.2000; editorial changes on 1.1.2005
Socialization-based acquisition	§85 AuslG (until end of 1999)	From 07/1993-12/1999: Acquisition by naturalization, entitlement if there are no particular circumstances (limited discretion): young persons between the age of 16 and 23 with 8 years of legal residence could acquire German nationality if they had an unlimited residence permit or a certain kind of limited residence permit, and if they attended a German school for 6 years (4 of which must have been a school of general education)	07/1993-12/1999
Family relation-based modes of acquisition of nationality			
Transfer of nationality to spouse	§9 StAG	Acquisition by naturalization (1 year residence prior to the marriage and 2 years' of marriage duration), entitlement if there are no particular circumstances (limited discretion); furthermore, the criteria of §8 StAG (see mode A06b) must be met. Is also applicable to so-called 'Lebenspartner' (i.e. registered homosexual partnerships)	amendment on 1.1.2000 and 1.8.2001 (for homosexual life partners)

Transfer of nationality to child	§5 StAG	Until 1.7.1998: acquisition of nationality ex lege by a child legitimized by a German national. Since 1.7.1998: acquisition of nationality by declaration if the child was born before 1.7.1993 and if the following conditions are met: his/her father is a German national and his/her mother is a foreign national, paternity is acknowledged or determined, the child has his/her legal habitual residence in Germany since 3 years, and the declaration is made before reaching the age of 23	amendment on 1.7.1998: former §10 RuStAG (entitlement) replaced by §5 StAG (declaration)
Transfer of nationality to parent of a minor national of a state under concern	NO		
Extension of acquisition to spouse of a foreign national who acquires nationality of a state concerned	§10 para. 2 StAG	Acquisition by naturalization (upon request), discretion: less than 8 years of legal habitual residence are sufficient	amendments on 1.1.2000; editorial changes on 1.1.2005; see also No. 5b above
Affinity-based modes of acquisition of nationality			
Reacquisition by former national	§13 StAG	Acquisition by naturalization, discretion: a former German national who has his/her habitual residence abroad may be naturalized if he/she is legally capable to act and if there is no reason for expulsion	editorial changes on 1.1.2005
	§12 (1) StAngRegG	Acquisition by naturalization, entitlement: a former German national who acquired a foreign nationality in connection with political, racial or religious persecution between 1933 and 1945, even if residence abroad is maintained	no (major) changes
	Art. 116 para. 2 of the German Basic Law	Acquisition by naturalization, entitlement: former German nationals whose nationality was withdrawn between 30 January 1933 and 8 May 1945 and their descendants are to be naturalized upon application	no (major) changes
Acquisition based on specific nationality:	§12 para. 2 StAG	Acquisition by naturalization, entitlement: 8 years of legal habitual residence in Germany (§§10 et seq. StAG, see mode A06a); special regulation in §12 para. 2 StAG for applicants from EU-member states only: loss or renunciation of former citizenship is not required in case of reciprocity	§12 para. 2 StAG introduced on 1.1.2000

Continued

Table A.5 Continued

Mode of acquisition of nationality	(Main) relevant article in law for this mode of acquisition	Brief description (criteria of eligibility, type of acquisition)	Changes since 1985
	§7 StAG	Acquisition of nationality ex lege: emigrants of German origin from Eastern European States having suffered from discrimination due to their descent ('Spätaussiedler', §7 StAG); requires admission to Germany and issue of a special certificate according to §15 BVFG ('Spätaussiedlerbescheinigung'). Since 2000, acquisition ex lege instead of entitlement to naturalization (see mode A19d)	amendments on 1.1.2000
	§40a StAG	Transitional regulation supplementing §7 StAG (mode A19a): acquisition of nationality ex lege on 1.8.1999 by 'Germans without German nationality' according to Art. 116 para. 1 of the German Basic Law	introduced on 15.7.1999; qualifying date for application of §40a StAG: 1.8.1999
	No. 8.1.3.4 StAR-VwV (admin. reg. only) in conj. with §8 StAG (mode A06b)	Acquisition by naturalization, discretion: German-speaking nationals from Liechtenstein, Austria or other areas in Europe where German is official or colloquial language: 4 years of legal habitual residence are sufficient (instead of 8 years: see mode A06b)	administrative regulation specified on 1.2.2001
	§6 StAngRegG	Acquisition by naturalization, entitlement: 'Germans without German nationality' (ethnic Germans within the meaning of Art. 116 para. 1 GG; since 1993: 'Spätaussiedler', see mode A19a); exception: if he/she endangers the security of the Federal Republic of Germany	replaced by §7 StAG (see mode A19a) on 1.1.2000
	§9 (1) StAngRegG	Acquisition by naturalization, discretion: ethnic German who is not an ethnic German within the meaning of Art. 116 para. 1 GG, that is, 'Vertriebener' (expellee) oder 'Aussiedler'; application may be handed in from abroad (before the 90s German authorities could have suspected that the applicants were discriminated)	no (major) changes
	§9 (2) StAngRegG	Acquisition by naturalization, entitlement: ethnic German who complies with the conditions of §9 para. 1 StAngRegG if he belonged to the German Wehrmacht, and if he did not acquire a foreign nationality after his displacement; application may be handed in from abroad	no (major) changes

	§11 StAngRegG	Acquisition by naturalization, discretion: persons having their permanent residence in Germany who were excluded from collective naturalizations within the meaning of §1 StAngRegG for racial reasons	no (major) changes
Cultural affinity-based acquisition: Person with cultural affinity to a state under concern (ethnicity, mother-tongue, and/or religion)	KfbG, BVFG – §2 para.1	The category of repatriate (Aussiedler) was created in BVFG in 1953, stipulating that 'A German citizen is a person who belongs to the German nation and who leaves the territories belonging now to foreign administration in the East; Gdansk, Poland, Lithuania, Latvia, Estonia, CSSR, Czech Republic, Hungary, Romania, Bulgaria, Yugoslavia, Albania' (Art. 1). Art. 6 stipulates that belonging to the German nation can be certified with: origin, language, upbringing, culture. The basic two principles upon which German citizenship was granted to this category of persons was: post-war fate (i.e. discrimination on the national ground) and belonging to the German nation. The BVFG act also stipulated that the repatriates receive various forms of financial support upon arrival.	BVFG introduced 1953, KfbG – amendments in 1992
	Aussiedleraufnahmegesetz 1990, KfbG, AufenthG (2005) Chapter 2 and 3	On 31.12.92 the category of repatriate was replaced by late-repatriate (Spaetaussiedler). The discrimination clause (post-war fate) was limited to the former CSSR territories. The law also introduced limits: 225.000 per year and only a person born before 1.1.93 can apply for the status. In principle it is possible to prove the German ancestry going back to the third generation (i.e. presenting the Deutsche Volks Liste),but there are limitations. A person born after 1.1.75 can acquire German citizenship only in case her/his parents already possess a German citizenship. The special status of repatriates diminishes with time: 2001 Spaetaussiedlerstatusgesetz stipulates that a person at the moment of application should be able to conduct a simple conversation in German. The status of a German national should be also 'binding' and leading to repatriation. Since 2005 (AufenthG) acquisition of the German citizenship is conditioned on the minimal knowledge of German . (B2 test) – both for the applicant and his non-German spouse. In addition, the marriage needs to last for at least 3 years.	

Continued

Table A.5 Continued

Mode of acquisition of nationality	(Main) relevant article in law for this mode of acquisition	Brief description (criteria of eligibility, type of acquisition)	Changes since 1985
dual citizenship			
Acquisition of the second citizenship at birth	§7 StAG (Nationality Law)	If a child born in Germany acquires a citizenship of the C2 state on the basis of *jus sanguinis* principle, she or he is obliged to choose between the citizenship of C2 and the C1 citizenship before reaching the age of 23. If the application is not submitted, the German citizenship is automatically withdrawn. As an exception, children of the repatriates already born in Germany (Spaetaussiedler) can keep the citizenship of their parents, without loosing the German one.	introduced 1999
Acquisition of the second citizenship after birth	§7, 12 StAG (Nationality Law)	Since 1999, German law allows to acquire an additional citizenship but only under certain circumstances. These are: (1) if renunciation of the prior citizenship causes 'particularly difficult conditions' (i.e. a foreign state does not allow that a person would be subject to humiliation, his civic rights would be affected or his economic property would be endangered, (2) reciprocity (if other EU state allows dual citizenship for the Germans). These countries are: Greece, UK, Ireland, Portugal, Sweden, Finland, France, Belgium, Italy, Hungary, Poland, Slovakia, Malta, Cyprus. Section 7 of Nationality Law also stipulates that the ethnic German repatriates and their family members do not have to give up their previous citizenship. Children of the repatriates born in Germany also have a right to maintain the citizenship of their parents (if that is passed on the basis of *jus sanguinis*). However, the general rule for the second generation is that upon reaching the age of 23 a person needs to choose between his parents' and the German citizenship; otherwise, it is automatically taken away.	introduced 1999

| loss of citizenship | §25–27 StAG (Nationality Law) | Loss of citizenship: (1) upon acquiring another citizenship, unless a person asks for permission to keep the German citizenship, (2) by voluntary application, but only if afterwards the person would not be stateless, (3) a person looses her/his second citizenship reaching the age of 23 unless exceptions apply, (4) a person looses German citizenship if she/he enlisted voluntarily with the military forces of the state whose citizenship that person possesses, unless there is an international agreement regulating that issue. In that case a person may be exempted from the military service in Germany or, if the service was shorter than in Germany – such a person would have to serve only to make up for the difference, (4) public service employers or persons having official relationship with public law functions may not be released from the German citizenship. Persons subject to compulsory military service can be released from the German citizenship only upon the consent from the Federal Ministry of Defence. | 1999 |

Source: Modified after Waldrauch (2006b).

Table A.6 National citizenship law in Hungary – legal changes since 1985

Mode of acquisition of nationality	(Main) relevant article in law for this mode of acquisition	Brief description (criteria of eligibility, type of acquisition)	Changes since 1985
BIRTHRIGHT-BASED MODES OF ACQUISITION OF NATIONALITY AT BIRTH (AUTOMATIC OR NON-AUTOMATIC)			
Jus sanguinis **at birth**			
Jus sanguinis at birth	§3 para. 1 and 2 in the Hungarian Citizenship Law (1993/LV)	A child acquires Hungarian citizenship if the parents are Hungarian citizens. If only one parent is a Hungarian citizen, Hungarian citizenship can be awarded retroactively in case of marriage, acknowledgement of paternity or determination of paternity.	New law on citizenship adopted in 1993 (but no substantial changes compared to the previous version from 1957), since then no changes.
	§5/A para c) in the Hungarian Citizenship Law	Those who have a mother of Hungarian citizenship and a non-Hungarian father, were born before 1 October 1957 and did not acquire Hungarian citizenship by birth, can acquire citizenship by sending a written statement to the President (no application procedure).	The amendment of 2003 added this paragraph.
Jus soli **at birth**			
Jus soli at birth (except foundlings or persons with unclear nationality)	§3 para. 3 in the Hungarian Citizenship Law	No, *only foundlings or children born to stateless parents with Hungarian residence.*	The Law from 1957 included (§2 para 2) that anyone who is not declared to be a citizen of another country but was born in the territory of Hungary should be regarded as a Hungarian citizen. This is not included in the 1993 Law. The 1993 Law was amended in 2003, but no substantial change (instead of 'child of stateless person' comes 'child of stateless parents')

MODES OF ACQUISITION OF NATIONALITY AFTER BIRTH and DUAL CITIZENSHIP STATUS

Residence-based acquisition not targeted at any special group	§4 para 1 in the Hungarian Citizenship Law	Acquisition by naturalization, entitlement: 8 years of legal habitual residence in Hungary. Complementary conditions: applicant has never been subject to criminal proceedings in Hungary, has sufficient means and a place to live in Hungary, his/her citizenship does not affect the interests of Hungary, and passed an exam on constitutional basics in Hungarian. The following are exempted from the exam: the incapable, those having a degree from a educational institution with education in Hungarian, and those older than 65. It is possible to acquire Hungarian citizenship in a shorter period of time and without the fulfilment of all complementary conditions (place and means to live and exam) upon Presidential decision if it serves the interests of Hungary.	The 1957 law required only 3 years of legal habitual residence. The 1993 Law was amended in 2001, 2003 and 2005 regarding the potential exemptions from the exam and the scope of the discretionary Presidential decision.
Socialization-based acquisition	§5/A para b) in the Hungarian Citizenship Law	Those who were born (and resided at birth) in the territory of Hungary and did not acquire the citizenship of parents, and have a legal habitual residence for at least 5 years in Hungary, can acquire citizenship by sending a written statement to the President (no application procedure). The statement can be made before the age of 19.	The amendment of 2001 added this paragraph.
	§4 para 4 in the Hungarian Citizenship Law	Acquisition by naturalization, entitlement: 5 years of legal habitual residence in Hungary and: being born in Hungary, (or) residence in Hungary started during minority, (or) being stateless, and all the complementary conditions listed above.	The amendment of 2001 added this paragraph.

Continued

Table A.6 Continued

Mode of acquisition of nationality	(Main) relevant article in law for this mode of acquisition	Brief description (criteria of eligibility, type of acquisition)	Changes since 1985
Family relation-based modes of acquisition of nationality			
Transfer of nationality to spouse	§4 para 2a in the Hungarian Citizenship Law	Acquisition by naturalization, entitlement: 3 years of legal habitual residence in Hungary and 3 years of marriage (or marriage ended due to death of partner); and all the complementary conditions listed above.	The 1957 Law had no requirement regarding the legal habitual residence. No substantial change since 1993.
Transfer of nationality to child of national of a state concerned	§4 para 2a and 6 in the Hungarian Citizenship Law	Adoption: Acquisition by naturalization, entitlement: 3 years of legal habitual residence in Hungary and being adopted by a Hungarian citizen; and all the complementary conditions listed above. In the case of minors who were adopted by a Hungarian citizen, there is no condition related to the legal habitual residence.	The 1957 Law had no requirement regarding the legal habitual residence in the case of children adopted by Hungarian nationals, and minors were automatically given Hungarian citizenship if the parent acquired one. Amendment of the 1993 Law in 2001 added 'or if parent already acquired Hungarian citizenship' in the case of minor applicants, and eased the conditions of naturalization for minors who were adopted by a Hungarian citizen.
	§4 para 5 in the Hungarian Citizenship Law	In the case of minors, there is no condition related to the legal habitual residence if they apply for citizenship together with parent or parent already acquired Hungarian citizenship.	
Transfer of nationality to a parent of minor, a national of a state concerned	§4 para 2b in the Hungarian Citizenship Law	Acquisition by naturalization, entitlement: 3 years of legal habitual residence in Hungary and having a child with Hungarian citizenship who is a minor; and all the complementary conditions listed above.	The 1957 Law had no requirement regarding the legal habitual residence. No substantial change since 1993.

Extension of acquisition to spouse of a foreign national who acquires nationality of a state concerned			
Affinity-based modes of acquisition of nationality			
Reacquisition by former national	§5 in the Hungarian Citizenship Law	A former Hungarian national can be renationalized by request if has never been subject to criminal proceedings in Hungary, has sufficient means and a place to live in Hungary, and his/her citizenship does not affect the interests of Hungary.	Renationalization was also possible before 1993. No substantial change since 1993.
	§5/A para a) in the Hungarian Citizenship Law	Those whose nationality was withdrawn by the acts 1947/X, 1948/XXVI, 1948/LX or 1957/V, or by the governmental decrees 7970/1946, 10515/1947 or 12200/1947, or lost their citizenship by exile between 15 September 1947 and 2 May 1990 can acquire citizenship by sending a written statement to the President (no application procedure).	The amendment of 2001 added this paragraph. Furthermore, before the 2003 amendment, the re-acquisition of nationality was based on the condition that the person in quotation did not act against Hungarian national security. This condition was deleted in 2003.
Acquisition based on specific nationality			
Cultural affinity-based acquisition: Person with cultural affinity to a state concerned (ethnicity, mother-tongue, and/or religion)	§4 para 3 in the Hungarian Citizenship Law	Acquisition by naturalization, entitlement: those who declare themselves as Hungarian nationals and who have ancestors with Hungarian citizenship and reside in Hungary can be naturalized without any condition related to the length of legal habitual residence.	Before 1993, only those could acquire Hungarian citizenship based on special rules (no requirement for the length of legal habitual residence), who had ancestors with Hungarian citizenship. After 1993, the condition to have at least 1 year of legal habitual residence in Hungary was added. The amendment of 2005 modified the condition related to the length of legal habitual residence, and now there is no condition related to the length of legal habitual residence.

Continued

Table A.6 Continued

Mode of acquisition of nationality	(Main) relevant article in law for this mode of acquisition	Brief description (criteria of eligibility, type of acquisition)	Changes since 1985
Mode of acquisition related to special status	§4 para 2d in the Hungarian Citizenship Law	Acquisition by naturalization, entitlement: 3 years of legal habitual residence in Hungary and having a refugee status; and all the complementary conditions listed above.	No such rules before 1993. No substantial change since 1993.
DUAL CITIZENSHIP Acquisition of the second citizenship at birth	§2 para 2 in the Hungarian Citizenship Law	This paragraph, which says 'A Hungarian citizen, who is at the same time a citizen of another state, should be regarded as a Hungarian citizen in the eyes of Hungarian law' is interpreted as a toleration of dual citizenship (de jure dual citizenship??). The abolishment of all bilateral treaties against dual citizenship also goes in this direction.	The Law on citizenship from 1957 explicitly tolerated dual citizenship, though preferred those applicants who withdrew or lost their other citizenship. However, bilateral treaties with other socialist countries regulated and banned dual citizenship (those who acquired dual citizenship due to the
Acquisition of the second citizenship after birth			parents' different citizenships had to choose or the citizenship was determined based on the place of residence). These treaties were abolished in 1990 (but not cancelled). In the 1993 Law, the referred paragraph was added.
LOSS OF CITIZENSHIP	§8 para 1 in the Hungarian Citizenship Law	Any Hungarian citizen who does not reside in Hungary can abdicate his/her citizenship through a written statement sent to the President if: the person has or will acquire another citizenship, is not subject to any criminal proceedings in Hungary and has no tax obligations or public debts. The citizenship can be re-acquired within one year if the other citizenship were not given.	Before 1993 these provisions were similar. The condition for re-acquiring citizenship was added by the 2001 amendment.

| §9 para 1 in the Hungarian Citizenship Law | Hungarian citizenship can be withdrawn from someone who acquired citizenship disregarding the legal rules, especially if citizenship was given based on false data. Citizenship cannot be withdrawn after 10 years. | No substantial change since 1993 (provisions introduced in 1993). |
| §2 para 2 in the Hungarian Citizenship Law | No-one can be arbitrarily deprived of his or her citizenship or of the right to choose his or her citizenship. | According to the 1957 Law (§15), it was possible to deprive someone of Hungarian citizenship because of disloyalty or serious crime. These provisions are no longer valid since 1993. |

Source: Own compilation.

Table A.7 National citizenship law in Poland – legal changes since 1985

Mode of acquisition of nationality	(Main) relevant article in law for this mode of acquisition	Brief description (criteria of eligibility, type of acquisition)	Changes since 1985
BIRTHRIGHT-BASED MODES OF ACQUISITION OF NATIONALITY AT BIRTH (AUTOMATIC OR NON-AUTOMATIC)			
Jus sanguinis at birth			
Jus sanguinis at birth	Act on Polish Nationality, 15.02.1962, Art.4 and 6	A child acquires Polish citizenship if at least one of his parent is a Polish citizen, regardless of the fact whether a child was born on the territory of the Poland or abroad. If parents wish to choose the other citizenship (i.e. the second parent's citizenship) for their child they should do so within 3 months after the child's birth.	No major changes since 1962 (including also the new bill on Polish Citizenship, 2006)
Jus soli at birth			
Jus soli at birth (except foundlings or person with unclear nationality)	Act on Polish Nationality, 15.02.1962, Art.5	no, only foundlings or children born to people with unclear nationality or the stateless.	No major changes since 1962 (including also the new bill on Polish Citizenship, 2006)
MODES OF ACQUISITION OF NATIONALITY AFTER BIRTH and DUAL CITIZENSHIP STATUS			
Residence-based acquisition not targeted at any special group	Act on Polish Nationality, 15.02.1962, Art. 9	Legal habitual residence for 5 years. It is possible to acquire Polish citizenship in a shorter period of time upon Presidential decision (discretionary). Acquisition of Polish citizenship may be also dependent on renunciation of the prior citizenship. *1997 AMENDMENTS*: a foreigner may apply for citizenship after 5 years of being granted a residence permit OR a long term/ unlimited residence permit for the EU citizens.	1997 Amendments, Art. 8

	A bill proposal to be debated in the Parliament. Act on the Polish Nationality, 2006, Art.29	Residence permit for 5 years (the EU citizens) OR residence permit for 7 years (non-EU) AND sufficient means to provide for one's living (apartment and a permanent work) AND passed a language test or attended a Polish school abroad. For other non-EU residents 10 years of legal habitual residence (other than long term/unlimited residence permit) AND sufficient means to provide for one's living AND a passed language test.	A new Bill on Polish Citizenship
Socialization-based acquisition	No		
Family relation-based modes of acquisition of nationality			
Transfer of nationality to spouse	Act on Polish Nationality, 15.02.1962, Art.10	Until 1999 a transfer of nationality was possible only from a man to a woman, upon application submitted within the three months after the marriage (enacted 1962). *Amended in 1999:* spousal transfer possible for men and women, conditions: 3 years of marriage, minimum 6 months of legal residence in Poland.	1999 Amendments – introduction of equality treatment of husbands and wives of Polish citizens with regard to acquisition of Polish nationality.
	A bill proposal to be debated in the Parliament. Act on the Polish Nationality, 2006, Art.28	2 years residence and 3 years of marriage duration for the EU citizens and stateless persons AND a language test AND sufficient means to provide for one's living. Non-EU citizens and legal residents, 5 years long uninterrupted residence and 3 years of marriage duration.	A new Bill proposal on Polish Citizenship

Continued

Table A.7 Continued

Mode of acquisition of nationality	(Main) relevant article in law for this mode of acquisition	Brief description (criteria of eligibility, type of acquisition)	Changes since 1985
Transfer of nationality to child of national a state concerned	Act on Polish Nationality, 15.02.1962, Art. 8, Art. 9 (in amended version from 1997)	Residence mode: 5 years' long legal residence requirement for a parent (applicant), automatic extension to a child. If only one parent acquires Polish nationality, it is automatically extended to minors upon the condition the second parent agrees that a child acquires other citizenship. A child that is over 16 years old has to agree personally to acquire Polish nationality. AMENDMENTS: additional condition introduced: Polish nationality can be extended to children unless they reside in Poland.	1997, 1999, minor amendments.
Transfer of nationality to parent of minor, national of a state concerned	No		
Extension of acquisition to spouse of a foreign national who acquires nationality of a state concerned	No		
Affinity-based modes of acquisition of nationality			
Reacquisition by former national	Act on Polish Nationality, 1962, Art.11, par 1, 2 Repatriation Act 9.11.2000, Art. 5 par. 2	Reacquisition of citizenship lost due to a marriage with a foreigner: according to the citizenship law from 1962 a procedure available only for women, from 1997 onwards – for both sexes. Reacquisition procedure has been also available since 1962 for the repatriates who prove their Polish origins with their lost citizen status in Poland (otherwise repatriation procedure can be initiated if an applicant proves his Polish nationality, not necessarily citizenship).	1962, 1997 – gender equality introduced. 2000 – a separate act regulating repatriation procedure and specifying the criteria for repatriation.

	A bill proposal to be debated in the Parliament. Act on the Polish Nationality, 2006, Art.3	Apart from the possibility to re-acquire Polish citizenship after a marriage with a foreigner is terminated, a person can reacquire citizenship if it has been lost before 04.06.1989 based on (1) Art.11 of the 20.01.1920 Act on the Citizenship of the Polish State, (2) Art.11 or 12 of the 8.01.1951 Act on Polish Citizenship or (3) Art.13, 14 or 15 of the 15.02.1962 Act on Polish Nationality in the version the Act had at the moment of the citizenship's loss. Polish citizenship shall not be reacquired by persons who (1) voluntarily entered the military service of a state being not in the anti-German alliance between 1.09.39 and 8.05.45, (2) accepted a public post in a state being not in the anti-German alliance between 1.09.39 and 8.05.45, (3) Is a threat to security, defence or public order in Poland, (4) acts against the Polish vital interests.	A new Bill on Polish Citizenship
Acquisition based on specific nationality Cultural affinity-based acquisition: Person with cultural affinity to a state concerned (ethnicity, mother-tongue, and/or religion)	No Act on Polish Nationality, 1962, Art. 12 (removed in the nineties). Repatriation Act 2000, Art.5	According to the Act on Polish Nationality from 1962 a person eligible to repatriate is a 'foreigner of a Polish nationality or origin, who comes to Poland in order to settle there'. Repatriation concerned the eastern territories belonging to Poland before 1945. *Repatriation Act 2000* concerns persons of Polish nationality or former Polish citizens who, as citizens of the Asiatic republics of the ZSRR, were not eligible to repatriate to Poland based on the repatriation program from late 40s/early 50s. Countries concerned in 2000 are: Armenia, Azerbaijan,	2000, a new, separate Act introduced.

Continued

Table A.7 Continued

Mode of acquisition of nationality	(Main) relevant article in law for this mode of acquisition	Brief description (criteria of eligibility, type of acquisition)	Changes since 1985
		Georgia, Kazakhstan, Kyrgyz Republic, Tadżykistan, Turkmenistan, Uzbekistan and the Asiatic part of the Russia. Persons of Polish nationality from other territories of the former ZSRR (i.e. former Polish territories) can repatriate only if they were subject to religious, national or political persecution. Conditions: an applicant needs to have at least one parent, one grandparent, or two great-grandparents of Polish nationality or citizenship. An applicant also needs to confirm his Polish origin by showing the ability to speak Polish and by cultivating Polish traditions and customs.	
Dual citizenship	Act on Polish Nationality, 1962, Art.2, Art. 8.1.3, Art. 13.1. Major Amendments in 2001	According to the Act on Polish Nationality from 1962 dual citizenship is not tolerated in Poland. Art.2 stipulates that 'A Polish citizen, in the light of the Polish law, cannot be simultaneously regarded as a citizen of another state'. Art.2 and Art. 8.1 par 3 have not been changed in the Amended version of the Act, Art.8.1.3 'Acquisition of the Polish citizenship may be conditioned upon presenting a certificate of the loss or renunciation of the foreign citizenship'. 1962: Art. 13.1'(.), a Polish citizen can acquire a foreign citizenship only after consent of a due institution. Acquisition of a foreign citizenship results in the loss of a Polish citizenship' in 2001:	Major amendments in 2001, introduction of voluntary renunciation of the Polish citizenship and de facto (though not de jure) toleration of dual citizenship

	A bill On the Polish Nationality, 2006. A new law to be debated soon in the Parliament. Art.3	Art 13.1 stipulates 'A Polish citizen looses Polish citizenship upon his/her application, having received a consent from the President of the Polish Republic to renounce his/her citizenship. The current law is being interpreted in favour of the de facto toleration of dual citizenship, given the biased meaning of Art.2 (which is interpreted in a following way: a dual citizen, when in Poland, is treated only as a Polish citizen). Art.3.1 stipulates that 'A Polish citizen who possesses a citizenship of another state, has exactly the same right and duties as a person who possesses only Polish citizenship.' De jure toleration of dual citizenship for the first generation.	A new Bill on Polish Citizenship
Acquisition of the second citizenship at birth	No A bill proposal to be debated in the Parliament. Act on the Polish Nationality, 2006, Art.3	Art.3.3 A child, whose parents (one Polish one foreign) chose a foreign citizenship for a child within one year after his birth, shall not acquire the second, Polish citizenship. No automatic, dual citizenship for the second generation.	A new Bill on Polish Citizenship
Acquisition of the second citizenship after birth	No A bill proposal to be debated in the Parliament. Act on the Polish Nationality, 2006, Art.17–28, 29–35	Neither the discretionary path of presidential decision to grant somebody the Polish citizenship, nor the naturalization procedure rule out possession of the dual citizenship.	
Loss of citizenship	Act on Polish Nationality 1962, Art.13,1, 14 and Art.15. Amended 2001	962: Art. 13.1'(,) a Polish citizen can acquire a foreign citizenship only after consent of a due institution. Acquisition of a foreign citizenship results in the loss of a Polish citizenship'.	1962, major amendments 2001

Continued

Table A.7 Continued

Mode of acquisition of nationality	(Main) relevant article in law for this mode of acquisition	Brief description (criteria of eligibility, type of acquisition)	Changes since 1985
		Art 13.1 stipulates since 2001 that 'A Polish citizen looses Polish citizenship upon his/her lapplication, having received a consent from the President of the Polish Republic to renounce his/her citizenship'.1962, Art 15.1 'A Polish citizen residing abroad can be deprived of the Polish citizenship if: (1) he has been disloyal towards the Polish People's Republic (PRL), (2) acted against the interests of the PRL, (3) left Poland illegally after 9.05.1945, (4) rejected to return to PRL upon the plea of the state's organ, (5) rejected to serve in the Polish army, (6) has been sentenced abroad for a crime that is also concerned but the Polish law'. In the 2001 version of the Act Art. 15 has been cancelled. Since 2001 a Polish citizen can loose Polish citizenship only upon his/her own voluntary decision.	

Source: Own compilation.

Table A.8 Quasi citizenship in Germany, Hungary and Poland

	Regulating Law	Definition of a quasi-citizen: Eligibility, territorial applicability and other conditions	Certifying document	Border crossing	Residence	Employment	Social security, healthcare	Educatioin	Voting rights
								What is guaranteed concerning	
Hungary	ACT LXII OF 2001 OF HUNGARIAN LIVING IN THE NEIGHBOURING COUNTRIES (STATUS LAW) ENTERED INTO FORCE 1 JAN. 2002, MODIFIED 23 JUNE 2003	Non-Hungarian citizens, declaring themselves to be of Hungarian nationality and: speaking fluent Hungarian, (or) being registered as Hungarian nationals in their country of residence, (or) being registered as Hungarian nationals at a church of their country or residence; not living in Hungary (have neither residence permit nor refugee status) but being residents of: Croatia, Romania, Serbia and Montenegro, Slovakia, Slovenia, and Ukraine. The act does not apply to non-Hungarian citizens who lost their Hungarian citizenship willingly or due to the fact that it was obtained by artifice.	Hungarian card, valid for five years (for children: valid up to the age of 18, unlimited validity for those older than 60)	Not regulated	Not regulated	Work-permit can be obtained the same way as in the case of other foreigners (no distinct treatment) unless regulated differently in international treaties. Hungarian card holders can apply for financial help to cover the costs of establishing eligibility for work.	Must pay employment taxes and insurance on work undertaken in Hungary unless international treaty orders otherwise; entitled to some healthcare provision in line with taxes paid; non-tax payers can also apply for help with healthcare costs in Hungary.	Entitled to higher education on the same rights as citizens of Hungary, including state financial support; those following non-state funded programmes can apply for maintenance funds; students in neighbouring states with Hungarian card are entitled to student privileges in the territory of Hungary; teachers working in neighbouring states are entitled to further training in Hungary, including financial support, can get financial support for training in their own country, and entitled to the privileges due to Hungary's teachers.	No

Continued

Table A.8 Continued

Regulating Law	Definition of a quasi-citizen: Eligibility, territorial applicability and other conditions	What is guaranteed concerning						
		Certifying document	Border crossing	Residence	Employment	Social security, healthcare	Education	Voting rights
	Applicant should be rejected if they are subject to an entry ban or have been deported from Hungary. Act applies also to a spouse and children, even if they are not of Hungarian nationality.							
Main changes in 2003	Being registered as Hungarian nationals at a church of their country or residence was included as a potential 'proof' of Hungarian nationality. Yugoslavia was changed to Serbia and Montenegro.		Before the amendment, only those were entitled to the Hungarian card who did not have a residence permit in Hungary. Furthermore, according to the original version, Hungarian card holders could enter and reside in Hungary under the most favourable conditions provided by and in line with international treaties; this statement was abolished by the amendment.		The amendment abolished the possibility of preferential treatment of Hungarian card holders (previously it granted work-permit for three months per calendar year, with possibility of extension)	No change	The amendment expanded the circle of potential beneficiaries: all students from neighbouring countries holding a Hungarian card can receive privileges regardless of the language of their school (before: they had to study in Hungarian); and all teachers working in neighbouring states holding a Hungarian card can receive privileges regardless of the language in which they teach (before: they had to teach in Hungarian).	No change

Poland	BILL PROJECT ISSUED BY SENATE FROM 22 APRIL 1999, REJECTED BY SEJM.	People who are neither citizens nor permanent residents of Poland but who are ex-citizens of Poland by virtue of emigration or post-1945 border changes, or who are descendants of such ex-citizens, or who have no connection to Polish citizenship but are 'attached to the Polish nationality'. CONDITIONS: Documentary evidence of Polish nationality or origin e.g. Polish identity, birth, marriage, school, military service certificates, evidence of former Polish nationality OR membership in Polish organizations; or involvement in 'the struggle for the Polish cause'; OR adherence to Polish culture in the family; or personal risks undertaken 'during the era of foreign rule' which prove 'solidarity with the Polish people'	POLISH CHART, UNLIMITED VALIDITY	Right to 'national visa', allowing multiple border crossings; exempt from requirements regarding possession of money to cover costs of stay	Unlimited residence	Access to services on same terms as Polish citizens during stay in Poland	Access to public schools on same terms as Polish citizens	No

Continued

Table A.8 Continued

				What is guaranteed concerning					
Regulating Law	Definition of a quasi-citizen: Eligibility, territorial applicability and other conditions	Certifying document	Border crossing	Residence	Employment	Social security, healthcare	Educatioin	Voting rights
	OR Command of Polish and conduct demonstrating that individual feels Polish AND no conviction for deliberate offence, unless performed for the cause of the Polish state. CHILDREN UNDER 18 AND SPOUSES INCLUDED.							
LAW 'ON POLISH ORIGIN VERIFICATION AND THE POLISH CHART' (O USTALANIU POLSKIEGO OBYWATELSTWA ORAZ KARCIE POLAKA), 21 OCT. 2007	The law introduces a category of a 'Foreign Pole', that is a person who can certify his Polish origin but who lives abroad and does not intend to repatriate to Poland (for that there is another procedure available). CONDITIONS: At least one parent OR one grandparent OR two great-grandparents who were Polish nationals or who had Polish citizenship. AND a link to Poland	POLISH CHART, valid for ten years, extending to minors and spouses	Visa allowing multiple border crossing, free from charge and a residence permit (a residence visa) granted for three months pro year or for longer. In the latter case an applicant should provide reasons for receiving an extended visa.	YES, unlimited	YES, unlimited	The law grants access to the necessary health and life saving treatment in case a person does not have a health insurance when residing in Poland.	Free access to all types of education (primary schools, universities, PhD studies, etc.). The *Foreign Poles* coming from the former ZSRR are entitled to extra provisions, which are not granted to *Foreign Poles* from the EU zone. These are: 37% discount for public transport, free entry to national museums, all sort of state's social stipends for students.	No

either by passive knowledge of Polish OR by cultivating Polish traditions and customs. CERTIFICATES: Documents proving Polish origin can be as follows: Polish ID, school or church certificates giving information on an applicant' nationality, documents certifying that an applicant was in the Polish military service, was deported or imprisoned as well as foreign ID stating Polish nationality of an applicant.

| Germany | ART. 116GG (GRUNDGESETZ, BASIC LAW) AND THE ACT ON EXPULSION FROM GERMANY 1956, REFORMED IN 1992 (BUNDERSVER-TRIEBENEN-GESTETZ, BVFG) | The category of 'Germans without a German citizenship' or 'belonging to the nation' (Volkszugehoerige). The GG, Art. 116 stipulates that a German is a person who: possesses a German citizenship or who was expelled; belongs to the German nation (or his spouse or ancestor does); or who lives on the territories that belonged to Germany on 31. 12. 1937. | For those external national who confirmed their citizenship – a German passport. Individuals who have not confirmed their citizenship but only declare German | Individuals who acquired German citizenship but who decided not to repatriate, are treated as other German citizens upon crossing the border. Germans without a German citizenship are treated as foreign citizens. | Individuals who acquired German citizenship but who decided not to repatriate, are treated as other Germans: they have unlimited residence, work permit and entitlement to social provisions. | Individuals who acquired German citizenship but who decided not to repatriate, are treated as other Germans: they have unlimited residence, work permit and entitlement to social provisions. | Individuals who confirmed their German citizenship and did not repatriate but later decided to study in Germany – are treated as German students who have a foreign *Abitur*. Germans without a German nationality can enjoy privileged status at German universities if they wrote their *Abitur* in German. The naturalization procedure is also shorter in their case – but not if they decide to take | No |

Continued

Table A.8 Continued

Regulating Law	Definition of a quasi-citizen: Eligibility, territorial applicability and other conditions	What is guaranteed concerning						
		Certifying document	Border crossing	Residence	Employment	Social security, healthcare	Educatioin	Voting rights
	The BVFG Act specifies the territorial applicability and the conditions upon which German nationality may be confirmed (Art. 6). Territories: Gdansk, Poland, Baltic States, CSSR, Czech Rep., Hungary, Romania, Bulgaria, Yugoslavia, Albania. Conditions: origin, knowledge of the German language, upbringing, culture. A person can also (re) acquire German citizenship upon presenting proofs of discrimination on the national/ ethnic ground, even if her knowledge of the language is not sufficient (since 2000 limited to former CSSR). 3 options: (1) confirm German nationality and automatically acquire		nationality and belong to German associations – do not obtain any official document.		Germans without a German citizenship are treated, in principle, as foreign citizens.	Germans without a German citizenship are treated, in principle, as foreign citizens.	up residence and employment in Germany.	

German citizenship – and repatriate (Overview Table), (2) acquire German citizenship and stay in the country of origin, (3) become a member of the German minority ass. in a country of origin without confirming citizenship but only by declaring to be a German national.

Source: Own compilation.

Notes

1 Citizenship in a Migratory World

1. Germany in 1945, Hungary in 1919 and Poland in 1945. More details are provided in Chapter 4.
2. Weil introduced four corresponding categories of states: (i) 'countries of immigrants' in which the majority of citizens are immigrants, such as the United States; (ii) 'countries of immigration' which received a lot of immigrants, such as Germany; (iii) 'countries of emigration' or the so-called sending states, such as Poland; and (iv) 'countries of emigrants' facing emigration of whole segments of the population to other countries, such as Israel.
3. European Convention on Nationality from 1997.
4. Hansen and Weil concentrated only on the selected provisions regulating naturalization as well as tolerance for dual citizenship.
5. This group of scholars draws only on the general principles of rational choice theory.

2 Comparative Citizenship Research: Competing Accounts Explaining Convergence and Divergence

1. Most of the scholars, like Joppke, would employ some assumptions from rational choice institutionalism, but would not rely solely on rational choice theory.
2. In his recent publications Christian Joppke (2006, 2007) abandons that position (see the 'Conclusion' section).
3. See Chapters 5 and 6.
4. These exclusionary practices concern ethnic Russians living permanently in Estonia and Latvia.
5. Furthermore, Latvia and Estonia continued to be monitored until 2001, while many states from the 'medium' group, such as Hungary and Poland, were entirely exempt from the OSCE monitoring.
6. In Latvia and Estonia the percentage of ethnic Russians amounts to ca. 30 per cent of the whole population.
7. For instance, Weil (2001) and Joppke (2001) analysed horizontal diffusion of aliens' rights in Western Europe and the United States, but did not focus specifically on the EU.
8. Details on the new citizenship law in Germany are to be found in Chapter 4.

3 National Parliaments As Deliberative Bodies

1. www.bundestag.de, www.sejm.pl, http://www.mkogy.hu/parl_en.htm (accessed 12 December 2007).
2. My special thanks to Anna Horvath, a PhD candidate from the Central European University in Budapest.
3. See Koopmans and Statham (2003) for a related approach (claims analysis).

4 Legislative Reforms of National Citizenship: Patterns of Convergence and Divergence in Germany, Hungary and Poland (1985–2007)

1. National legislation specifies conditions under which exemptions are allowed, for instance when the other state does not allow renunciation or if renunciation of the other citizenship would expose the person to persecution.
2. *Staatsangehörigkeit Gesetz*, §4 para. 1, s.2, StAG 2000.
3. Applies to children born out of wedlock as well.
4. §4 para. 1 s. 2 amended on 1 July 1993 and 1 July 1998; exception in §4 para. 4 StAG introduced on 1 January 2000.
5. *Bundesgesetz über die österreichische Staatsbürgerschaft* (*Staatsbürgerschaftsgesetz* 1985 – StbG), last amended 2006, §7 (3).
6. §4 para. 3 StAG, introduced on 1 January 2000; amendments on 1 January 2005 resulting from the new German Immigration Act.
7. §4 para. 1 StAG, introduced on 1 January 2000; amendments on 1 January 2005.
8. §§10 *et seq.* StAG, introduced on 1 January 1991; entitlement since 1 July 1993; further amendments on 1 January 2000; editorial changes on 1 January 2005.
9. B1 stands for intermediate knowledge of the language, recognized as being necessary to enter the job market.
10. AufenthG, §44a, introduced on 30/07/2004.
11. '[*Wenn*] *er in besonderer Weise integrationsbedürftig ist und die Ausländerbehörde ihn zur Teilnahme am Integrationskurs auffordert*', AufenthG, §44a, (3).
12. AufenthG, §44a, introduced on 30 July 2004.
13. Information provided by the German Ministry of the Interior: www. eu2007.bmi.bund.de/cln_028/nn_164892/Internet/Content/Themen/ Staatsangehoerigkeit/DatenundFakten/Was__aendert__sich__durch__ das__Richtlinienumsetzungsgesetz.html (accessed 4 January 2008).
14. Written enquiry and reply from 16 June 2006. Frank Fischer, *Stadtamt Bremen, Staatsangehörigkeits- und Namensrechtsbüro*.
15. §9 StAG amendment on 1 January 2000 and 1 August 2001 (for homosexual life partners).
16. §10 para. 2 StAG amendments on 1 January 2000; editorial changes on 1 January 2005; see also No. 5b above.

17. §5 StAG amendment on 1 July 1998: former §10 RuStAG (entitlement) replaced by §5 StAG (declaration).
18. §85 AuslG (until end of 1999), July 1993 – December 1999.
19. §13 StAG, §12 (1) StAngRegG, Article 116 para. 2 of the German Basic Law, §12 para. 2 StAG KfbG, BVFG- §2 para.1, *Aussiedleraufnahmegesetz* 1990, KfbG, AufenthG (2005) Chapters 2 and 3, §7 StAG, §40a StAG, No. 8.1.3.4 StAR-VwV (admin. reg. only) in conj. with §8 StAG (mode A06b), §6 StAngRegG, §9 (1) StAngRegG, §9 (2) StAngRegG, §11 StAngRegG.
20. The first and second categories of the DVL were regarded as equivalent to German citizenship, because they 'certified' membership of the German nation.
21. §7 StAG (Nationality Law) §7, 12 StAG (Nationality Law), introduced 1999.
22. One parent is a German citizen. *Jus sanguinis* dual citizenship.
23. §25–27 StAG (Nationality Law).
24. ART. 116 GG (Grundgesetz) and the Act on expulsion from Germany 1956 reformed in 1992 (*Bundesvertriebenengesetz*, BVFG).
25. §3 paras 1 and 2 in Hungarian Citizenship Law (1993/LV).
26. §5/A para. (c) in Hungarian Citizenship Law.
27. §3 para. 3 in Hungarian Citizenship Law.
28. §4 para. 1 in Hungarian Citizenship Law.
29. Ibid.
30. §4 para. 2a in Hungarian Citizenship Law.
31. §5/A para. (b) in Hungarian Citizenship Law.
32. §5 in Hungarian Citizenship Law, §4 para. 3 in Hungarian Citizenship Law.
33. §2 para. 2 in the Hungarian Citizenship Law, 1957, changes 1993.
34. §8 para. 1 in the Hungarian Citizenship Law, §9 para. 1 in the Hungarian Citizenship Law, §2 para. 2 in the Hungarian Citizenship Law.
35. Act LXII of 2001 on Hungarians Living in The Neighbouring Countries (STATUS LAW). Entered into force 1 January 2002, modified 23 June 2003.
36. That is, such as Hungarian citizens working as teachers.
37. Act on Polish Nationality, 15 February 1962, §4 and 6.
38. Act on Polish Nationality, 15 February 1962, §9.
39. 1997 Amendments, §8.
40. Foreigners' Law, 13 June 2003, Chapter 5.
41. Foreigners' Law, 13 June 2003, Chapter 5, §64.1–3.
42. A bill proposal to be debated in Parliament. Act on Polish Nationality, 2006, §29.
43. Act on Polish Nationality, 15 February 1962, §10, 1999 Amendments – introduction of equal treatment of husbands and wives of Polish citizens with regard to acquisition of Polish nationality.
44. A bill proposal to be debated in Parliament. Act on Polish Nationality, 2006, §28.
45. Act on Polish Nationality, 15 February 1962, §8, §9 (in amended version from 1997). 1997, 1999, minor amendments.

46. Act on Polish Nationality, 1962, §12 (removed in the 1990s). Repatriation Act 2000, §5.
47. Repatriation Act 2000, §5.
48. Act on Polish Nationality, 1962, §2, §8.1.3, §13.1. Major Amendments in 2001.
49. A bill proposal to be debated in Parliament. Act on Polish Nationality, 2006, §17–28, 29–35.
50. Act on Polish Nationality, 1962, §13.1, 14 and §15. Amended 2001.
51. Bill proposal issues by Senate from 22 April 1999, rejected by Sejm. Bill proposal 'On Polish Origin Verification and The Polish Card' (*O Ustalaniu Obywatelstwa Polskiego oraz o Karcie Polaka*).
52. Dual citizenship practice, *de jure* dual citizenship is not allowed in Hungary.
53. Dual citizenship practice, *de jure* dual citizenship is not allowed in Poland.
54. Until the 1980s in Poland one could not easily obtain a passport. Those who did were not allowed to keep it at home after returning from abroad: they had to leave it at the local police office. In order to get the passport back, one had to write an application and attach a confirmation concerning the destination of the trip. It was particularly difficult to obtain a passport and permission if one wanted to travel to Western Europe.

5   Explaining Convergence and Divergence of National Citizenship Legislation: A Comparative Analysis of Parliamentary Debates

1. Before World War II possession of dual citizenship was forbidden by the European states. Furthermore, ethnic Germans living on the former German territories (i.e. Silesia) were deprived of German citizenship (and granted Polish citizenship) if they decided to stay in Poland.
2. *Bundestag* and *Bundesrat*.
3. *Asylbewerberleistungsgesetz* (AsylbLG) http://www.gesetze-im-internet.de/bundesrecht/asylblg/gesamt.pdf (accessed 27 November 2007) Entered into force in 1993.
4. StAG, §3.
5. Central European Forum for Migration Research, '*Zmiana paradygmatu w niemieckiej polityce imigracyjnej w latach 1998–2004? Wnioski dla Polski*' (A new policy paradigm in the German immigration policy 1998–2004? Consequences for Poland), in: CEFMR Working Paper, February 2006.
6. See Chapter 5.
7. The CDU was collecting signatures against dual citizenship.
8. For details see the sub-chapter analysing parliamentary debates in Hungary.
9. 1993–1997.
10. At about the same time the Hungarian Status Law found itself under the Commission's scrutiny.

11. The number of Polish experts' statements is not very high in comparison with the leading political parties; however, experts' opinion still played an important role, that is, experts were usually presenting a government's position on a bill.
12. Political parties in Germany. Left-wing; the Social Democratic Party (SPD), the Greens (*Bündnis 90/die Grünen*), the Left (*die Linke*), Party of Democratic Socialism (PDS). Right-wing parties: Christian Democratic Union/Christian Social Union (CDU/CSU), Free Democratic Party (PDF).
13. Hungarian political parties. Left-wing and liberal parties; Hungarian Socialist Party (MSZP), the Alliance of Free Democrats (SZDSZ). Right-wing and conservative parties: Hungarian Civic Forum (Fidesz), Hungarian Democratic Forum (MDF), Hungarian Truth and Life Party (MIEP), Christian Democratic People's Party (KDNP). Agrarian: Independent Party of Smallholders, Agrarian Workers and Citizens (FKGP).
14. More details are provided in the section presenting justificatory strategies.
15. Political parties in Poland. Right-wing parties: Freedom Union (UW), Solidarity Election Action (AWS), Movement for the Reconstruction of Poland (ROP), Law and Justice (PIS), Conservative Party (SK), Civic Platform (PO), League of Polish Families (LPR). Left-wing: The Left Wing Alliance (SLD). Agrarian: Polish Peasant Party (PSL). Populist: Self-defence (Samoobrona, S).
16. See the section on justificatory strategies.
17. *In den meisten europäischen Ländern [...] z. B. in Schweden, in Italien und in den Niederlanden, wird die Staatsangehörigkeit nach einer Kombination von Abstammungs- und Territorialprinzip vergeben. Vor allem das britische und das französische Recht stehen in dieser Tradition. Das deutsche Blutsprinzip ist im europäischen Rahmen wirklich ein außerordentlicher Anachronismus, und zwar aus der Wilhelminischen Zeit.*
18. *Auch in der Weimarer Republik vollzog sich der Erwerb der Staatsangehörigkeit ohne nationale Komponente. Das änderte sich grundlegend im Dritten Reich. [...] Zugang zur deutschen Volksgemeinschaft fanden nur Volksdeutsche. Fremdvölkische wurden als Arbeitssklaven ins Reich geholt oder verschleppt, Juden wurden ausgebürgert und vergast. [...], die Reinerhaltung deutschen Blutes war vorrangiger Staatszweck.*
19. *die Bundesrepublik Deutschland also war schon nach der Erkenntnis jener Bundesregierungen und ist auch für die heutige Bundesregierung kein Einwanderungsland und kann es auch nicht sein. Wir sind kein Einwanderungsland, und wir können es nicht werden!*
20. *Ob Sie dies wollen oder nicht: Es gibt Menschen, die leben seit ein oder zwei Generationen hier und haben nicht den Willen, sich zu integrieren. Einen solchen Menschen werden Sie auch durch die Verleihung eines deutschen Passes nicht integrieren. Ich sage deshalb: Die Paßverleihung hat für mich nicht automatisch eine Integrationswirkung. Sie steht nach meinem Dafürhalten am Ende des Integrationsprozesses.*
21. *Wann werden Sie endlich begreifen, dass sich ein lebendiges und demokratisches Zusammenleben in unserer Gesellschaft niemals auf völkisch-nationalem*

Bewusstsein gründen kann, sondern einzig und allein darauf, dass alle, die in diesem Land auf Dauer leben, gleiche Rechte haben und sich auf dieser Grundlage über ihre verschiedenen politischen, kulturellen, wirtschaftlichen und sozialen Interessen auseinandersetzen?

22. *Was wir vielmehr wollen, ist eine wirkliche Integration. Deswegen wollen wir die Einbürgerungsfristen verkürzen. Wir wollen mehr Anspruchseinbürgerungen schaffen. Voraussetzung der Einbürgerung sind aber insbesondere ausreichende Sprachkenntnisse, damit wir uns verstehen. Wir wollen, dass die Ausländer Art. 3 des Grundgesetzes akzeptieren: Männer und Frauen sind gleichberechtigt.*

23. *[...] höhere Hürden in das Gesetz eingebaut werden, das kann und darf nicht übersehen werden. Ich nenne die Tatsache, dass man jetzt die deutsche Sprache ausreichend beherrschen muss. Ich frage Sie, was ist ausreichend? Wer bestimmt, was ausreichend ist? Auch wer angeblich seine Arbeitslosigkeit oder Sozialhilfesituation selbst verschuldet hat, wird nicht eingebürgert.*

24. The previous Card gives detailed information on that issue.

25. See section on 'Germany: an immigration state?' in this chapter.

26. *Wir wollen, auch wenn die Finanzsituation noch so schwierig ist, dass die Opfer der Naziherrschaft, zu denen ebenfalls die Vertriebenen gehören, die Entschädigung noch als Lebende sehen.*

27. *Ein Spätaussiedler soll Deutscher sein, weil er der Definition gemäß ein deutscher Volkszugehöriger ist. Ein deutscher Volkszugehöriger ist jemand, der sich in seiner Heimat zum deutschen Volkstum bekannt hat, sofern dieses Bekenntnis durch bestimmte Merkmale wie Abstammung, Sprache, Erziehung, Kultur bestätigt wird. Diese Definition bedeutet in meinen Augen eine ethnische Ausgrenzung und Privilegierung bestimmter Bevölkerungsgruppen mit ausländischer Staatsangehörigkeit und Wohnort in einem anderen Staat.*

28. *Wie sehr die Probleme der doppelten Staatsangehörigkeit in Deutschland überdramatisiert werden, zeigen nicht zuletzt die durchweg positiven Erfahrungen anderer Länder. Schauen wir auf diesem Gebiet nach Frankreich, Großbritannien und den Niederlanden. Nehmen Sie als Beispiel die überaus beliebte niederländische Königin Beatrix. Sie besitzt nicht eine, nicht zwei, nicht drei, sie besitzt vier Staatsbürgerschaften, neben der niederländischen auch die deutsche, die englische und die kanadische; man höre und staune. (Erwin Marschewski [CDU/CSU]: Das ist wirklich erstrebenswert!) Kein Niederländer, Herr Marschewski, hat jemals ernsthaft bezweifelt, dass seine Königin Beatrix eine loyale, staatstreue Holländerin sei.*

29. *Mit der von Ihnen vorgesehenen Regelung müssen Sie diejenigen Menschen, die in diese Gesellschaft absolut nicht passen und alles getan haben, um sich an den Rand dieser Gesellschaft zu begeben, auf Dauer behalten.* (Sebastian Edathy [SPD]: *Dass wir Sie auf Dauer behalten, finde ich viel schlimmer!*) *Meine Damen und Herren, ich habe gesagt: Kriminalität ist auch ein Aspekt, den wir berücksichtigen müssen.*

30. *Der deutsche Paß ist nicht irgendein Papier, [...] sondern er setzt eine bewusste Hinwendung zum deutschen Staat voraus.*

31. *A magyar állampolgárság a kontinentális jogrendszerekhez hasonlóan és hagyományainknak megfelelően vérségi alapon, az ún. leszármazás jogcímén keletkezik.*

32. Azok számára álljon könnyen elérhetővé a magyar állampolgárság, akiket ehhez az országhoz valóságos kapcsolat fűz. A most tárgyalt törvény sajnálatos módon nem szolgálja ezt a célt. Azt a jelenlegi gyakorlatot tartósítja, melynek eredményeként a valamikor kivándorolt magyarok sok generáción keresztül örökítik a magyar állampolgárságot, még azokra az utódaikra is, akik az országgal semmiféle kapcsolatban nem állnak, akár magyarul sem tudnak. Természetesen helyénvaló, hogy külföldön született magyarok gyermekei öröklik a magyar állampolgárságot, amennyiben az anyaországgal valamiféle kapcsolatban állnak. Indokolatlan azonban, hogy akik erre nem tartanak igényt, azok is automatikusan örököljék a magyar állampolgárságot, s ezzel a magyar állam felelősségét, annak ellenére, hogy más államnak is állampolgárai.

33. Az állampolgárság intézményének leértékelődése elkerülése érdekében a javaslat az európai szabályokhoz közelítő vagy azokkal közel azonos, a jelenleginél szigorúbb feltételeket támaszt az állampolgárság megszerzése elé. Megkívánja azt, hogy az állampolgárságért folyamodó meghatározott ideig Magyarország területén éljen, büntetlen előéletű legyen, és integrálódjon a magyar társadalomba. Hatályos törvényünknek előírása, hogy a magyar állampolgárság megszerzése előtt legalább három évig letelepedett, bevándorolt külföldiként éljen Magyarországon a kérelmező. Ez a szabály – a hároméves időtartam – sem mai viszonyainknak, sem a mai európai gyakorlatnak nem felel már meg. Kevés ahhoz ez az idő, hogy a leendő magyar állampolgár beilleszkedéséről, társadalmi viszonyaink elfogadásáról, integrálódásáról egyáltalán beszélhessünk.

34. A státustörvényt a kormány a Ház elé terjesztve azzal a XX. századi örökséggel nézünk szembe, hogy ma államhatárok osztják meg az egykor egy testet alkotó magyarságot. A határokat nem változtathatjuk meg, de felülemelkedhetünk, átívelhetünk a megosztottságon. A státustörvény szembenézés azzal, hogy az államhatárok egy időben és még ma is részlegesen, lelki határokká is váltak. Az anyaország jelentős része félt közösséget vállalni a határon túli nemzetrészekkel. És ahol félelem van, ott nincs szabadság. A Fidesz-Magyar Polgári Párt meggyőződése, hogy mi, magyarok, Magyarországon és a határon túl immáron szabadok vagyunk, szabadon vállalhatjuk az együttműködést azokkal, akik velünk összetartozónak vallják magukat. A végeken élő magyar közösségek határon túliak maradnak, de a nemzeti szolidaritásnak immáron nem lehetnek határai.

35. Ami leginkább kritikaként vagy problémaként merült fel, tulajdonképpen az, hogy a legtöbb ágazatban, a legtöbb szakmában ezek a munkavállalók – mivel a környező országok döntő többségében az életszínvonal és a bér lényegesen elmarad a magyarországi helyzethez képest – nagyon sokszor alulkínálják a magyar munkavállalók ajánlatait, tehát egyfajta bérletörő szerepet is játszanak sajnálatos módon. Ez egy nagyon súlyos probléma, amellyel szembe kell néznünk. A bizottságunk ülésén is megfogalmazódott, hogy mindenképpen garanciákat kell beépíteni a törvénybe a tekintetben, hogy a határon kívül élő magyarok legalább olyan bért kapjanak egy-egy ágazatban, egy-egy szakmában, mint ami itt, Magyarországon általános.

36. A magyar állampolgárság kedvezményes honosítás útján történő megadása tehát nem ellentétes az Európai Unió szabályaival és elveivel. Az Európai Unió csaknem valamennyi tagországa ismeri és alkalmazza a kettős állampolgárság

intézményét. Hosszan lehetne sorolni az egyes uniós tagországok gyakorlatában meglévő hasonlóságokat és különbözőségeket, így a német, a portugál, a görög, a spanyol, az olasz, a francia, a skandináv államok vagy a britek gyakorlatát, de az észtek és a lettek hasonló gyakorlatát is. [...] Ha tehát egy kicsit közelebb nézünk... [...] Szlovákia ismeri és alkalmazza a kétoldalú megállapodásokon alapuló kettős állampolgárság intézményét. [...] Ráadásul, például Romániában semmiféle törvény nem tiltja a kettős állampolgárságot. A külföldi állampolgár viszonylag egyszerűen megkaphatja a román állampolgárságot is, elég, ha akármilyen távoli rokonság útján bizonyítja román származását.

37. *A kettős állampolgárság alapján azok, akik mint külföldi állampolgárok, eddig munkavállalási engedéllyel végezhettek munkát Magyarországon, most a magyar állampolgárság jogán engedély nélkül lesznek foglalkoztathatók bármilyen munkahelyen. Úgy gondoljuk, hogy súlyos feszültségek alakulhatnak ki a munkaerőpiacon, különösen az érintett országhatárok melletti keleti és északi megyékben és a fiatalabb generációkban. Az újonnan állást keresők kiszoríthatják a jelenlegieket, a már foglalkoztatottakat. Minden 100 ezer új álláskereső [...] évi 50 milliárd forint többletterhet jelenthet annak a kasszának, amelyből ma a munkanélküli-ellátásokat és -támogatásokat fedezzük.*

38. AWS, 22 September 1999.

39. *W dalszym ciągu też jako uzupełniająca pozostaje zasada ius soli, czyli zasada ziemi. Ma ona skutecznie zapobiegać, tak jak dotychczas starała się czynić, przypadkom bezpaństwowości dzieci.*

40. *Polska jest członkiem Rady Europy, konwencję o obywatelstwie ma zamiar ratyfikować w najbliższym czasie i dlatego też ta ustawa poprzedza jakby ratyfikację tej konwencji. [...] Są to więc pewne reguły, które są w tej chwili wypracowane i dlatego są to tak zwane standardy.*

41. *Cudzoziemcowi można nadać obywatelstwo na jego wniosek, jeżeli zamieszkuje w Polsce na podstawie zezwolenia na osiedlenie przez co najmniej 5 lat. Senat był nawet skłonny skrócić ten okres, lecz w głosowaniu końcowym został on wydłużony. W ustawodawstwach państw europejskich jest różnie, można powiedzieć, że najczęściej stosowany jest rzeczywiście okres 5-letni. Istniały także obawy przed zbyt szybką naturalizacją cudzoziemców.*

42. *Jeśli natomiast chodzi o kryterium językowe, to wprowadza się je w tej chwili w różnych krajach. Będziemy nad tym myśleć przy okazji trwających prac nad nową ustawą o obywatelstwie polskim i przewidywaną na koniec tego roku nowelizacją ustawy o cudzoziemcach.*

43. See Chapter 4.

44. *Następna sprawa związana jest z przepisem dotyczącym przywracania obywatelstwa. [...] naszym zamiarem było to, aby przywrócić obywatelstwo jednak tym, dla których jego utrata była krzywdą, była wynikiem prześladowania. [...] Po burzliwych dyskusjach w komisji sejmowej uznano, że te osoby, które wyjechały świadomie i z czysto ekonomicznych przyczyn dokonały takiego, a nie innego życiowego wyboru – i to wprost wynika z dokumentów czy z materiałów – nie powinny być tą zasadą objęte.*

45. *[...] czas najwyższy, by po 10 latach wolnej Rzeczypospolitej Polskiej upomnieć się o tę część narodu polskiego. O tę część, która przez tyle lat odczuwa*

niesprawiedliwość, ma poczucie krzywdy, odosobnienia. Tak jak wielu posłów podkreślało w poprzedniej debacie, często zapewniamy tych Polaków werbalnie o miłości, o wdzięczności, o współczuciu ich losowi. [...] Obrazowo rzecz ujmując: Matka mająca na przykład pięcioro dzieci nie powie, że ma za mało chleba. Może dać skromne porcje, ale chleb musi się znaleźć dla wszystkich dzieci. Szczególnie dotyczy to dzieci, które złożyły swoją ofiarę w postaci ciężkiego życia, deportowania, tak jak w Kazachstanie.

46. *W projekcie tym, wydaje się, szerokie są zobowiązania władz centralnych do zapewnienia pracy i mieszkania, uznania uprawnień emerytalnych i zdobytych za granicą wykształcenia i kwalifikacji. Nie wiemy dziś, czy budżet państwa jest w stanie przyjąć na siebie całość tych zobowiązań. Jak pokazują doświadczenia niemieckie, masowy napływ repatriantów niesie ze sobą poważne obciążenia finansowe, w tym także dla budżetu centralnego. W ostatniej dekadzie, w latach 1989–1998, w Niemczech przybyło około 2 milionów repatriantów, a rząd federalny przeznaczał rocznie na ten cel około miliarda marek.*

47. *Pewne kontrowersje i spory [...] wzbudził art. 4 ustawy, który stanowi: Obywatel polski nie może być równocześnie uznawany przez władze Rzeczypospolitej Polskiej za obywatela innego państwa. W moim przekonaniu, brzmienie tego artykułu jest w pełni słuszne i logiczne. Jest to rozwiązanie liberalne, które nie zabrania obywatelowi polskiemu posiadania obywatelstwa innego państwa, ale jednocześnie wymaga od tego obywatela w sposób wyraźny, aby na terenie Rzeczypospolitej podporządkowywał się tylko przepisom prawa polskiego.*

48. *[...]w mniej więcej połowie tych państw obowiązuje zasada wielokrotnego obywatelstwa, a w drugiej połowie – zasada jednokrotnego. Państwa, które przyjmują zasadę wielokrotnego obywatelstwa, to przede wszystkim państwa o charakterze postkolonialnym [...] bądź państwa emigracyjne, takie jak Australia, USA, Francja czy Anglia. Charakterystyczne jest również to, że nasz najbliższy sąsiad zachodni – Niemcy, a także kraje skandynawskie, stosują zasadę pojedynczego obywatelstwa. Pomimo kontrowersji związanych z zasadą, przemawia do mnie argument, że nie leży w interesie Polski stwarzanie możliwości podwójnego obywatelstwa.*

6   Towards Convergence: Horizontal Europeanization of National Citizenship Legislation

1. Maria Vicente Micheletti and Others v. Delegacion del Gobierno en Cantabrie (C-369/90) and Kaur case (C-192/99).
2. www.curia.europa.eu/jurisp/ (accessed 2 August 2008).
3. Ibid.
4. See Chapter 5.
5. The Status Law regulates the relation between ethnic Hungarians living abroad and the Hungarian state.
6. As a clarification: what is meant here is not immigration, but naturalization law.

Appendix

1. The detailed description of the NATAC approach, as well as the operationalization of the dependent variable with its components, is provided in Chapter 3.
2. C1 – country in question, C2 – other country (After NATAC glossary).
3. This category was absent in the NATAC typology. This research project included the 'quasi citizenship' due to its importance in the countries under study.
4. Ein Spätaussiedler soll Deutscher sein, weil er der Definition gemäß ein deutscher Volkszugehöriger ist. Ein deutscher Volkszugehöriger ist jemand, der sich in seiner Heimat zum deutschen Volkstum bekannt hat, sofern dieses Bekenntnis durch bestimmte Merkmale wie Abstammung, Sprache, Erziehung, Kultur bestätigt wird. Diese Definition bedeutet in meinen Augen eine ethnische Ausgrenzung und Privilegierung bestimmter Bevölkerungsgruppen mit ausländischer Staatsangehörigkeit und Wohnort in einem anderen Staat.

Bibliography

Aleinikoff, A.; Klusmeyer, D. (2000) *From Migrants to Citizens* (Washington, D.C.: Carniege).

Aleinikoff, A.; Klusmeyer, D. eds (2001) *Citizenship Today: Global Perspectives and Practices* (Washington, D.C.: Carnegie).

Aleinikoff, A.; Klusmeyer, D. (2002) *Citizenship Policies for an Age of Migration* (Washington, D.C.: Carnegie).

Bade, K. J.; Oltmer, J. (2003): *Aussiedler: deutsche Einwanderer aus Osteuropa*, Schriften des Instituts für Migrationsforschung und Interkulturelle Studien (IMIS), Vol. 8 (Osnabrück: V&R Unipress).

Bader, V. (2005a), 'Reasonable Impartiality and Priority for Compatriots. A Criticism of Liberal Nationalism's Main Flaws', *Ethical Theory and Moral Practice*, vol. 8 (1–2): 83–103.

Bader, V. (2005b), 'The Ethics of Immigration', *Constellations*, vol. 12 (3): 331–361.

Barry, K. (2006) 'Home and Away: The Construction of Citizenship in an Emigrant Context', *New York University Law Review*, vol. 81 (1):11–60.

Bauböck, R. (1994a) *From Aliens to Citizens. Redefining the Status of Immigrants in Europe* (Aldershot: Ashgate).

Bauböck, R. (1994b) *Transnational Citizenship* (Aldershot: Edward Elgar).

Bauböck, R. (2005a) 'Citizenship Policies: International, State, Migrant and Democratic Perspectives' *Global Migration Perspectives*, Research Paper no. 19, available at http://www.gcim.org/attachements/GMP%20No%2019.pdf (accessed 6 February 2011).

Bauböck, R. (2005b), 'Expansive Citizenship-Voting beyond Territory and Membership', *PS-Online*, October 2005, available at http://journals.cambridge.org/action/displayAbstract?fromPage=online&aid=342364&fulltextType=RA&fileId=S1049096505050341 (accessed 6 February 2011).

Bauböck, R. ed. (2005c), 'Migration and Citizenship: Legal Status, Rights and Political Participation' *State of the Art Report IMISCOE Cluster B 3*, Available at: www.imiscoe.org/publications/workingpapers/documents/migration_and_citizenship.pdf (accessed 6 April 2007).

Bauböck, R. ed. (2006) *Migration and Citizenship* (Amsterdam: Amsterdam UP).

Bauböck, R. (2007a), 'Stakeholder Citizenship and Transnational Political Participation: A Normative Evaluation of External Voting', *Fordham Law Review*, vol. 75 (5): 2393–2447.

Bauböck, R. (2007b), 'Why European Citizenship? Normative Approaches to Supranational Union', *Theoretical Inquires in Law*, vol. 8 (2): 452–488.

Bauböck, R. (2010) 'Studying Citizenship Constellations', *Journal of Ethnic and Migration Studies*, vol. 36 (5): 847–859.

Bauböck, R.; Ersbøll, E; Groenendijk, K.; Waldrauch, K. (2006) *Acquisition and Loss of Nationality. Policies and Trends in 15 European States* (Amsterdam: Amsterdam UP, IMISCOE).

Bauböck, R.; Perchinig, B.; Sievers, W. eds (2007) *Citizenship policies in the new Europe* (Amsterdam: Amsterdam UP, IMISCOE).

Bauböck, R.; Perchinig, V.; Sievers, W. eds (2009) *Citizenship Policies in the New Europe*, 2nd updated and enlarged edition (Amsterdam: Amsterdam UP).

Bauder, H. (2008) 'Media Discourse and the New German Immigration Law', *Journal of Ethnic and Migration Studies*, vol. 34 (1): 95–112.

Bellamy, R. (2008) 'Evaluating Union citizenship: belonging, rights and participation within the EU', *Citizenship Studies*, vol. 12 (6): 597–611.

Benhabib, S. (2004) *The Rights of the Others: Aliens, Residents and Citizens* (Cambridge: Cambridge UP).

Benhabib, S.; Resnik, J. (2009) *Migrations and Mobilities. Citizenship, Borders and Gender* (New York and London: New York UP).

Blondel, J. (1973) *Comparative Legislatures* (Englewood Cliffs, NJ: Prentice-Hall).

Blotevogel, H. H.; Mueller, U.; Wood, G. (1993) 'From Itimerant Worker to Immigrant? The Geography of Guestworkers in Germany' In: King, R. ed., *Mass Migration in Europe: The Legacy and the Future* (London: Belhaven).

Brubaker, R. (1992) *Citizenship and Nationhood in France and Germany* (Cambridge, MA: Harvard UP).

Brubaker, R. (1996) *Nationalism Reframed. Nationhood and the National Question in the New Europe* (Cambridge: Cambridge University Press).

Brubaker, R. (2004) *Ethnicity without Groups* (Cambridge, MA: Harvard UP).

Calder, G.; Cole, P.; Seglow, J. eds (2010) *Citizenship Acquisition and National Belonging. Migration, Membership and the Liberal Democratic State* (Basingstoke: Palgrave Macmillan).

Caporaso, J.; Cowles, M.; Risse, T. eds (2001) *Transforming Europe: Europeanization and Domestic Change* (Ithaca, NY: Cornell UP).

Carens, J. (1992) 'Migration and Morality: A Liberal Egalitarian Perspective' In: Berry, B.; Goodin, R. eds, *Free Movement: Ethnical Issues in the Transnational Movement of People and Money* (London: Harvester Wheatshead).

Carens, J. (2000) *Culture, Citizenship and Community. A Contextual Exploration of Justice as Evenhandedness* (New York, Oxford University Press).

Checkel, J. (1999) 'Norms, Institutions, and National Identity in Contemporary Europe', *International Studies Quarterly*, vol. 43 (1): 83–114.

Checkel, J. (2001a), 'The Europeanization of Citizenship?' In: Caporaso, J.; Cowles, M.; Risse, T. eds, *Transforming Europe: Europeanization and Domestic Change* (Ithaca, NY: Cornell UP).

Checkel, J. (2001b), 'Why Comply? Social Change and European Identity Change' *International Organization*, vol. 55 (3): 553–88.

Chilton, P. (2004) *Analyzing Political Discourse. Theory and Practice* (London and New York: Routledge).

Chwaszcza, C. (2009) 'The unity of the people, and immigration in liberal theory', *Citizenship Studies*, vol. 13 (5): 451–473.

Coenders, M.; Scheepers, P. (2008) 'Changes in Resistance to the Social Integration of Foreigners in Germany 1980–2000: Individual and Contextual Determinants', *Journal of Ethnic and Migration Studies*, vol. 34 (1): 1–26.

Dahl, R. (1989) *Democracy and its Critics* (New Haven, CT: Yale UP).

Dell'Olio, F. (2005) *The Europeanization of Citizenship: Between the Ideology of Nationality, Immigration and European identity* (Aldershot: Ashgate).

Diez, T.; Squire, V. (2008) 'Traditions of Citizenship and the Securitisation of Migration in Germany and Britain', *Citizenship Studies*, vol. 12 (6), 565–81.

Dryzek, J. (1990) *Discursive Democracy: Politics, Policy and Political Science* (Cambridge: Cambridge UP).

Elrick, J.; Frelak, J.; Hut, P. (2006) *Polen und Deurschland gegenüber ihren Diasporas im Osten* (Warsaw: WEMA).

Eriksen, E. O.; Fossum, J. (2002) 'Democracy through Strong Publics in the European Union?' *Journal of Common Market Studies*, 40(3): 401–424.

Ette, A. (2003) *Germany's Immigration Policy 2000–2002: Understanding Policy Change with a Political Process Approach* (Centre for Migration, Citizenship and Development, Working Paper no. 3).

Evans, G.; Heath, A. (1995) 'The Measurement of Left-Right and Libertarian-Authoritarian Values: A Comparison of Balanced and Unbalanced Scalles' *Quality and Quantity*, 29 (2): 191–206.

Faist, T. ed. (2007) *Dual Citizenship in Europe: From Nationhood to Societal Integration* (Aldershot: Ashgate).

Faist, T.; Gerdes, J.; Rieple, B. (2004) *Dual Citizenship as Path-Dependent Process* (Centre for Migration, Citizenship and Development, Working Paper no.7).

Favell, A. (2001) *Philosophies of Integration: Immigration and the Idea of Citizenship in France and Britain* (London: Macmillan).

Fowler, B. (2004) 'Fuzzying Citizenship, Nationalizing Political Space: A Framework for Interpreting the Hungarian 'Status Law' as a New Form of Kin-State Policy in Central and Eastern Europe' In: Jeda, O.; Kántor, Z.; Majtenyi, B.; Halász, I. eds, *The Hungarian Status Law: Nation Building and/or Minority Protection* (Budapest and Sapporo: Slavic Research Center).

Gellner, E. (1993) *Nations and Nationalism* (Ithaca, NY: Cornell University Press).

George, A.; Bennett, A. (2005) *Case studies and Theory Development in the Social Sciences* (Cambridge, MA: MIT Press).

Goodman, S. W. (2010) 'Integration Requirements for Integration's Sake? Identifying, Categorising and Comparing Civic Integration Policies', *Journal of Ethnic and Migration Studies*, vol. 36 (5): 753–772.

Górny, A.; Koryś. P. eds (2007) *Obywatelstwo wielokrotnego wyboru. Interdyscyplinarne ujęcie kwestii podwójnego obywatelstwa w Polsce* (Warszawa: Wydawnictwo Uniwersytetu Warszawskiego).

Górny, A. (2009) 'Same Letter, New Spirit: Nationality Regulations and their Implementation in Poland' In: Bauböck, R.; Perchinig, B.; Sievers, W. eds, *Citizenship Policies in the New Europe*, 2nd updated and enlarged edition (Amsterdam: Amsterdam UP).

Graziano, P.; Vink, M. (2007) *Europeanization. New Research Agendas* (Basingstoke: Palgrave MacMillan).

Hailbronner, K. (2003) 'Rights and Duties of Dual Nationals: Changing Concepts and Attitudes' In: Martin, D.; Hailbronner, K. eds, *Rights and Duties of Dual Nationals – Evolution and Prospects* (The Hague: Kluwer Law International).

Hall, P. and Taylor, R. (1996) 'Political Science and the Three New Institutionalisms', *Political Studies*, vol. 44 (5): 936–57.

Hammar, T. (1990) *Democracy and the Nation State* (Avebury: Aldershot Gower Publishers).

Hansen, R.; Weil, P. (2001) *Towards a European nationality: Citizenship, Immigration and Nationality Law in the EU* (New York: Palgrave).

Hansen, R.; Weil, P. (2002) *Dual Nationality, Social Rights and Federal Citizenship in the U.S. and Europe: The Reinvention of Citizenship* (New York, Oxford: Berghahn Books).

Hay, C. (2006) 'Constructivist Institutionalism', In: Rhodes, R.A.W.; Binder, S.; Rockman, B. eds (2006) *The Oxford Handbook of Political Institutions* (Oxford: Oxford UP).

Hedwig, R. (1996) 'Die Dynamik der Einwanderung im Nichteinwanderungsland Deutschland' In: Fassmann, H.; Münz, R. eds, *Migration in Europa. Historische Entwicklung, aktuelle Trends, politische Reaktionen* (Frankfurt/Main: Campus).

Heinrich, A. (2002) 'The Integration of Germans from the Soviet Union', In: Rock, D.; Wolff, S. eds, *Coming Home to Germany? The Integration of Ethnic Germans from Central and Eastern Europe in the Federal Republic* (New York: Bergham Books).

Honohan, I. (2010) 'Republican Requirements for Access to Citizenship' In: Calder, G.; Cole, P.; Seglow, J. eds, *Citizenship Acquisition and National Belonging. Migration, Membership and the Liberal Democratic State* (Basingstoke: Palgrave Macmillan).

Hooghe, L.; Marks, G.; Wilson, C. (2002) 'Does Left/Right Structure Party Positions on European Integration?' In: *Comparative Political Studies*, vol. 35 (8): 965–89.

Howard, M. M. (2005) 'Variation in Dual Citizenship Policies in the Countries of the EU', *International Migration Review*, vol. 39 (3): 697–720.

Howard, M. M. (2006) 'Comparative Citizenship: An Agenda for Cross-National Research', *Perspectives*, vol.4 (3): 443–455.

Howard, M. M. (2009) *The Politics of Citizenship in Europe* (New York: Cambridge UP).

Howard, M. M. (2010) 'The Impact of the Far Right on Citizenship Policy in Europe: Explaining Continuity and Change', *Journal of Ethnic and Migration Studies*, vol. 36 (5), 735–751.

Ieda, O.; Kantor, Z.; Majtenyi, B.; Vizi, B.; Halasz, I. (2004) *The Hungarian Status Law: Nation Building and/or Minority Protection* (Sapporo, Budapest: Slavonic Research Center).

Isin, E. F.; Turner, B. S. (2007) 'Investigating Citizenship: An Agenda for Citizenship Studies', *Citizenship Studies*, vol. 11 (1): 5–17.

Janoski, T. (2009) 'The Difference that Empire Makes: Institutions and Politics of Citizenship in Germany and Austria', *Citizenship Studies*, vol. 13 (4): 381–411.

Järve, P. (2009) 'Estonian Citizenship: Between Ethnic Preferences and Domestic Obligations', In: Bauböck, R.; Perchinig, B.; Sievers, W. eds, *Citizenship Policies in the New Europe*, 2nd updated and enlarged edition (Amsterdam: Amsterdam UP).

Joppke, C. (2007) 'Beyond National Models: Civic Integration Policies for Immigrants in Western Europe', In: *West European Politics*, 30 (1), 1–22.

Joppke, C. (1999) *Immigration and the Nation-State: the United States, Germany and Great Britain* (Oxford: Oxford UP).

Joppke, C. (2001) 'The Evolution of Alien Rights in the United States, Germany, and the European Union', In: Aleinikoff, A.; Klusmeyer, D. eds, *Citizenship Today: Global Perspectives and Practices* (Washington, D.C.: Carnegie).

Joppke, C. (2002) 'The Legal-Domestic Sources of Immigrant Rights: The United States, Germany, and the European Union', *Comparative Political Studies*, vol. 34 (4): 339–366.

Joppke, C. (2005a) *Selecting by Origin. Ethnic Migration in the Liberal States* (Cambridge, MA: Harvard UP).

Joppke, C. (2005b), 'Exclusion in the Liberal State. The Case of Immigration and Citizenship Policy', *European Journal of Social Theory*, vol. 8 (1): 43–61.

Joppke, C. (2007) 'Transformation of Citizenship: Status, Rights, Identity', *Citizenship Studies*, vol. 11 (1): 37–48.

Joppke, C.; Morawska, E. (2003) *Towards Assimilation and Citizenship: Immigrants in Liberal Nation-States* (Basingstoke: Palgrave Macmillan).

Kemp, W. (2002) 'Applying the Nationality Principle: Handle with Care', *Journal of Ethnopolitics and Minority Issues in Europe*, Issue 4, http://*.ecmi.de/jemie/download/Focus4-2002_Kemp_Kymlicka.pdf.

Kiss, B.; Zahoran, C. (2007) 'Hungarian Domestic Policy in Foreign Policy', *International Issues & Slovak Foreign Policy Affairs*, Issue 02: 46–64.

Klekowski von Koppenfels, A. (2002) 'The Legal Background to the Migration of Ethnic Germans', In: Rock, D.; Wolff, S. eds, *Coming Home to Germany? The Integration of Ethnic Germans from Central and Eastern Europe in the Federal Republic* (New York: Bergham Books).

Klopp, B. (2002) *German Multiculturalism. Immigrant Integration and the Transformation of Citizenship* (Westpoint, CT/London: Praeger).

Knill, C.; Lehmkuhl, D. (1999) 'How European Matters: Different Mechanisms of Europeanization', *European Integration online Papers (EIoP)* vol. 3 (7) http://eiop.or.at/eiop/texte/1999–007a.htm (accessed 12 January 2007).

Kohn, H. (1944) *The Idea of Nationalism: A Study of its Origins and Background* (New York: Macmillan).

Koopmans, R.; Statham, P. (2003) 'How National Citizenship Shapes Transnationalism: Migrant and Minority Claims-making in Germany, Great Britain and the Netherland', In: Joppke, K.; Morawska, E. eds, *Towards Assimilation and Citizenship: Immigrants in Liberal Nation-States* (Basingstoke: Palgrave Macmillan).

Koopmans, R.; Erbe, J. (2003) *Towards a European Public Sphere? Vertical and Horizontal Dimensions of Europeanised Political Communication,* WZB Discussion Paper SP IV 2003–403.

Koslowski, R. (2000) *Migrants and Citizens. Demographic Change in the European State System* (Ithaca, NY and London: Cornell University Press).

Koslowski, R. (2005) *International Migration and the Globalisation of Domestic Politics* (London and New York: Routledge).

Kostakopoulou, D. (2001) *Citizenship Identity and Immigration in the European Union* (Manchester: Manchester UP).

Kostakopoulou, D. (2010) 'Matters of Control: Integration Tests, Naturalisation Reform and Probationary Citizenship in the United Kingdom', *Journal of Ethnic and Migration Studies,* vol. 36 (5): 829–846.

Kovacs, M. (2006) 'The politics of dual citizenship in Hungary', *Citizenship Studies,* vol. 10 (4): 431–451.

Kovacs, M; Tóth, J. (2007) 'Citizenship and nationality law – the case of Hungary', In: Bauböck, R.; Perchinig, B.; Sievers, W. eds, *Citizenship policies in the new Europe* (Amsterdam: Amsterdam UP, IMISCOE).

Kreuzer, C. (2003) 'Double and multiple nationality in Germany after the citizenship reform act of 1999', In: Martin, D.; Hailbronner, K. eds, *Rights and Duties of Dual Nationals – Evolution and Prospects* (The Hague: Kluwer Law International).

Krippendorff, K. (2004) *Content Analysis. An Introduction to its Methodology* (Thousand Oaks, CA: Sage).

Krūma, K. (2009a) 'Lithuanian Nationality: Trump Card to Independence and its Current Challenges' In: Bauböck, R.; Perchinig, B.; Sievers, W. eds, *Citizenship Policies in the New Europe,* 2nd updated and enlarged edition (Amsterdam: Amsterdam UP).

Krūma, K. (2009b), 'Checks and Balances in Latvian Nationality Policies: National Agendas and International Frameworks', In: Bauböck, R.; Perchinig, B.; Sievers, W. eds, *Citizenship Policies in the New Europe,* 2nd updated and enlarged edition (Amsterdam: Amsterdam UP).

Kuisma, M. (2008) 'Rights or privileges? The challenge of globalization to the values of citizenship', *Citizenship Studies,* vol. 12 (6): 613–27.

Kymlicka, W. (1995) *Multicultural Citizenship* (Oxford: Clarendon).

Kymlicka, W.; Norman, W. (1994) 'Return of a Citizen: a Survey of a Recent Work on Citizenship Theory', *Ethics,* vol. 104 (2): 352–381.

Lavanex, S. (2007) 'Asylum Policy', In Graziano, P.; Vink, M. eds, *Europeanization. New Research Agendas* (Houndmills: Palgrave MacMillan).

Levy, D. (2002) 'Integrating Ethnic Germans in West Germany: Early Postwar Period' In: Rock, D.; Wolff, S. eds, *Coming Home to Germany? The Integration of Ethnic Germans from Central and Eastern Europe in the Federal Republic* (New York: Bergham Books).

Liebert, U. (1995) *Models of Democratic Consolidation: Parliaments and Organized Interests in the Federal Republic of Germany, Italy and Spain (1948–90)* (Opladen: Leske und Budrich).

Liebert, U. (2004) 'European Social Citizenship. Preconditions for Promoting Inclusion', In: Magnusson, L.; Strath, B. eds, *A European Social Citizenship?*

Preconditions for Future Policies from Historical Perspective (Brussels: P.I.E. Peter Lang).

Liebert, U. (2007) 'The European Citizenship Paradox: Negotiating Equality and Diversity in the New Europe' In: Siim, B.; Squires, J. eds, *Negotiating Diversity within Equality: Comparative Citizenship Analyses*, Critical Review of International Social and Political Philosophy (CRISPP), vol. 10 (special issue): 417–441.

Liebich, A. (2007) "Altneuländer or the Vicissitudes of Citizenship in the New EU States", In: Bauböck, R.; Perchinig, B.; Sievers, W. eds, *Citizenship Policies in the New Europe* (Amsterdam: Amsterdam UP).

Liebich, A. (2009) "Altneuländer or the vicissitudes of citizenship in the new EU states", In: Bauböck, R.; Perchinig, B.; Sievers, W. eds, *Citizenship policies in the new Europe. Expanded and Updated Edition* (Amsterdam: Amsterdam UP, IMISCOE).

Lister, R. (2003) *Citizenship, Feminist Perspectives* (New York: Palgrave Macmillan).

Maas, W. (2008) 'Migrants, States, and EU Citizenship's Unfulfilled Promise', *Citizenship Studies*, vol. 12 (6), 583–596.

Mann, M. (1987) 'Ruling Class Strategies and Citizenship', *Sociology*, vol. 21 (3), 339–354.

March, J. and Olsen, P. (2004) 'The logic of appropriateness', In: ARENA Centre for European Studies, University Oslo, Working Papers WP 04/09, www.arena.uio.no/publications.wp04.9.pdf (acccessed 3 May 2007).

Marshall, T. H. (1949/1965) 'Citizenship and Social Class', *Class, Citizenship and Social Development. Essays by T.H. Marshall* (New York: Anchor Books).

Martin, D.; Hailbronner, H. eds (2003) *Rights and Duties of Dual Nationals – Evolution and Prospects* (The Hague: Kluwer Law International).

Martin, D.; Heilbronner, K. (2003) *Rights and Duties of Dual Nationals. Evolutions and Prospects* (The Hague: Kluwer Law International).

Miller-Idriss, C. (2006) 'Everyday Understandings of Citizenship in Germany', *Citizenship Studies*, vol. 10 (5): 541–570.

Nozick, R. (2002) *Anarchy, State and Utopia* (New York: Basic Books).

O'Brennan, J.; Raunio, T., eds (2007) *National Parliaments Within the Enlarged European Union. From 'Victims' of the Integration to Competitive Actors?* (Abingdon: Routledge).

Palmowski, J. (2008) 'In Search of the German Nation: Citizenship and the Challenge of Integration', *Citizenship Studies*, vol. 12 (6), 547–563.

Perczyński, P.; Vink, M. (2002) 'Citizenship and Democracy: A Journey to Europe's Past', *Citizenship Studies*, vol. 6 (2): 183–199.

Rawls, J. (1999) *The Law of Peoples* (Cambridge, MA: Harvard UP).

Reiter, B. (2008) 'The Perils of Empire: Nationhood and Citizenship in Portugal', *Citizenship Studies*, vol. 12 (4): 397–412.

Rock, D.; Wolff, S. eds (2002) *Coming Home to Germany? The Integration of Ethnic Germans from Central and Eastern Europe in the Federal Republic* (New York: Bergham Books).

Rubio-Marin, R. (2000) *Immigration as a Democratic Challenge: Citizenship and Inclusion in Germany and the United States* (Cambridge: Cambridge UP).

Rubio-Marin, R. (2006) 'Transnational Politics and the Democratic Nation-State: Normative Challenges of Expatriate Voting and Nationality Retention of Emigrants', *New York University Law Review*, vol. 81 (1): 117–148.

Sartori, G. (1984) *Social Science Concepts. A Systematic Analysis* (Beverly Hills, CA: Sage).

Schmidt, V. (2005) 'Institutionalism and the State', In: Hay, C.; Marsh, D.; Lister, D. eds, *The State: Theories and Issues* (Basingstoke: Palgrave).

Schmidt, V.; Radaelli, C. (2004) 'Policy Change and Discourse in Europe: Conceptual and Methodological Issues', *West European Politics*, vol. 27 (2): 183–210.

Sedelmeier, U. (2005) 'The EU and Eastern Enlargement: Risk, Rationality, and Role-Compliance' In: Schimmelfennig, F.; Sedelmeier, U. eds, *The Politics of European Union Enlargement: Theoretical Approaches* (London: Routledge).

Sedelmeier, U.; Schimmelfennig, F. (2002) 'Theorising EU enlargement: research focus, hypotheses and the state of research', *Journal of European Public Policy*, vol. 9 (4): 500–528.

Shaw, J. (2007) *The Transformation of Citizenship in the European Union* (Cambridge: Cambridge UP).

Shorten, A. (2010) 'Linguistic Competence and CitizenshipAcquisition' In: Calder, G.; Cole, P.; Seglow, J. eds, *Citizenship Acquisition and National Belonging. Migration, Membership and the Liberal Democratic State* (Basingstoke: Palgrave Macmillan).

Soysal, J. (1994) *The Limits of Citizenship* (Chicago, IL: University Press).

Tyler, I. (2010) 'Designed to Fail: A Biopolitics of British Citizenship', *Citizenship Studies*, vol. 14 (1): 61–74.

Vink, M. (2001) 'The Limited Europeanization of Domestic Citizenship Policy: Evidence from the Netherlands', *Journal of Common Market Studies*, vol. 39 (5): 875–96.

Vink, M. (2002) 'Negative and Positive Integration in European Immigration Policies', *European Integration Online Papers* (EIoP), vol. 6 (13), http://eiop.or.at/eiop/pdf/2002-013.pdf.

Vink, M. (2005) 'Patterns of Citizenship Liberal Trends, Convergence and the Politics of Nationhood', http://www.personeel.unimaas.nl/m.vink/patterns_of_citizenship.html (accessed 15 August 2006).

Vink, M.; de Groot, G.-R. (2010) 'Citizenship Attribution in Western Europe:International Framework and Domestic Trends', *Journal of Ethnic and Migration Studies*, vol. 36 (5): 713–34.

Waldrauch, H. (2006a), 'Acquisition of Nationality', In: Bauböck, R; Ersbøll, E; Groenendijk, K.; Waldrauch, K. eds, *Acquisition and Loss of Nationality. Policies and Trends in 15 European States* (Amsterdam: Amsterdam UP, IMISCOE).

Waldrauch, H. (2006b), 'Methodology of Comparing Acquisition and Loss of Nationality', In: Bauböck, R; Ersbøll, E; Groenendijk, K. and Waldrauch, K. eds, *Acquisition and Loss of Nationality. Policies and Trends in 15 European States* (Amsterdam: Amsterdam UP, IMISCOE).

Weil, P. (2001) 'Access to Citizenship: A Comparison of Twenty-Five Nationality Laws' In: Aleinikoff, A; Klusmeyer, D. eds, *Citizenship Today: Global Perspectives and Practices* (Washington, D.C.: Carnegie).

Weis, P. (1956) *Nationality and Statelessness in International Law* (London: Stevens and Sons).

Wiedemann, M. (2003) 'Development of Dual Nationality Under German Law' In: Martin, D.; Hailbronner, K. eds, *Rights and Duties of Dual Nationals – Evolution and Prospects* (The Hague: Kluwer Law International).

Wodak, R.; Meyer, M. eds (2001) *Methods of Critical Discourse Analysis* (London: Sage).

Wodak, R.; van Dijk, T. A. eds (2000) *Racism at the top. Parliamentary Discourses on Ethnic Issues in Six European States* (Klagenfurt: Drava).

Index